D0777171

Praise for *The Quest for Prosperity*

"This is a must-read for anyone interested in the emerging consensus on development policy. Justin Yifu Lin makes a powerful case for a 'new structural economics' grounded in a very persuasive analysis of the evolution of ideas in economics. It will resonate especially well with practitioners familiar with the practical constraints of policymaking in developing countries."

Montek Ahluwalia   deputy chairman of the Planning Commission of the Republic of India

"In this masterpiece, Justin Yifu Lin weaves together 250 years of economic thought with his own wisdom acquired during China's economic rise. He dares to envision the end of world poverty and spells out—thoughtfully, sensibly, and pragmatically—how this can be accomplished. It is impossible for an economist to write a better, or a more important, book."

George A. Akerlof   Nobel Laureate in Economics

"Combining valuable insights from his experience in China, his time as the World Bank's chief economist, and the 2008 financial crisis, Justin Yifu Lin's recommendations for development policy reflect an impressive and unique personal journey."

Kemal Dervis   vice president of the Brookings Institution and former executive head of the UN Development Programme

"*The Quest for Prosperity* is an important book. Written with verve and clarity, it reflects a deep understanding of global economic issues, and proposes practical solutions that anyone concerned with the plight of the world's poor would be wise to read."

Robert Fogel   Nobel Laureate in Economics

"Justin Yifu Lin's life journey has been one of discovery driven by insatiable curiosity. His invaluable contributions to economic theory and policy in these turbulent times are distinctive because of the sharpness of his observations, his willingness to rigorously test a hypothesis, and his courage to posit emerging views. *The Quest for Prosperity* builds on his already substantial contribution to development economics. It is a must-read for all policymakers and students."

Trevor Manuel   minister in the presidency of the National Planning Commission of South Africa

"Justin Yifu Lin lays out an innovative framework for understanding the mystery of economic growth, drawing insightful conclusions about the experience of successful economies that should provide important inspiration to developing countries as they seek to expand their comparative advantages and design their own growth strategies."

Ngozi Okonjo-Iweala   finance minister of Nigeria

"Justin Yifu Lin cracks the code of economic development in this extraordinary tour de force—offering a rare combination of personal experience, rigorous analysis, and empirical investigation. His powerful recipe will become an enduring feature of future development efforts."

Stephen S. Roach   former chairman of Morgan Stanley Asia
and author of *The Next Asia*

"Part personal narrative, part sophisticated economic analysis, this important book offers a new approach for accelerating economic development around the world. Justin Yifu Lin's exceptional grounding in Chinese realities and Chicago economics, as well as his extensive experience, shine throughout."

Dani Rodrik   author of *The Globalization Paradox: Democracy and the Future of the World Economy*

"This is a truly exciting book. Speaking directly to the reader and quoting Lewis Carroll as easily as Simon Kuznets, Justin Yifu Lin proposes a new approach to development economics that makes great sense."

Thomas C. Schelling   Nobel Laureate in Economics

"This book is a tour de force: a seminal contribution to development studies that is engagingly, even entertainingly, written. Lin uses words, not statistics, to carry his arguments; and he illuminates abstract ideas with the dicta of people as diverse as Winston Churchill, Deng Xiaoping, and Mick Jagger."

Robert Wade   London School of Economics and Political Science

THE QUEST FOR PROSPERITY

THE
QUEST
FOR
PROSPERITY

How Developing Economies Can Take Off

JUSTIN YIFU LIN

PRINCETON UNIVERSITY PRESS

Princeton and Oxford

Published by Princeton University Press, 41 William Street, Princeton, New Jersey 08540
In the United Kingdom: Princeton University Press, 6 Oxford Street, Woodstock, Oxfordshire OX20 1TW
press.princeton.edu

Library of Congress Cataloging-in-Publication Data

Lin, Justin Yifu, 1952–
    The quest for prosperity : how developing economies can take off / Justin Yifu Lin.
      p. cm.
    Includes bibliographical references and index.
    ISBN 978-0-691-15589-0 (hardback : alk. paper)
    1. Developing countries—Economic conditions.   2. Developing countries—Economic policy.   I. Title.
    HC59.7.L41863   2012
    338.9009172′4—dc23   2012016049

British Library Cataloging-in-Publication Data are available

This book has been composed in Minion Pro with Knockout display by Princeton Editorial Associates Inc., Scottsdale, Arizona

Printed on acid-free paper. ∞

Printed in the United States of America

10 9 8 7 6 5 4 3 2 1

CONTENTS

PROLOGUE

WHEN A SENIOR WORLD BANK OFFICIAL PHONED ME from Washington, D.C., in January 2008 to offer me the position of senior vice president and chief economist of the World Bank Group, I was in the middle of spring break, busy preparing my teaching and research priorities for the next semester and attending to various economic policy matters. I was not expecting the call, but it was not a total surprise—two months before, I had met with World Bank President Robert Zoellick in his hotel room in Beijing for an hour and a half, an hour longer than scheduled, when he was visiting China. It was not a formal job interview—at least it did not feel like one at the time. The stated purpose was to discuss China's inflation, widening income disparities, rural development, and other domestic issues. In response to Zoellick's inquisitive mind, polite manner, and eyes burning with intensity, I gradually extended the discussion to the main challenges facing the world economy, the way to achieve more inclusive growth and reduce poverty, the potential role of foreign aid and multilateral organizations, and many other issues. At the end of the meeting, I gave him a copy of my Marshall Lectures delivered at Cambridge University a year earlier.[1] It summarized my research on economic development and transition issues in China and other countries.

An Intriguing Offer

The job offer was both exciting and humbling. Being asked to serve presented an extraordinary opportunity and was a sign of changing times. For the first time since the World Bank was created in 1944, a national from a developing country was being invited to serve as its chief economist, guide its intellectual leadership, and shape the economic research agenda of the institution. To meet the challenges of development, the institution had to be an agent of change. To be effective in this role it must combine its finance with ideas and knowledge. The development economics vice presidency, which I was being asked to lead, increases understanding of development policies and programs by providing intellectual leadership and analytical services to the Bank and the broader development community. Its aim is to improve the effectiveness of Bank operations and meet the needs of its client countries for high-quality services.

But giving up my exciting work—even momentarily—was not easy. I had served for 15 years as professor and founding director of the China Centre for Economic Research at Peking University. In those years I had developed strong and fruitful relations with many students, colleagues, and friends, some of whom counted on me in pursuing fascinating research questions. I had also been closely involved in economic policy discussions in China since coming back home in 1987 after four years completing a Ph.D. at the University of Chicago and a year of postdoctoral research at Yale University. Our remarkable economic success was a source of both pride and intellectual curiosity. I was eager to continue working on the increasingly challenging issues facing China. In an environment in which many prominent economists were predicting difficult times ahead, it was quite tempting to stay home and contribute to the debate and search for solutions.

At the same time, the World Bank offer was a lifetime opportunity to work on development issues in many different contexts, and perhaps to shape the global conversation on growth and poverty reduction strategies. The broad responsibilities of the position include helping accelerate poverty reduction and contribute to progress toward the Millennium Development

Goals by providing countries with the knowledge necessary to make more informed policy choices. That knowledge has also been used over the years to inform global public advocacy initiatives. And developing it involves research, data, analysis, global monitoring, projections, statistical capacity building, and policy review and advice.

The development economics vice presidency covered all these dimensions, sponsored research projects in other parts of the Bank, and produced flagship reports to set the agenda of international development as well as two top scholarly journals in the field. It had among its staff some of the world's best-known development economists. And economists who had been World Bank chief economists were among the most respected names in the field: Nobel laureate Joseph Stiglitz, Larry Summers, Stanley Fischer, Anne O. Krueger, Hollis B. Chenery, Michael Bruno, Lord Nicholas H. Stern, and François Bourguignon. Following in the footsteps of such people would be a great honor—and a daunting responsibility.

Helping countries to attain sustained dynamic growth to eliminate poverty and achieve prosperity has been my life's pursuit since I was a child. I realized that joining the World Bank would allow me to share my insights on this subject with many others, undertake an ambitious research program to examine unresolved challenges in economic development, and shed new light on the causes of economic take-off or lagging growth in poor regions.

Indeed, the Bank had made an intriguing offer, one I could not refuse.

I asked for a week to think through what moving to Washington would mean for my personal and professional life. I needed to organize a leave of absence from the university and to make arrangements for my Ph.D. students and my successor. But I was ready for the challenge.

Strange Childhood Memories from Africa

A week after I took the position in June 2008, I was on a flight to South Africa, Rwanda, and Ethiopia. It was not my first trip on the continent, but in many ways it was an initiatory journey. Why not go to Latvia, Mexico, or Nepal for my first official trip?

Why Africa? Probably because I saw the continent as the last frontier for development economics, the place where new knowledge and new solutions could yield the greatest payoffs. Thanks to much-improved macroeconomic policies, higher commodity prices, and significant increases in aid, capital flows, and remittances, economic growth south of the Sahara had accelerated from 3.1 percent in 2000 to 6.1 percent in 2007. Similarly, per capita growth in gross domestic product (GDP) had increased from 0.7 percent a year over 1996–2001 to 2.7 percent a year over 2002–08. The proportion of Africans living on less than $1.25 a day had fallen from 58 percent in 1996 to 50 percent in 2005. The prevalence of deadly diseases such as AIDS was stabilizing and even declining in some countries. Sixty percent of the children were completing primary school, and child mortality was falling in a large group of countries.

A new wave of empirical research by development agencies, academic institutions, and leading economists from various backgrounds even suggested that several African economies were on the verge of an unprecedented economic take-off.[2] The strong performance and resilience of these economies were not accidents but the results of sustained efforts in most countries in the past two decades. At least five fundamental changes were at work: more democratic and accountable governments; more sensible economic policies; the end of the debt crisis and changing relationships with donors; the spread of new technologies; and the emergence of a new generation of policymakers, activists, and business leaders.[3] And the security situation was also improving.[4]

True, the development challenges were still overwhelming. Many African economies still exhibited signs of limited structural transformation, reflecting the slow progress since independence. The region was overwhelmingly rural in 1960, with agriculture accounting for some 40 percent of GDP and 85 percent of the labor force. Although the rural share of the population fell steadily over the past five decades, it was still 63 percent in 2000, significantly higher than in other regions. A World Bank study noted:

Economic growth has not been accompanied by an increase in productive employment—particularly troubling since 7–10 million young

Africans enter the labor force every year. A skills deficit hinders Africa's ability to compete in the global economy, and opportunities for African entrepreneurs, especially women, remain constrained by limited access to information, innovation, and adequate tools to create viable businesses. . . . Because of its high dependence on rainfed agriculture, Africa is vulnerable to extreme weather events such as faster desertification, rising sea levels, and more frequent droughts. Africa may be the continent worst hit by climate change. The delivery of basic services continues to fail poor people—with high degrees of teacher absenteeism in schools and money often failing to reach frontline service providers.[5]

The continent also performed poorly on governance indicators and lagged behind on infrastructure development, with major deficits in transport, roads, water, telecommunications, and energy. Private investment averaged only 15 percent of GDP due to the continent's infrastructure deficit and business regulations. Africa's market share of global exports had declined from 3.5 percent in the 1970s to 1.5 percent in 2008. In addition, the global economic crisis, coming on the heels of the food and fuel price crises of 2008, was threatening the hard-won progress. Still, I felt there was ground for optimism about the continent's economic future. Looking beyond the complex difficulties at hand, I had a sense that hope was back and that perhaps a little push in the implementation of good policies could bring the same positive results observed elsewhere in the developing world, most notably in Asia.

I started my field trip in South Africa by attending the Annual Bank Conference on Development Economics, a gathering of academic and policy researchers working on development issues. President Thabo Mbeki opened the meeting, with some 800 researchers from all over the world in attendance. I gave a speech based on my Marshall Lecture at Cape Town University. I argued that the best way to reduce poverty and to have dynamic, inclusive growth is to take a country's comparative advantage as the guiding principle in its economic development. That allows the economy to be most competitive and to create the most jobs for the poor. Trevor Manuel, minister of finance of South Africa, chaired the session, commented on my speech, and became a supportive friend.

I then went to Rwanda to explore the constraints and opportunities for harnessing the country's potential for growth, especially in the rural sector. In the eastern province I visited farmers' cooperatives for agribusiness, mushroom production, and technology extension. I also met with government officials, including President Paul Kagame, a tall, serious former military man with a calm demeanor and hearty voice. We discussed agricultural modernization, especially irrigation in Rwanda. I suggested that although it was important to mobilize international funding and donor support for building microdams, it was also important to mobilize farmers in the off-peak seasons to build small ponds near each household farm through their own efforts in order to harvest rain. They could then buy small diesel or electronic pumps to extract underground water and to turn rainfed agriculture into irrigated agriculture. The country could produce pumps, starting with assembly and foreign direct investment, to serve the rural market. The president was quite interested in this basic suggestion. He was perhaps thinking about the African proverb "One does not use a sword to kill a snail," similar in spirit to China's proverb "One need not use an ox butcher's knife to kill a chicken."

In Ethiopia I spent the first few days in the Nazareth and Rift Valley areas, holding seminars and discussions with agricultural extension workers and women farmers and visiting export-oriented agricultural and cooperative union members. In Addis Ababa I met with business leaders, academics, and policymakers. I also met with Prime Minister Meles Zenawi, another former military leader with a sharp mind and unmatched intellectual curiosity. Prior to our three-hour brainstorming session, I had collected a series of simple items ordinarily sold in local stores, all produced overseas. These included a box of matches made in Nepal and a plastic electric switch and other basic products made in China.

After discussing the traditional issues of macroeconomic stabilization, such as inflation and the balance-of-payments deficit, on which we quickly agreed, I showed Zenawi the items I had purchased in local markets and asked him why Ethiopia—a country with some 85 million inhabitants and an old and sophisticated business tradition, a proud nation that had withstood all kinds of foreign invasions throughout its long history and had never been colonized by any foreign power—could still afford in the twenty-first century to import such basic light manufacturing products, including matches from Nepal, another poor but smaller and landlocked country. As for the products "made in China," which required few skills and little technology to make but were still imported by Ethiopia, I indicated that I was proud as a Chinese citizen to see our industries dominate world markets, even for very basic goods. But as the World Bank chief economist and as a citizen of the world concerned with the fight against poverty in Ethiopia, I was puzzled by the many costly missed opportunities that each of these imported products represented.

Besides costing the economy large sums of foreign exchange that could be used to purchase crucial capital goods, new technology, or cutting-edge medicines, the country's development strategy was contributing to high underemployment and fueling poverty. I proposed that the government, in addition to continuing its export-promotion efforts, encourage industries that substitute their own goods for imports of simple manufactured goods. The potential benefits were obvious: the savings from import substitution would have the same effect as earning foreign exchange from export promotion. Further, the substitution industries would create jobs for the poor and train entrepreneurs for further industrial development. The key was to design and roll out the strategy in a way that would avoid government involvement and the waste of public money in industries inconsistent with Ethiopia's comparative advantage—industries that would be uncompetitive, unviable, and costly. And that was indeed possible.

Traveling in these three African countries, I could see everywhere images from my childhood. I was touched by the farmers longing to improve their lives and build better futures for their children. Their eyes reminded me of the eyes of farmers I had seen when I was a young child in Taiwan, China, in the 1960s and 1970s, and when I first went to the mainland in 1979. It was a strange feeling to go back in time in my own country in my mind while visiting these distant places. I was impressed not only by their national leaders' commitments for their nations' futures and their thirst to understand and learn from the experiences of other countries but also by the excitement and thirst for knowledge of junior professionals, academics, students, and businesspeople. The many difficulties they faced daily did not seem to reduce their enthusiasm for and commitment to working for a better future.

Rwanda, Ethiopia, and even South Africa in some respects have an old Asian flavor in their current economic and sociopolitical complexion: their population density, traditional agriculture, small and weak industrial sector, pervasive poverty, and yet strong and committed governments and stable societies, with diligent people everywhere are similar to the conditions in much of East Asia a generation ago.

I had the same feeling well beyond Africa. My trips to other developing countries in the following months and years also brought back memories of Asian countries from several decades ago, when they were struggling with poverty, poor governance, and weak capacity—and were considered basket cases by many top economists.

Yes, I always had the strange feeling of being back in my childhood. The images that struck me everywhere, the energy and the optimism of the people, and the intensity of my interaction with various development stakeholders convinced me that with good ideas, the right development strategies, and some financial means, these poor countries could achieve Asian-type economic performance in the coming decades and become newly industrialized economies. Talking to policymakers, I quickly came to the conclusion that my responsibility was to draw lessons from world history, policy experiences in other countries, and economic analysis to help them formulate appropriate strategies—strategies that would take into account their visions, strengths, constraints, and goals.

This would have to be done with conviction and humility, recognizing the differences in circumstances and possibilities in each place. Just like Europe, Latin America, or Asia, Africa is not a country. It is a diverse continent with more than 50 different countries, each with its own history, culture, strengths, and weaknesses. Embarking on the task of economic development, policymakers should keep in mind what Deng Xiaoping, the architect of China's reform and opening, told Ghana's President Jerry Rawlings in 1985: "Please don't try to copy our model. If there is any experience on our part, it is to formulate policies in light of one's own national conditions."[6] The main purpose of this book is to outline a road map for such country-centered development strategies.

THE QUEST FOR PROSPERITY

ONE

New Challenges and New Solutions

SINCE BECOMING THE WORLD BANK'S CHIEF ECONOMIST, I have had ample opportunity to reflect on an old American saying: "Be careful what you wish for, you might just get it!" For better or worse, the beginning of my tenure coincided with the eruption of the most serious financial and economic crisis, both in magnitude and in scope, since the Great Depression. No country has been immune to the economic slowdown. Most economic and financial experts severely underestimated its timing, speed, and severity. As a result, despite strong macro policy responses, the current situation remains full of uncertainties.

This crisis, unlike many other crises preceding it, was not the fault of developing countries. It was an unexpected setback to and challenge for their macro management. Some of them had little exposure to the financial derivatives that triggered the crisis and had the fiscal space and the foreign reserves to apply strong policy stimulus programs. But many others had enormous short-term capital inflows through multinational bank branches, large current account deficits, overpriced housing markets, or limited fiscal space for countercyclical measures.

The amplitude, brutality, and unfairness of the crisis was perhaps most obvious in Sub-Saharan Africa. Despite being the global economy's least integrated region, it was perhaps the worst hit by the crisis. Each channel for the crisis to affect the continent has had a particularly nefarious impact. The decline in commodity prices, though a benefit to oil-importing countries, has led to a substantial decline in exports and government revenue for many commodity exporters. Even countries that saved their windfalls when prices were high suffered because their nonoil sectors are small and highly dependent on government spending.[1]

Private capital flows, which had surged to record levels prior to the recession (and exceeded foreign aid to the continent) declined abruptly. African stock markets fell by an average of 40 percent, with some, such as that of Nigeria, falling by more than 60 percent.[2] Workers' remittances, which had also been on the rise and had become a major source of growth for labor-exporting countries, also declined substantially. Only foreign aid continued to rise, but it remained well short of the commitments made by G-8 countries at the Gleneagles Summit in 2005, when the global economy was more robust. With mounting pressures in donor countries to stimulate their own economies and plan for fiscal consolidation, it could be expected that the volumes of aid they gave to Africa would be lower in the years ahead. Such developments were likely to slow their growth rates and derail progress toward the Millennium Development Goals.[3]

Luckily, through a joint effort, the world has avoided the worst. Policymakers quickly understood the almost unprecedented scale and dangers of the crisis. Other post–World War II economic crises occurred either in some individual developing country or region (East Asia, Latin America, Mexico, or the Russian Federation) or in only one or two high-income countries (Japan, Sweden). Their impact was a small fraction of global GDP. This time, the crisis struck almost all advanced and developing economies at the same time, making it impossible for one country to escape high unemployment and large excess capacity through individual actions on monetary, exchange rate, or trade policies.

Thanks to the strong policy coordination of the G-20 countries, the world escaped another Great Depression. Policymakers responded swiftly and creatively to the crisis, using various instruments, including credible pledges to free trade, large-scale fiscal stimulus packages, very accommodative mone-

tary policy, and decisive and often innovative support for the financial sector (liquidity provision, recapitalization, asset purchases, and guarantees on
various types of assets and liabilities).[4] The objectives were to cushion the
direct effects of the credit crunch and financial turbulence on the developed
economies and to reduce the virulence of the adverse feedback loop in which
economic weakness and financial stress were mutually reinforcing.

The Bane of Excess Capacity

These swift actions by international financial institutions and governments
prevented a global economic meltdown and buffered the impact of the crisis. But although the short-term effects of the policy response have helped
the world economy avoid a depression, they have not addressed the underlying issues of heightened systemic risks, falling asset values, and tightening
credit—which have taken a heavy toll on business and consumer confidence
and aggravated a sharp slowing in global economic activity. Central bank
provision of liquidity to banks and primary dealers has not always been very
effective because, with large excess capacity in housing, construction, and,
to a large extent, the manufacturing sector as well, the business environment
in developed countries is dominated by concerns about capital, asset quality,
and credit risk. These concerns limit the willingness of many intermediaries
to extend credit, even when liquidity is available. As a result, the global
recovery has been fragile. Moreover, growth is not expected to be fast enough
to make big inroads into high unemployment and spare capacity. Besides,
the downside risks have increased, not least those related to potential currency conflicts and the attendant risks of protectionism.

Indeed, the world has had a two-track recovery, and most high-income
countries, which still constitute 70 percent of the global economy, continue
to struggle with high unemployment, large excess capacity, towering public
debts, slow growth, and volatile financial markets. In my view, the global crisis was triggered by the financial sector, but the main challenge for a sustained global recovery lies in the real sector. Excess capacity could have

persistent negative effects on corporate profits, private-sector investment, and household consumption. And it could eventually render traditional monetary policies ineffective, especially in rich countries.

When capacity is underused, low interest rates may not stimulate private investment and consumption due to a lack of profitable investment opportunities and a lack of job security that hurts household consumption.[5] Excess capacity also creates a vicious circle in financial markets: asset prices (real estate), private investment, and household consumption are likely to remain sluggish, so the excess capacity will persist. This dynamic puts additional downward pressure on asset prices and corporate profits and increases the volumes of nonperforming loans. In addition, wages in many industries are still flat or declining, further curtailing personal consumption. Deteriorating household balance sheets tend to add to the uncertainty. The wait-and-see attitude of investors and consumers may sustain the downward spiral in output decline in some large countries: the reduction in consumption due to the concerns about job security and low confidence about the future causes even more excess capacity.

The crisis-hit advanced countries need structural reforms in their labor markets, welfare systems, and financial institutions to regain competitiveness and dynamic growth. Structural reforms are recessionary in general and politically infeasible when excess capacity is large and unemployment is high in a country. The way out is not traditional monetary and fiscal policies but a large-scale, coordinated, global productivity-enhancing, bottleneck-releasing infrastructure program to create enough demand to absorb the excess capacity and space for structural reforms in advanced countries. I called this "Beyond Keynesianism" in a speech I gave at the Peterson Institute of International Economics in February 2009.[6] Without it, the weak growth in advanced countries—known as the "new normal"—may persist. In the face of excess capacity, "cheap money" may not stimulate private demand.[7] Instead, cheap credit will encourage speculative profit-seeking ventures and fuel the surge in some asset prices, notably in emerging markets, through carry trade and other short-term capital flows. Given the low profitability in the real economies of many countries, such surges may not be sustainable. Fiscal policy is indeed more promising if the challenges of rising debt are addressed.[8] If governments and private-sector leaders can identify and make investments in key areas that present binding constraints to growth, the spending today will not only have a short-run effect of boosting demand and jobs—it may also pave the way toward a brighter future of sustained strong economic growth. That would help overcome the debt sustainability problem that may occur when a fiscal stimulus does not increase future productivity.[9]

When the global crisis erupted, the World Bank, under the leadership of President Bob Zoellick, quickly formed a three-pillar package of crisis responses to help client countries: strengthening the social safety net to avoid a long-term adverse impact on the vulnerable, supporting small and medium enterprises for job generation, and investing in bottleneck-releasing infrastructure projects as countercyclical interventions. No matter how the global economy evolves, it is imperative for developing countries to continue their dynamic growth. Growth and jobs are essential for them to maintain social stability and reduce poverty today and to achieve their development aspirations in the future. If they can do so, they will also contribute to a sustained global recovery. How? The global crisis provides a good opportunity for the development community to rethink many tenets of economics and policy.

The Apparent Mystery of Economic Success

In the wake of global crisis, "rethinking" has been one of the most frequently used terms in the media and among professional economists. The Institute for New Economic Thinking, founded with an endowment from George Soros, held its inaugural conference, "The Economic Crisis and the Crisis in Economics," at Cambridge University in April 2010. Delighted to be one of the 200-plus participants from around the world, I observed that renowned economists, government officials, and journalists challenged much accepted wisdom in economics. I was also encouraged to see Olivier Blanchard, my counterpart at the International Monetary Fund, doing something many skeptics thought was impossible—showing humility on behalf of economists and acknowledging mistakes in judgment. He wrote: "It was tempting for macroeconomists and policymakers alike to take much of the credit for the steady decrease in cyclical fluctuations from the early 1980s on and to conclude that we knew how to conduct macroeconomic policy. We did not resist temptation. The crisis clearly forces us to question our earlier assessment."[10]

Summarizing the long-standing conventional wisdom, he also observed: "We thought of monetary policy as having one target, inflation, and one instrument, the policy rate. So long as inflation was stable, the output gap was likely to be small and stable and monetary policy did its job. We thought of fiscal policy as playing a secondary role, with political constraints sharply limiting its de facto usefulness. And we thought of financial regulation as mostly outside the macroeconomic policy framework."[11] Other prominent researchers such as Akerlof (2009), Krugman (2009), and Stiglitz (2009) have also questioned some fundamental tenets of mainstream macroeconomics, notably the assumption that competitive markets are enough to produce strong business incentives, efficient outcomes, and wealth.

In the domain of development economics, which became a field of research only after World War II, the failure of several waves of theories to provide successful policy prescriptions has been even more obvious. To be sure, development economics has provided us with some remarkable insights. But as a subdiscipline of economics, it has so far been unable to provide a convincing intellectual agenda for generating and distributing wealth in poor countries, evidenced by the persistence of poverty in many parts of the world.

Several decades from now, when economic historians look back on the story of the past 100 years, it is very likely that they will be more intrigued by the mystery of diverging performances by various countries, especially in the second half of the twentieth century. They will be amazed by the rapid-growth path followed by a small number of countries such as Brazil, China, India, Indonesia, the Republic of Korea, Malaysia, Mauritius, Singapore, Thailand, and Vietnam, where the industrialization process quickly transformed their subsistence agrarian economies and lifted several hundred million people out of poverty in a single generation.

Even more perplexing may be the unusual intellectual route that many of these successful countries followed: few, if any, actually adopted the dominant policy prescriptions of the time. Leaving aside the United States, which ranks third, the four most populous countries (Brazil, China, India, and Indonesia), have made great strides, averaging annual growth rates well over 6 percent a year. That vastly improved the standards of living for more than 40 percent of the world's people. The same is taking place in other South American countries (Chile, Colombia, and Peru) and in some African countries (Ethiopia, Ghana, and Mauritius). These countries hardly adopted standard recommendations from prevailing development theories.

But future economic historians will be puzzled by the apparent inability of many other countries, with more than one-sixth of humanity (the "bottom billion," as Paul Collier famously put it), to escape the trap of poverty. They will also notice that, except for the few successful economies, there was little economic convergence between rich and poor countries before the global crisis erupted in 2008—this despite the many efforts of developing countries and the assistance of many multilateral development agencies. Also puzzling may be the realization that some countries grew from low to middle incomes but have stayed there for decades, if not centuries. Argentina, the Philippines, Russia, South Africa, and the Syrian Arab Republic are well-known examples of countries caught in the "middle-income trap," with growth slowing after they reach a certain income level.

How can we make sense of economic success—or failure? Economists have conjectured about that seminal question for centuries—most recently with the help of the Growth Commission Report.[12] But beyond a consensus on broad principles and a rejection of one-size-fits-all approaches, economists still have trouble identifying actionable policy levers directly relevant to specific countries.

The global financial and economic crisis confirmed the observation that countries with sustained high rates of growth have also performed well despite the global meltdown. With its heavy human, financial, and economic costs, the crisis provides a unique opportunity to reflect on knowledge from several decades of growth research and development thinking, draw policy lessons from successful countries, and explore new approaches going forward. In a more global world where fighting poverty is not only a moral responsibility but also a strategy for confronting some of the major problems that ignore boundaries and contribute to global insecurity (diseases, malnutrition, insecurity, violence), thinking about new ways of generating and sustaining growth is a crucial task for economists.

Taking Einstein's Joke Seriously: A New Structural Economics

Albert Einstein once joked: "Theory is when you know everything but nothing works. Practice is when everything works but nobody knows why. We have put together theory and practice: nothing is working . . . and nobody knows why!"

As strategies for achieving sustainable growth in developing countries are being reexamined in light of the global crisis, it is critical to refocus development research efforts on the nature of economic development, which, from what I see, is a process of continuous structural change including not only industrial and technological upgrading and economic diversification but also changes in employment structure (with labor moving into high-productivity sectors) and changes in "hard" (tangible) and "soft" (intangible) infrastructure. The economic literature has devoted much attention to technological innovation but not enough to these equally important issues.

Taking Einstein's joke seriously, this book focuses on the long-term development challenges facing policymakers and attempts to provide a road map for policymakers engaged in the quest for prosperity. First it discusses the evolution of development thinking since the end of World War II and the rise and fall of the dominant paradigms. Taking into account lessons from development history and economic analysis and practice, it then explains why a few countries have succeeded in their quest for growth and prosperity while many others have failed. Finally it suggests a framework to enable developing countries to achieve sustainable growth, eliminate poverty, and narrow their income gap with the developed countries.

The conclusion is optimistic: although specific country circumstances and history have often played important roles, there is nothing truly mysterious about the stellar economic performance of China, Korea, Singapore, and other countries such as Mauritius. I believe that all developing countries, including those in Sub-Saharan Africa, can grow at 8 percent or more continuously for several decades in an increasingly global world, significantly reduce poverty, and become middle- or even high-income countries in the span of one or two generations. But they can do this only if their governments have the right policy frameworks to facilitate the private sector's development in a market economy along the lines of their comparative advantage as determined by their endowments and to tap into the latecomer advantage provided in the global economy.[13]

The book proposes a new framework—a new structural economics—that builds on lessons from history and economic practice. It emphasizes the idea that structural features need to be taken into account in the economic development analysis and policymaking. And it sees the state as a facilitator that helps a developing country convert its backward structure to a modern structure in an open market economy.

The new approach also considers structural differences between countries at different levels of development and tries to explain them. Those differences do not result from the distribution of global power among nations or from other exogenously determined rigidities as assumed by the earlier development theories. In large part they are endogenous to country endowment structures (defined as the relative abundance of such production factors as natural resources, labor, human capital, and physical capital) and are determined by market forces. The analysis rejects the deterministic economic philosophy of proponents of "old structuralism," who considered poor countries necessarily victims of an unequal world order and recommended distortive government interventions to build inward-looking economies. It also rejects blind faith in the magical virtues and infallibility of free markets in a world where business development requires overcoming externalities and exploiting synergies among firms and industries.

The new structural economics described in this book is organized around three ideas:

- First, an economy's structure of factor endowments (the amount of land, labor, and capital that a country possesses)—which is given at any specific time and is changeable over time—determines its total budget, relative factor prices, and comparative advantages and evolves from one level of development to another. So the industrial structure of a given economy will differ at different levels of development. Each industrial structure requires the corresponding infrastructure (both "hard," or tangible, and "soft," or intangible) to facilitate its operations and transactions.

- Second, each level of economic development is a point along the continuum from a low-income agrarian economy to a high-income industrialized economy, not a dichotomy of two economic development stages ("poor" or "rich," "developing" or "industrialized"). Industrial upgrading and infrastructure improvement targets in developing countries should not necessarily draw from those in high-income countries.

- Third, at each given level of development, the market is the basic mechanism for effective resource allocation. However, economic development is a dynamic process that requires industrial upgrading and diversification along with corresponding improvements in "hard" and "soft" infrastructure at each new level. Such upgrading entails large externalities to firm transaction costs and the returns to capital investment. So, in addition to an effective market mechanism, the government should coordinate or provide the improvements in infrastructure and compensate for the externalities to facilitate industrial upgrading and diversification.

These ideas should not be overly controversial because they come from historical and contemporary evidence showing that governments facilitate industrial upgrading and diversification in all successful countries. But the suggestion that governments should be active in designing and implementing industrial policies to boost economic development has long been mired in controversy.

Many economists who agree with the general notion that government intervention is indispensable for structural transformation still oppose a proactive public role for government in assisting industrial upgrading and diversification. The main reason for such opposition is the lack of a general framework to guide policymaking. It is therefore useful to draw on the theories of comparative advantage and the potential benefits of backwardness—as well the successful and failed experiences of industrial policies—to codify some basic principles to guide successful government intervention. Going beyond the discussion of development theory, this book also suggests a user-friendly growth identification and facilitation framework to help policymakers around the world fulfill humanity's collective quest for prosperity and peace.

As the world emerges from the Great Recession, we need to remind ourselves that the interdependence of nations is an essential feature of the multipolar growth world. Going forward, the key challenges on the international agenda will be to accelerate the recovery with adequate macroeconomic policies, to increase future productivity in developing countries, and to enhance the regulatory framework of the financial sector to prevent new crises and avoid asset bubbles.

The economic incentives and "payoffs" for cooperation between rich and poor countries are numerous and increasing. There is a need for win-win solutions to achieve sustainable global growth and a more stable world. The world must avoid zero-sum game approaches such as currency wars, trade wars, or costly and abrupt rebalancing policies that seem appealing but may do more harm than good. Responding effectively to the new multipolar world order entails new international financial arrangements along with structural reforms in both high-income and developing countries.

In difficult times, great leaders have expressed hope. Winston Churchill, in his speech to the British Parliament on becoming prime minister at the beginning of World War II in 1940, bluntly said to his fellow countrymen: "I have nothing to offer but blood, toil, tears, and sweat. . . . But I take up my task with buoyancy and hope." He later wrote: "The pessimist sees difficulty in every opportunity. The optimist sees the opportunity in every difficulty." Former Czech president and acclaimed writer Vaclav Havel suggests that a distinction should be drawn between optimism, which he finds too naïve or opportunistic, and hope, which is a desire for the morally right thing to be done: "Hope is definitely not the same thing as optimism. It is not the conviction that something will turn out well, but the certainty that something makes sense, regardless of how it turns out."

Today's global economic challenges require both optimism and hope. Fortunately, we have learned useful lessons from history, economic analysis, and policy to enable us to tackle them. My expectation is that this book will contribute to the search for solutions.

TWO

A Battle of Narratives and Changing Paradigms

A S I WAS DOING MY POSTDOCTORAL STUDY at Yale's Economic Growth Center in 1986, I gave a seminar at Harvard University, and while there I visited the Museum of Fine Arts in Boston. Paul Gauguin's famous painting *Where Do We Come From? What Are We? Where Are We Going?* left a deep impression. Gauguin considered it his masterpiece and the summation of his ideas. In the painting he tried to address the old question of the meaning of life. Sprawled across the wide frame of the painting are various figures, each engaged in a particular and significant act. One of them is a man wearing a simple loincloth and picking an apple. In the background two women walk with their arms around one another. At the far left side of the painting, a dark-skinned, unclothed old woman sits on the verge of death, her head in her hands.

Gauguin, who had migrated to Tahiti "in search of a society more unspoiled than his native France," offered in that 1897–98 piece his representation of questions of human existence. The whole atmosphere of the painting reflects a kind of pessimism and even nihilism that marked intellectual life in Europe at the end of the nineteenth century, despite the Industrial Revolution that was lifting large fractions of populations out of poverty. The figures in the painting were confronting not economic misery but more existential issues of self-worth.

Giving Meaning to One's Life

The poor people I grew up with in Taiwan, China, and observed on the mainland never approached life with the pessimism Paul Gauguin's figures seem to display in his painting. As a child from a postwar, devastated former colony living my early years through the difficult and uncertain times of sociopolitical and economic turbulence, I approached issues of human dignity primarily through the lenses of history and economics. And yes, hunger seemed to be a crucial aspect of human suffering that existed in the memory of Chinese society. Instead of saying, "'Hello," "Good morning," "Good afternoon," or "Good evening," Chinese people on both sides of the Taiwan Strait greeted their friends by asking, "Have you had your meals?"

Coming home from school for lunch, my brothers would not even ask our mother for a meal if the stove was cold. But the pessimism, disillusionment, and hopelessness in Paul Gauguin's work were never part of the collective psyche of the people around me. On the contrary, human powerlessness was a source of motivation and inspiration. I saw it in the people I grew up with. And I observed it repeatedly in the people of the countries of Africa, South Asia, and many other poor places I visited in recent years. It persuaded me that every country is bestowed with the seeds of prosperity.

As a teenager I learned about the lives of two men who became my personal sources of inspiration and whose stories helped me to make major life choices. One was Li Bing, a governor of Qin Kingdom in China's Warring States Period more than 2,200 years ago, in what is now Sichuan Province. After witnessing the suffering of his people from frequent flooding of the Min River, he built the Dujiangyan irrigation system, "the largest, most carefully planned public works project yet seen anywhere on the eastern half of the Eurasian continent."[1] Despite daunting technical and geological difficulties, Li Bing personally led tens of thousands of workers for eight years to gouge a 20-meter-wide channel through hard rocks in the mountain and build an irrigation system on the river banks. That infrastructure project, still fully operational today, turned one of the poorest regions of the country into a fertile and rich place called "the land of heaven." After my return to the mainland from Taiwan, China, in the summer of 1979, one of the first places I visited was Dujiangyan. Standing on a cliff overlooking the narrow water channel, I was dazed and inspired by the thundering sound and the scene of water rushing through the channel below my feet—a flow that has never stopped for more than 2,200 years—to irrigate the fertile plain downstream.

Another hero of mine is Wang Yangming (1472–1529), the great Ming Dynasty thinker, Confucian philosopher, administrator, and general. Like his European contemporary Martin Luther (1483–1546), Wang established his own philosophical system, the Neo-Confucian School of Mind, through a revolutionary reinterpretation of Confucian classics and freed people from the rigid behavior code of the prevailing Confucian thinking espoused by the 12th-century Neo-Confucian philosopher Zhu Xi. He is best known for his teaching on the unity of knowledge and action, which posits that "knowing is the beginning of action; action is the completion of knowing." His philosophy influenced East Asian society for centuries. Wang was also an outstanding governor and a gifted military commander. He was exiled several times and banned from the imperial court because of his fight for justice and his revolutionary teaching. But his personal sufferings never compromised his inner sense of duty. Despite his political setbacks and the scant military support he had as governor, he prevailed over a prince's revolt and several other peasant rebellions, brought peace, and promoted education in the region where my forefathers lived before migrating to Taiwan, China, 250 years ago.

I have always believed that a man should be like Li Bing, doing something to promote prosperity for his land through generations, and that an intellectual should be like Wang Yangming, thinking independently and integrating knowledge and action for the benefit of people, even under unfavorable or adverse personal circumstances. Such efforts offer a good sense of purpose to one's life. Wang Yangming's philosophy of integrating knowledge and action is especially helpful to me in fulfilling my responsibilities at the World Bank, a knowledge bank whose mandate is to help create "a world free of poverty." While life is obviously about more than material concerns, solving basic human needs and giving economic opportunities to everyone are good ways to escape pessimism and nihilism. Creating the conditions for people to make the best of their gifts and to adjust their mental models to the reality surrounding them is indeed what Li Bing and Wang Yangming were able to do. In their own ways, they helped their fellow citizens improve their human condition—and in so doing, give meaning to their lives.

I have been lucky to receive a good education at top universities on both sides of the Taiwan Strait and in the United States. I have also been doubly fortunate to observe Taiwan, China, where I was born, turn from a poor agrarian society to an industrial power during my growing-up years and to participate in the mainland's miraculous transformation from a poor, centrally planned economy to a vibrant market economy. My many travels to poor, remote villages around the world as World Bank chief economist always remind me of the first time that I went from Guangzhou, the capital of Guangdong Province, to Shenzhen, one of four newly designated special economic zones, in 1980. It took more than 10 hours by car and ferries to travel the 300 kilometers of poor road and to cross several rivers. Then Shenzhen was a small fishing village across the border from Hong Kong Special Administrative Region (SAR), China. Today it has been transformed into one of the highest-income modern cities in China, with 15 million residents. Today the trip from Guangzhou to Shenzhen by highway takes only about 2 hours by car and 1 hour by high-speed train. Now when I meet young, innocent students on those trips in my new capacity, I cannot stop asking myself if they will be as lucky as I have been. From my readings I understand that most economists believed in the 1960s that Africa had much better conditions and opportunities for economic development than did the economies of East Asia. And I wonder: will the destiny of poor countries in Africa, South Asia, and other regions change in the coming decades?

Looking back at the historical context of Dujiangyan, which had significant economic, military, and even psychological implications, it is difficult to underestimate Li Bing's achievements—especially after learning from the work of British-born economic historian Angus Maddison, who calculated that, prior to the eighteenth century, it had taken about 1,400 years for the Western world to double its per capita income.[2] And, measured by today's living standards, all countries in the world were poor at the beginning of the eighteenth century.

The Evolution of Growth

Economic historians who have examined the evolution of growth throughout history tend to divide it into three periods. The first, spanning most of human history up to the middle of the eighteenth century, was marked by static living standards, despite population growth—the Malthusian conditions. The second, from about 1750 to the 1820s, saw some improvement in living standards and changes in demographic trends (higher fertility rates and lower mortality rates). The third, observed initially in England at the end of the first quarter of the nineteenth century and continuing to the present, has been one of modern economic growth.[3]

Deciphering the mystery of modern economic growth and explaining convergence and divergence are important topics for research. Economic growth is indeed the main source of divergences in living standards across countries and regions of the world. As Barro and Sala-i-Martin (1995) observe, "If we can learn about government policy options that have even small effects on long-term growth rates, we can contribute much more to improvements in standards of living than has been provided by the entire history of macroeconomic analysis of countercyclical policy and fine tuning."[4]

Simon Kuznets, who pioneered the search for rigorous analytical tools with which to observe growth patterns, in his Nobel Prize lecture defined a country's economic growth as "a long-term rise in capacity to supply increasingly diverse economic goods to its population, this growing capacity based on advancing technology and the institutional and ideological adjustments that it demands. All three components of the definition are important. The sustained rise in the supply of goods is the *result* of economic growth, by which it is identified."[5] That process of sustainable increases in per capita income, characterized by continuous technological innovation, industrial upgrading, and institutional adjustment, is a modern phenomenon.

Before the eighteenth century, most countries were in the development stage of a relatively backward agrarian economy—disturbed from time to time by war and natural calamities and afflicted by the Malthusian trap (the idea that, because population growth is ahead of agricultural growth, there must be a stage when the food supply cannot feed the population). Except for the ruling classes, craftsmen, and merchants—a minority of the population—most people worked in subsistence agriculture, animal husbandry, or fishery. Given the technologies and industries at the time, the allocation of resources, developed through generations of practice in such economies, was close to optimal. So the gains from improving the allocation of resources were small.[6] Further economic development was feasible only with some technological innovations, as an exogenous shock to the system or an improvement from experience.[7] In this premodern era, economic development was mainly in the form of population increase and the aggregate size of the economy. Growth was extensive, but per capita income did not change much.[8] At that time, the income gap between areas that today would be considered developed and those that would be considered developing was fairly small from today's viewpoint—at most 50 percent.[9] Indeed, some of today's developing countries—such as China and part of India—were believed to be richer than Europe at that time.[10] Until the late eighteenth century, the overall performance of markets—in terms of integration—in China and Western Europe was comparable.[11]

After the Industrial Revolution began in England in the mid-eighteenth century, laboratory experiments became the major source of technological invention and innovation.[12] This was especially true in the case of the major inventions, which consisted of radical new ideas and involved large, discrete, novel changes.[13] For developed countries at the global technological frontier, such a transformation of invention enabled them to accelerate their technological advances through investments in research and development, and technological invention and innovation became endogenous.[14] With increas-

ing investments in research and development, technological change accelerated, industrial structures were upgraded continuously, and productivity
increased. As a result, developed countries in the Western Hemisphere began
to take off, and the divergence between the North and the South appeared.[15]

Lant Pritchett documented that phenomenon, which he calls "divergence,
big time," in a seminal article.[16] Looking at the evolution of productivity and
living standards, he estimated that from 1870 to 1990 the ratio of per capita
incomes between the richest and the poorest countries increased by roughly
a factor of five and that the difference in income between the richest country
and all others increased by an order of magnitude. Bradford DeLong (1997)
observed the same pattern when he noted: "We live today in the most
unequal—in terms of the divergence in the life prospects of children born
into different economies—age that the world has ever seen."[17]

The divergence is all the more puzzling in that throughout the past century, developing and middle-income countries have attempted to catch up
with the most advanced economies, with few successes. In the late nineteenth
and early twentieth centuries, many countries in Latin America, Europe, and
Asia (most notably, countries of the former Soviet Bloc and China) launched
ambitious economic catch-up strategies, often based on modern capital-
intensive heavy industries. The emergence of colonies or semicolonies as
newly independent states, first in Asia and the Middle East and later in
Africa, was also accompanied by strong nationalist sentiments and bold
dreams. Compared with developed countries, these developing countries had
an extremely low economic growth rate and per capita gross national products, high birth and death rates, low average educational attainments, and
very backward infrastructure. Heavily specialized in the production and
export of primary commodities, they relied on imports of modern manufactured goods. Thus it was central to every developing government's national
agenda to launch technologically sophisticated industries to reduce reliance
on imports of modern products, achieve a rapid economic take-off, and eliminate poverty. But most of these countries failed to reach their goals.

Sustained acceleration of economic growth was indeed achieved by a few
successful economies, and more recently in a small number of countries

such as Chile, China, India, Mauritius, or Vietnam.[18] But many low-income countries have remained poor, and a large number of middle-income countries could not move closer to the living standards of the United States or Western Europe. As a result, more than a sixth of humanity (the "bottom billion," in Collier's words) has remained trapped in poverty.[19]

A well-known fact, confirmed by the recent crisis, is that countries with sustained high rates of growth before the crisis also performed well after the crisis despite the global meltdown. Their dynamic performance has made them more resilient. With strong external balance sheets and ample fiscal room before the crisis, they were able to implement countercyclical policies to combat external shocks.

In an increasingly global world where fighting poverty is not only a moral responsibility but also a strategy for confronting some major problems (disease, malnutrition, insecurity, and violence) that ignore boundaries and contribute to global insecurity, thinking about new ways of generating and sustaining growth is a crucial task for economists. That makes it essential to continue searching for new ideas on the mechanics of wealth creation.

This chapter briefly surveys the evolution of knowledge on economic growth and development thinking. A quick review of intellectual progress and challenges, it highlights the many changes that have occurred in that long quest—especially during the past 60 years—and the fact that no successful country followed policy prescriptions from constantly changing dominant paradigms. It concludes by stating the need for fresh thinking derived from lessons of history, practice, and economic analysis.

Deciphering the Mystery of Poverty and Wealth

From Qin Shi Huang, the first emperor of Qin Dynasty, and his Great Wall to the pharaohs of Egypt and their pyramids, from Macedonia's King Alexander and the entire cities he built to France's Louis XIV and his shining palaces, world political leaders have often been obsessed with achieving greatness through political victories and infrastructure that would survive them and, perhaps, improve their people's lives. Yet intellectuals and scholars started to think systematically about economic growth strategies only at the end of the eighteenth century.

It took a Scottish moral philosopher with no training in economics to set the course of modern economics and challenge researchers to provide answers to what is arguably the most fundamental question in public policy: what is the recipe for growth, job creation, and poverty reduction? Indeed, since Adam Smith started his inquiry into the secrets of wealth creation in 1776, economists have behaved like detectives in mystery novels, imagining theories, exploring hypotheses, examining facts, tracking evidence, following leads. They have had some successes and many disappointments.

Most progress has been in identifying systematic differences between high-growth and low-growth countries in their initial conditions and policy and institutional variables. But in terms of actionable policy levers, much remains left to conjecture. In fact, more than 200 years after Smith's seminal work, economic growth is still a "mystery" to many and an "elusive quest" to others—to use metaphors offered by Elhanan Helpman and William Easterly.

David Hume, who Walt Rostow claims was "the first modern economist," placed economic analysis at the center of his analysis of the human condition. He also offered economic concepts considered to "form a reasonably coherent and consistent theory of the dynamics of growth." Classical economists who followed in his footsteps—such as Adam Smith, Alfred Marshall, David Ricardo, and Allyn Young—were also obsessed with economic growth. Perhaps because of their fascination with the idea of human progress celebrated during the Enlightenment, they explored the nature and determinants of economic development and how policymakers could foster prosperity. Their pioneering work highlighted factor accumulation, factor substitution, technical change, and specialization, still at the core of modern growth theory.

"Nothing matters more to the long-term economic welfare of a nation than its rate of economic growth," Robert Barro noted in his Lionel Robbins Memorial Lectures, delivered at the London School of Economics in February 1996. "Compounded over many years, seemingly small differences in annual growth rates can lead to vast differences in standards of living."[20] Yet growth analysis slowed after the Great Depression as the intellectual focus shifted from long-run to short-run issues. Economists were conflicted between the dynamics of business cycles and the study of long-term growth—both important for human welfare.

And then something rather strange happened in the 1940s: four researchers working independently came up with the various building blocks of the first analytical framework for understanding why some countries grow faster than others. Following initial work by Roy Harrod and Evsey Domar, Robert Solow and Trevor Swan produced the Solow–Swan model, sparking the first major wave of systematic growth analysis. Their objective was to understand the mechanics of growth, identify its determinants, and develop techniques of growth accounting that would explain the role of economic policy.

Irish comedian Spike Milligan once said, "Money can't buy you happiness, but it does bring you a more pleasant form of misery." His dark humor was perhaps widely shared by the first generation of growth researchers, who highlighted the centrality of capital in their work. Their models featured neoclassical forms of production functions with specifications that relied on constant returns to scale, diminishing returns, and some elasticity of substitution between inputs. To present a general equilibrium model of the economy, they adopted a constant saving-rate rule. This was a crude assumption but a major step forward in tool building because it offered a clear demonstration that general equilibrium theory could be applied convincingly to real-world issues. One important prediction from these models was the idea of conditional convergence, derived from the assumption of diminishing returns to capital—poor economies with less capital per worker (relative to their long-run or steady-state capital per worker) will grow faster.[21]

The major strength of that line of growth research was the explicit introduction of technology—in addition to capital and labor—into the theoretical and empirical analysis. But the limited toolkit available at the time created a major shortcoming to that approach: technology was presented as an exogenously given public good. The major prediction of the model based on the assumption of diminishing returns to capital was the idea that per capita growth will cease in the absence of continuous improvements in technology. Although that assumption allowed the model to maintain its key prediction of conditional convergence, it also seemed odd: technology, the main determinant of long-run growth, was kept outside the model.[22]

Researchers from the so-called Cambridge–England tradition distinguished themselves among early growth theorists. Led by economists such as James Meade, Roy Harrod, Michal Kalecki, Richard Kahn, Nicholas Kaldor, and Joan Robinson, among others, they laid down the foundations of what is known as the monopolistic competition revolution. Contrary to what was conventional wisdom among economists from the 1930s through the 1960s, their work suggested that one central feature of growth analysis should be the recognition that most industries are neither perfectly competitive nor complete monopolies. They also challenged the idea that capital could be measured and aggregated in growth models, which was at the core of the traditional neoclassical view developed at the time by Robert Solow and Paul Samuelson. Although the views from the Cambridge–England group were highly controversial initially and even perceived as leftist or ideologically motivated, their contribution to the evolution of the economics of growth was subsequently acknowledged by mainstream economics.[23]

Despite the burgeoning of that new field of research in the 1940s and 1950s, macroeconomists showed more interest in the study of the business cycles that characterized the postwar period. As they tried to better understand stabilization policies—monetary and fiscal measures to avoid disruptive and costly inflation—they devoted few resources to the analysis of the long-run determinants of growth. Moreover, the mainstream had to face the challenge of evolutionary economics, which was launched in a series of articles published in the 1970s and synthesized by Nelson and Winter (1982). These authors and their followers focused their critique on the basic question of how firms and industries change over time. They raised significant objections to the fundamental neoclassical assumptions of profit maximization and market equilibrium, which they found ineffective in the analysis of technological innovation and the dynamics of competition among firms. To replace these assumptions they suggested that economics borrow from biology the concept of natural selection and construct a more accurate evolutionary theory of business behavior. They acknowledged that films are generally motivated by profit and search for ways of improving profits, but they did not consider these ways profit maximizing. Likewise, they emphasized the tendency for the more profitable firms to drive the less profitable ones out of business. The implications of their new paradigm and analytical framework were far reaching. Not only were they able to develop more coherent and powerful models of competitive firm dynamics under conditions of growth and technological change, but their approach was also perceived to be compatible with findings in psychology and other social sciences. Finally, their work also had important implications for welfare economics and for government policy toward industry. It was therefore natural that it later became another source of inspiration for many other economists who rejected the neoclassical framework.

Within the neoclassical tradition, things changed only in the 1980s, when a new group of prominent researchers decided to return their attention to differences in economic performance among countries. Their motivation was probably the availability of new cross-country data that revealed major differences in country performances and allowed for comparative empirical analysis. New work from economic historians such as Angus Maddison also raised awareness of the importance of growth. The numbers were puzzling and have remained so. Surveys of economic growth and levels of performance in different parts of the world economy show that growth has indeed been uneven across countries and regions. Between 1900 and 2001, per capita GDP in Western Europe increased by a factor of 6.65 (6.7 in Western offshoots), above 5.2 in Latin America, 4.2 in Eastern Europe, and only 2.5 in Africa.[24] The number of people living in high-growth environments or in countries with per capita incomes equal to those of Organisation for Economic Co-operation and Development (OECD) countries has increased in the past 30 years by a factor of four, from 1 billion to about 4 billion.[25]

A new wave of growth analysts and modelers had to come up with a convincing theory of technological change—one that frees the neoclassical model from the exogeneity of the main determinant of long-term growth. A first step was to design a theory of continuous growth fueled by non-diminishing returns to investment in a broad class of physical and human capital. The process could go on indefinitely if returns do not diminish as economies grow.[26] A second and more effective approach was to move away from the straightjacket of perfect competition and incorporate imperfect competition and research and development (R&D) theories in growth modeling. Such bold methodological moves helped explain why the economy would not run out of new ideas and why per capita income growth could be kept positive in the long run.[27]

Endogenous growth theory, as it came to be known, maintained the assumption of nonrivalry because technology is indeed a very different type of factor than capital and labor—because it can be used indefinitely by others at zero marginal cost.[28] But it was important to take the next logical step and to better understand the public good characterization of technology and think of it as a partially excludable nonrival good. The new wave therefore reclassified technology not just as a public good but as a good that is subject to a certain level of private control. By making it a partially excludable nonrival good and therefore giving it some degree of excludability or appropriability, it was possible to ensure that incentives for its production and use matter. The necessary move away from perfect competition has yielded large methodological payoffs. Although neoclassical models of growth took technology and factor accumulation as exogenous, endogenous growth models can explain why technology grows over time through new ideas, providing the microeconomic underpinnings for models of the technological frontier.

Another puzzling question for economists has been how technological diffusion takes place in some countries to generate or sustain growth—and why it does not take root in others. Chile, Japan, and Singapore successfully adopted technologies available from more advanced countries to launch their industrial upgrading, while the Democratic Republic of Congo, Jamaica, and Nepal have had difficulties doing the same. Beyond differences in initial endowments and historical and sociopolitical itineraries, what has prevented the latter from performing as well as the former?

Various interesting possibilities have recently been explored in an attempt to answer that critical question. One option has been to add an avenue for technology transfer as a new component to the endogenous growth model— that is, "endogenizing" the mechanism by which different countries use various intermediate capital goods.[29] Another popular route has been to try to identify the fundamental determinants of growth through political-economy models. Contrary to previous waves of growth modeling, this line of research focuses not on the proximate determinants of growth but on the impact on growth of such factors as institutions and the quality of governance.[30] Several other approaches are being explored in the economic literature but so far have yielded few insights that can explain the mystery of economic growth across countries and time.[31]

Robert Lucas and the Drycleaner's Daughter

What happened? How can one explain "the mystery of economic growth"? Why did some countries do so well and others so poorly?

"The most beautiful thing we can experience is the mysterious," said Albert Einstein. Many economists must have thought the same way, since an increasingly large number of them have devoted their efforts to solving the puzzle of economic growth. My former University of Chicago professor Robert Lucas, whose research revolutionized the study of business cycles and landed him the Nobel Prize in economics, wondered: "How can an economist not be interested in the wealth of nations?"[32] Looking at diverging trends in GDP per capita among countries, he also observed: "I do not see how one can look at figures like these without seeing them as representing *possibilities*. Is there some action a government of India could take that would lead the Indian economy to grow like Egypt's or Indonesia's? If so, *what,* exactly? If not, what is it about the "nature of India" that makes it so? The consequences for human welfare involved in questions like these are simply staggering: Once one starts to think about them, it is hard to think about anything else."[33]

Following Theodore Schultz and Gary Becker—two of my mentors at Chicago—and others, Lucas believes that the successful transformation from an economy of traditional agriculture to a modern, growing economy depends crucially on an increase in the rate of accumulation of human capital. He has tried to show how that idea, embodied in aggregative models of economic growth, produces behavior that conforms "better to the facts of economic development than the behavior predicted by models centered on other visions of the engine of growth."[34]

Acknowledging that "the sources and perhaps even the character of this increase in human capital growth remain somewhat ill understood, a *deus ex machina,* an invisible cause to which important visible effects are attributed," Lucas has developed a general theory of how growth could be sustained and why growth rates might differ in different countries.[35] The framework in his work is a model with the accumulation of both physical and human capital, with emphasis on the external benefits of human capital through the diffusion of new knowledge or on-the-job learning, often stimulated by trade.[36] He makes his case that for a lesser developed country to transform to a modern, growing economy, it must experience an increase in the rate of the accumulation of human capital. Societies and their citizens must be open to the "new possibilities that development creates."[37]

Lucas stresses the preeminence of accumulating human capital through interesting real-life anecdotes. For instance, he tells the story of his dry-cleaner's daughter in his neighborhood in Chicago. When he takes his shirts to the laundry, operated by a Korean woman, recently arrived, "whose English is barely adequate to enable her to conduct her business," he observes that her 3-year-old daughter is seated on the counter and being drilled in arithmetic—which she is very good at and clearly enjoys enormously. He conjectures that 15 years in the future that girl will be pursuing her studies at the University of Chicago or the California Institute of Technology, alongside the children of professors and Mayflower descendants!

While I fully agree with the importance of human capital accumulation in sustaining growth, I also believe that what truly distinguishes modern economic growth from premodern growth is the way that innovation is integrated into business practices and development and the speed at which this is happening. Beginning in the eighteenth century, some economies were able to move from experience-based *exogenous* innovation to science- and experiment-based *endogenous* innovation. Such change accelerated technological innovation, structural transformation, and income growth.[38]

That observation has different implications for different groups of countries: to benefit from the new mechanism of technological innovation, an advanced country needs to invest in research, invent new technology and products, and invest in human capital. The increase in human capital enhances the capacity of its scientists to carry out R&D—and allows its labor force to integrate new technology into production processes.

To fully exploit the potential unleashed by new technology and industries, a developed country must also improve its institutions constantly and thereby provide adequate funding and incentives for new inventions and infrastructure in order to reduce transaction costs and maintain its productive capacity on the production-possibility frontier. Why is this so? Because industrialized high-income economies tend to have comparative advantage in capital-intensive industries with economies of scale in production. The various types of "hard" infrastructure (power supplies, telecommunications networks, roads and port facilities, and so on) and "soft" infrastructure (regulatory and legal frameworks, cultural value systems, and so on) they need must comply with the evolving necessities of national and global markets, where business transactions are long in distance and large in value.

As these countries keep moving up the industrial ladder in the process of industrial and technological development, they also increase their scale of production—because of the indivisibility of capital equipment. Their firms become larger and often need larger markets, which in turn necessitate corresponding changes in power, transportation, and other forms of infrastructure. As firms reach the global technology frontier, they increasingly need to invent new technologies and products by themselves, so they face the greater risk arising from the uncertainty of technological breakthroughs and the acceptance of markets for their new products. With changes in the sizes of firms, the scope of the market, and the nature of risk along the way to the upgrading of the industrial structure, the requirements for infrastructure services, both hard and soft, also change. If the country's infrastructure is not improved simultaneously, the upgrading in various industries will be inefficient or stalled.[39]

Things are quite different—and frankly easier—for developing countries, which have the advantage of backwardness to innovate in their choices of technology, industries, and institutions. They can simply imitate or license existing technology, industries, and institutions from high-income industrial countries. If developing countries' leaders can figure out an effective way of working with the private sector to create a policy framework that allows private agents to tap into that potential and catch up with advanced economies, their economies will enjoy much faster rates of innovation and growth than do those of more advanced ones.

Explaining Convergence and Divergence

On both the theoretical and the empirical fronts, there has been some progress in our understanding of growth in recent decades. On the theoretical front, the analysis of endogenous technical innovation and increasing returns to scale has provided economists with a rich general framework for capturing the broad picture and the mechanics of economic growth in high-income industrial countries and for explaining why their economic growth rates have consistently been higher than their population growth rates. From Solow's work we know the importance of capital accumulation (both physical and human) and technical change in the growth process. From contributions by Becker, Heckman, Lucas, Schultz, and many others we have also learned about the importance of human capital through the diffusion of new knowledge or on-the-job learning, often stimulated by trade, and the college wage premium.[40] From work by North (1981), with supporting theoretical and empirical analyses exemplified by the works of Greif (1993), Acemoglu,

Johnson, and Robinson (2001), and Glaeser and Shleifer (2002), we have learned that growth is largely driven by innovation and institutions that have evolved in countries where innovative activity is promoted and conditions are in place for change. From Romer, Lucas, and the endogenous growth theorists we have understood the need to apply growth theory on accumulation to knowledge creation and innovation. In sum, we know quite a lot about some of the basic ingredients of growth, especially in advanced countries.

On the empirical front, the availability of standardized data sets—especially the Penn World tables—has stimulated interest in cross-country work that highlights systematic differences between high-growth and low-growth countries in:

- Initial conditions such as productivity, human capital, demographic structure, infrastructure, financial development, or inequality.

- Policy variables of various sorts, such as trade openness, macroeconomic stability, levels and composition of public spending, taxation, and regulation.

- Institutional variables such as general governance indicators, administrative capacity, rule of law, protection of property rights, and corruption.

Various studies based on cross-country regressions have confirmed the idea of conditional convergence: that is, a low initial level of income is generally associated with a high subsequent growth rate when other determinants of growth are held constant. And the share of output allocated to investment and various measures of human capital, such as enrollment rates in primary and secondary schools, is often positively associated with growth. By contrast, population growth (or fertility) and political instability (as measured by the frequency of revolutions, coups, or wars) are negatively associated with growth in income per person. And countries with more distorted markets, measured by the black market premium on foreign exchange or other impediments to trade, tend to have lower growth rates, while those with better-developed financial markets—measured, say, by the size of liquid assets relative to income—tend to have higher growth rates.[41]

But perhaps because "doubt grows with knowledge," as Johann Wolfgang von Goethe once noted, growth research still faces significant methodological difficulties and challenges in identifying actionable policy levers to accelerate and sustain growth in specific countries. Deaton (2009) expresses the general sentiment of despair among economists when he notes that "empiricists and theorists seem further apart now than at any period in the last quarter century. Yet reintegration is hardly an option because without it there is no chance of long-term scientific progress."[42] Many decades of theoretical advances and the development of new techniques have yielded elegant and often abstract models but no concrete methodology for policy-makers to use to stimulate growth.

Moreover, contrary to the predictions of most neoclassical models, convergence among world economies has been limited. In 2008, in the United States (the largest and one of the world's richest countries), GDP per capita, measured in purchasing power parity, was 3 times higher than in neighboring Mexico, 16 times higher than in India, and 145 times higher than in the Democratic Republic of Congo. That gap is still widening. For most of the past century, incomes in developing countries have fallen far behind those in developed countries, both proportionately and absolutely.[43] Yet empirical observation reveals that divergence between industrial and developing countries is not inexorable: in the past two centuries, some countries have been able to catch up with the most advanced economies (in the late nineteenth century, France, Germany, and the United States; in the twentieth century, the Nordic countries and the 13 economies, including Japan, analyzed in the Growth Commission Report).

Japan achieved the most impressive growth record of the past century. According to Maddison, its per capita GDP in 1900 was barely 29 percent that of the United States (measured in 1990 Geary–Khamis dollars). In 2008 it was 73 percent. Other countries made progress in the direction of catching up with the United States. Sweden improved its GDP per capita relative to the United States from 54 percent to 78 percent. France's GDP per capita remained above 70 percent that of the United States. By contrast, the countries of the former Soviet Union recorded a decline in their GDP per capita relative to the United States from 30 to 25 percent.[44]

Historical evidence suggests that the growth process in successful economies followed a similar pattern: front-runners such as England or the United States devoted ingenuity to the production of innovative new products, industries, and ways of doing business, allowing them to make productivity gains and grow at a rapid pace. Latecomers such as France, Germany, and Japan could simply imitate the successful countries, like flying geese, and catch up. That is why the West took 300 years to innovate and industrialize but Japan less than 100 years and East Asia (most notably Hong Kong SAR, China; Taiwan, China; Korea; and Singapore, which converged to the income levels of advanced Western countries in the second half of the twentieth century) only 40 years. More recently, a new group formed by Brazil, Russia, India, and mainland China (the BRICs) also took off. The story of almost any other successful economy—from Chile to Mauritius—can be understood through that same pattern.

Yet except for that select group, most developing countries have failed to achieve their economic growth ambitions since World War II. In fact, many have encountered frequent crises despite efforts by their governments and assistance from international development agencies. These pervasive experiences of failure highlight the need to understand how developing countries can create the conditions necessary to facilitate the flow of technologies and unleash growth, even with suboptimal macroeconomic policies, weak institutions, and the absence of full-fledged private property rights.

The inability of growth research to predict divergence on a large scale ("big time," to use Pritchett's words) indicates that the proposed theories did not capture the fundamental factors that determine whether a developing country will converge. Some researchers have recently argued that the evolution of the economic performance of nations is determined by conditional convergence—the idea that countries converge when all other macroeconomic variables that proxy for differences in steady-state characteristics are held constant. Or, to put it differently, the distribution of world income reveals the existence of convergence clubs among countries.[45]

The puzzle of diverging performances may be more easily sorted out through comparative analysis based on in-depth country studies and historical experience. The key reasons for convergence of successful economies seem to lie in their ability to change their human as well as physical capital endowments, increase the pace of adoption of new ideas, speed the process of industrial upgrading, and improve soft infrastructure (such as institutions) and hard infrastructure (such as transportation and telecommunications networks). But intellectual progress has been even slower in the domain of development economics. Understanding and replicating the economic strategies and policies that allowed latecomers to catch up with the most advanced economies is still a major challenge for economists and policymakers around the world.

Development Thinking:
A Tale of Progress, Waves, Fads, and Fashion

Swiss linguist Ferdinand de Saussure, who developed a branch of linguistics called structural linguistics in the late nineteenth and early twentieth centuries before dying in 1913, would probably have been amazed to see the wide range of meanings that were subsequently associated with the word *structuralism* in all the social sciences and the humanities. His goal was to elaborate a mode of thinking and a method of analysis that focus on examining the relations and functions of the smallest constituent elements of large systems such as human languages and cultural practices. Specifically, Saussure's linguistic inquiry was centered not on speech itself but on the underlying rules and conventions enabling language to operate. He often said he was mainly "concerned with deep structures" rather than surface phenomena and interested in the infrastructure of language that is common to all speakers and that functions on an unconscious level. He was quite successful in his endeavor, leaving behind an intellectual legacy that laid the foundations for many developments in his field.

Following in Saussure's footsteps, researchers in other fields expanded the structuralist tradition. French anthropologist Claude Levi-Strauss (1963) specified four criteria for structural analysis: first, it examines unconscious infrastructures of cultural phenomena; second, it regards the elements of infrastructures as "relational," not as independent entities; third, it explores entire systems, not single elements; and fourth, it offers general laws to explain the underlying organizing patterns of phenomena.

Structuralism emerged in economics with the publication of a very influential 1943 article by Austrian economist Paul Rosenstein-Rodan.[46] His concerns at the time were not the difficulties facing poor countries such as Brazil, China, and Nigeria but "problems of industrialisation of Eastern and South-Eastern Europe"—the title of his work. His article suggested that the virtuous circle of development depended essentially on the interaction between economies of scale at the level of individual firms and the size of the market. Specifically, it assumed that modern methods of production can be more productive than traditional ones only if the market is large enough for their productivity edge to compensate for the necessity of paying higher wages. But the size of the market depends on the extent to which these modern techniques are adopted. Therefore, if the modernization process can be started on a very large scale, the process of economic development will be self-reinforcing and self-sustaining. If not, countries will be indefinitely trapped in poverty. The article ignited a flurry of similar ideas, which came to be known as the structuralist approach to economic development.

In the 1940s and 1950s, various works with similar theoretical foundations were published by a diverse group of researchers who argued forcefully and convincingly that the very nature of the problems facing small, low-income countries were fundamentally different from those of the larger, industrialized countries. In doing so, they sought to locate economics in the broader intellectual ethics of structuralism and rejected minimalist and reductionist approaches to social theory. Focusing on the constraints that shape human choice rather than the choice itself, they identified three interlinked structural features that slowed down industrialization in the Third World: the impossibility for developing countries to compete on the world stage with advanced economies, despite the large wage differentials; the propensity of rich countries to erect trade barriers to protect their markets and limit the exports of low-income countries; and the dependency of output in developing countries on imported capital equipment.

Just as American poet Wallace Stevens suggested that there are at least "thirteen ways of looking at a blackbird," it can be said that there are many ways of approaching early structuralism in the economic discipline. Some critics have suggested that Stevens's poem was structured not primarily to present a peculiar and unique literary aesthetics but to question the reader's way of thinking on various themes. By using the signifier *blackbird,* repeated in each of the thirteen stanzas, the poet forces and guides us through a process of self-questioning. Similarly, economic structuralism was meant to bring about enlightenment not necessarily by enunciating a finite theory of how poor countries should be understood but to challenge orthodox thinking about them. In fact, no comprehensive survey could do justice to the often quite different brands of economic thoughts that subsequently became lumped together under the label "structuralism." Therefore, the few paragraphs below only give the reader a taste of the most representative works and draw common themes from that approach.

Economic structuralism eventually became a broad theme of analysis for several generations of researchers and thinkers of often different ideological inclinations. Their attempt to study systematically the entire range of problems of developing countries started in the particular historical and intellectual context of the post–World War II era. Their work was done against the background of the rise of Keynesian interventionism in economics, the experience of state planning in the Soviet Union (which seemed to yield remarkable results at the time), the political independence of many formerly colonized countries and territories, and the desire of new nationalist governments to prove their capabilities by modernizing their new nations.

The intellectual tradition ignited by Rosenstein-Rodan's work evolved into three overlapping phases.[47] Despite their differences, these first-generation structuralists (also referred to as "old structuralists" in this book) argued that modern, advanced industries were unable to develop spontaneously in a developing country precisely because of structural rigidities and the coordination problems in their markets. This market-failure thesis became the core of "development economics," which emerged after World War II.[48] It held that the market encompassed insurmountable defects and that the state was a powerful supplementary means to accelerate the pace of economic development. Many development economists then advocated that the state overcome market failures by playing a leading role in the industrialization push, directly allocating the resources for investment, and setting up public enterprises in the large modern industries to control the "commanding heights."

The first phase of economic structuralism, from 1945 to the mid-1950s, highlighted the fact that poor economies were characterized by low savings, low investment rates, and high population growth rates, all primarily caused by market failures due to scale economies and external effects.[49] Other leaders of that first group of thinkers stressed the dual-economy nature of these countries—that is, the existence of a large subsistence agriculture sector with virtually unlimited labor supply, together with a much smaller modern industrial sector.[50]

A second wave extended from roughly the mid-1950s to the late 1960s and was dominated by contributions from Myrdal (1957), Hirschman (1958), Chenery and Bruno (1962), and Furtado (1964). In addition to earlier themes, the second wave of thinkers highlighted the structural differences between rich and poor countries. They pointed to the many supply constraints in particular sectors, such as the agricultural sector, which they saw as the hostage of a rigid import ratio. Lifting these constraints required importing more modern equipment and machinery from rich countries— and that was beyond the means of poor countries with low levels of domestic savings and foreign exchange.

Moreover, that second group of early structuralists believed that trade could not be relied on as an engine of growth because any attempt to increase exports would be met with inelastic world demand for commodities and hence worsening terms of trade. The slump of international trade in the Great Depression seemed to validate such export pessimism. In Latin America, political leaders and social elites were influenced strongly by the deterioration in the terms of trade, the economic difficulty encountered during the Great Depression in the 1930s, and the thesis developed independently by two economists, German Hans Singer (1950) and Argentine Raul Prebisch (1959). Singer and Prebisch believed that the decline in the terms of trade against the export of primary commodities was secular and resulted in the transfer of income from resource-intensive developing countries to capital-intensive developed countries. They argued that the way for a developing country to avoid being exploited by developed countries was to develop domestic manufacturing industries through a process known as import substitution.

Although there was broad agreement on the diagnostics in the first two generations of these old structuralist economists, there was divergence over what specific policies to implement to break out of the trap and start the virtuous cycle. Rosenstein-Rodan seemed to indicate that a "big push" (a large and coordinated government investment program) was the solution. Estonian-born economist Ragnar Nurkse also saw the main obstacles to development in the narrow market and suggested that only new investments realized simultaneously could create the needed demand. In his "balanced growth" theory, he identified the shortage of capital as the binding constraint to development, understood as an expansion of the market and an increase in production.

Others, such as Hirschman, thought that the problem was not the shortage of capital but the lack of entrepreneurial abilities, itself a reflection of institutional factors. They suggested an "unbalanced growth approach" in which investments would not be spread evenly in poor economies but would be concentrated in selected projects in key economic sectors with strong backward and forward linkages.[51] In sum, many developing-country governments regarded economic growth as their direct and prime responsibility.

In many cases, the results were disappointing. Instead of converging to the developed countries' incomes, those in developing countries stagnated or even deteriorated, and those countries' income gap with developed countries widened. In many developing countries, well-intended government interventions failed. This was the case across African, Latin American, and South Asian countries in the 1960s and 1970s, when import substitution and protection were essential features of the development strategy.

As government-led economic development strategies based on the old structuralist teachings failed in many countries, the free-market approach appeared to triumph and to influence development thinking. That trend was reinforced by a new revolution in macroeconomics: the prevailing Keynesian macroeconomics was challenged by the stagflation in the 1970s, the Latin American debt crisis, and the collapse of the socialist planning system in the 1980s. The rational expectations revolution emerged and refuted the theoretical foundation for the state's role in using fiscal policy and monetary policy for economic development.

Things became even worse for Latin American economies that followed the old structuralist paradigm when they faced a major debt crisis in 1982. That happened when international financial markets realized that the collapse of the Bretton Woods system had put some countries with unlimited access to foreign capital in situations in which they could not pay back their loans. The crisis was precipitated by interrelated exogenous shocks that toppled Mexico and several other Latin American economies, already overburdened with a substantial percentage of the world's outstanding debt. It prompted multilateral lending institutions and bilateral lenders—especially the United States—to call for a comprehensive set of reforms of Latin American economies and to advocate a set of free-market policies that followed the canons of the neoclassical paradigm. A new wave of development thinking was born, known later as the Washington Consensus.

Proponents of the old structuralism at the time must have felt like nineteenth-century American engineer Alfred Holt, who said at a meeting of an engineering society, "It is found that anything that can go wrong at sea generally does go wrong sooner or later"—which sounds like an earlier version of the famous Murphy's Law. The last nail in the coffin of old structuralist theories of economic development was the collapse of socialist economies in the latter half of the 1980s, which led Francis Fukuyama to proclaim "the end of history." That momentous event seemed to mark the complete victory of free-market economics over defenders of state interventions and centrally planned economic systems. Most mainstream economists concluded that almost any government intervention in the economy was bound to fail because of the inevitable distortion of the allocation of resources, supplies, and prices and the absence of a viable incentive system for economic agents.

In the early 1980s, structuralists made a new attempt to respond to criticism from neoclassical economists and to modify and adjust development economics to the actual experience of poor countries.[52] It drew inspiration both from growth theorists of the Cambridge–England tradition and from evolutionary economics and attempted to reconcile some of the initial findings of structuralism with advances in rigorous economic analysis. It has evolved in recent years to include important contributions—most notably by Ocampo and Taylor (1998), Dutt and Ross (2003), and Ocampo, Rada, and Taylor (2009). Taylor's particular brand of "neostructuralism," dubbed "late structuralism" by Gibson (2003), generated quite a bit of attention. But it could not really compete with the *new* neoclassical views that dominated policy circles at the time, fueled the sense of triumph of the free-market approach, and centered development thinking on the Washington Consensus policies.

These dominating views were presented by John Williamson, the economist who coined the term *Washington Consensus* as "a summary of what most people in Washington believed Latin America (not all countries) ought to be undertaking as of 1989 (not at all times)." The new consensus quickly came to be perceived as

a set of neoliberal policies that have been imposed on hapless countries by the Washington-based international financial institutions and have led them to crisis and misery. . . . The three big ideas here are macroeconomic discipline, a market economy, and openness to the world (at least in respect of trade and foreign direct investment). These are ideas that had long been regarded as orthodox so far as OECD countries are concerned, but there used to be a sort of global apartheid which claimed that developing countries came from a different universe which enabled them to benefit from (a) inflation (so as to reap the inflation tax and boost investment); (b) a leading role for the state in initiating industrialization; and (c) import substitution. The Washington Consensus said that this era of apartheid was over.[53]

Did the Washington Consensus represent a strong wave of truly new ideas, or was it just another fad in development thinking? One thing is sure: in terms of growth, employment generation, and economic stability, its results were disappointing, and some economists referred to the 1980s and 1990s as "lost decades" for developing countries.[54] Not surprisingly, the ideas of the Washington Consensus quickly became highly controversial, too.[55] Some even observed that there had been no consensus in the first place and that economists in Washington had always held different views of economic policy. Antiglobalization critics argued that high-income countries and multilateral organizations should not be setting a neoliberal economic agenda for the world.

Even among mainstream economists, the new policy agenda had its discontents. Commenting on the economic and social cost of the structural adjustment programs that underpinned the Washington Consensus, Joseph Stiglitz observed that serious mistakes had been made in their design: "Today, in many people's minds there is recognition that there will be social consequences if social safety nets are not provided and the social consequences will overwhelm the short-run economic consequences. Indonesia [for instance] was more hurt from the riots that resulted from cutting off those subsidies than it would have possibly been helped by a slight improvement in budgetary position."[56] Dani Rodrik noted: "The one thing that is generally agreed on about the consequences of these reforms is that things have not quite worked out the way they were intended. Even their most ardent supporters now concede that growth has been below expectations in Latin America. . . . Not only were success stories in Sub-Saharan Africa few and far in between, but the market-oriented reforms of the 1990s proved ill-suited to deal with the growing public health emergency in which the continent was embroiled."[57]

Many critics interpreted the Washington Consensus to represent neo-liberal policies such as capital account liberalization (which Williamson says he quite consciously excluded from his list), monetarism, supply-side economics, or a minimal state (getting the state out of welfare provision and income redistribution). But the main reason for its failure to deliver on its promises was that it really advocated a set of idealized market institutions, some of which may even be missing from advanced market economies. It was not an effective economic strategy for most developing countries, which typically are trapped in multiple levels of distortions and need to gradually organize their transition out of these second-, third-, or nth-best situations. The Washington Consensus framework also ignored the requirement that developing countries' governments play a key role in overcoming the issues of coordination and externality in the process of technological innovation, industrial upgrading, and structural change.[58]

Another related but different strand of thought in development thinking was the new institutional economics, which built on work by Ronald Coase and Douglass North.[59] It emphasized the importance of property rights, good governance, enabling business environments, and other institutions, all seen as the foundations for a well-functioning market economy. The basic foundation of the theory was the recognition that transactions are never costless—and that various alternatives, all of which are flawed, must be considered in policy design and implementation. It was an attempt to explain the formation and evolution of social institutions using the language and tools of economics.

Coase and North identified four levels of institutions. Level 1 consists of embedded informal institutions such as traditions, customs, values, and religion. At level 2, formal rules are created—the strongest one of which in the judicial order is a country's constitution. Level 3 is the level of governance or implementation of the formal rules, often made necessary by the failures of level-2 institutions to operate as planned; it is also the level at which agents interact formally with each other and contracts are signed, making good governance in contracts essential in its key role: to "craft order, thereby to mitigate conflict and realize mutual gains."[60] And finally, level 4 is the level of the market, where transactions actually occur and prices adjust.

The new institutional economics provided good insights on the genesis and importance of transaction costs and the need to design rules that ensure business incentives. But it also prescribed sustained (and generally slow) investments in the "soft" infrastructure that allows markets to work properly. Its main weakness was its very broad approach to economic development, which resulted in rigid recommendations for policy: its proposals were generally so basic and diffuse that they could overwhelm developing countries' governments, which are often short on resources, capacity, and time.

In a landmark report on the lessons of the 1990s, the World Bank highlighted the complexity of economic growth and recognized that it is not amenable to simple formulas. It noted that the reforms in many developing countries in the 1990s focused too narrowly on the efficient use of resources, not on the expansion of capacity and growth. Although these reforms enabled better use of existing capacity, establishing the basis for sustained long-run growth, they did not provide sufficient incentives for expanding that capacity.[61] This led to the conclusion that "there is no unique universal set of rules. . . . [We] need to get away from formulae and the search for elusive 'best practices.'"[62]

The Frustrating Search for New Answers

"Let's go. Yes, let's go. (They do not move)." Samuel Beckett, in his celebrated play *Waiting for Godot,* depicts the meaninglessness of life in a repetitive plot in which nothing much ever happens. Vladimir, the main character, who has a stronger sense of moral judgment than the others, is also bestowed with an acute sense of indecisiveness. Constantly suffering from guilt, he ponders on his own shortcomings. "Was I sleeping, while the others suffered?" he wonders. Thinking that he has done little or perhaps nothing to improve the miseries of others, he feels the stigma of shame and disgrace. He fears that "tomorrow," when he "wakes up," he will have nothing useful to recollect from his today. "Where do you go from here?" he asks others.

Many economists have felt the same after so many years of research. The disappointments of development thinking in general and growth research in particular—most notably from the perspective of policymakers seeking specific action plans to generate prosperity—have led to a reassessment of the validity and usefulness of existing knowledge and to a search for radically new approaches. The new consensus seems to have less faith in simple formulas and the search for "best practices" but greater reliance on deeper economic analysis to identify each country's one or two most binding constraints on growth.

That line of research is exemplified by the Growth Diagnostics framework proposed by Ricardo Hausmann, Dani Rodrik, and Andrés Velasco. It aims to identify the one or two most binding constraints on any developing economy and then focus on lifting them. The main rationale is to ensure that economic reforms are contingent on the economic environment: "Presented with a laundry list of needed reforms, policymakers have either tried to fix all of the problems at once or started with reforms that were not crucial to their country's growth potential. And, more often than not, reforms have gotten in each other's way, with reform in one area creating unanticipated distortions in another area. By focusing on the one area that represents the biggest hurdle to growth, countries will be more likely to achieve success from their reform efforts."[63]

The proposed approach offers a decision-tree methodology to help identify the relevant binding constraints for each country. Although it does not specifically identify the political costs and benefits of various reform strategies, its focus on alternative hypotheses can help clarify the options available to policymakers for responding to political constraints. "We are concerned mainly with *short-run* constraints," the authors write. "In this sense, our focus is on igniting growth and identifying constraints that inevitably emerge as an economy expands, not on anticipating *tomorrow's* constraints on growth."[64]

A key lesson from that approach is the notion that different countries (or even the same country at different points in time) require different policy choices to facilitate growth; that the "big principles" that growth requires—sound money, property rights, openness, free markets—can take many forms; and that achieving them requires a country-specific context and information. In particular, these principles need not take any one precise institutional or policy form. Each country is assumed to have some binding constraints to its growth potential, and failure to identify and remove them would impede economic performance even if all other production factors were satisfactory. The Growth Diagnostics approach is certainly an important advance in growth analysis. But its model does not fully flesh out the notion of "binding constraint."[65] The variable definitions are deliberately left quite imprecise, making it challenging to operationalize them.

Another influential new approach is that of Poverty Lab researchers at the Massachusetts Institute of Technology, who suggest that the quest for growth be recentered on assessing the impact of a development project or program (against explicit counterfactual outcomes). Starting with the idea that credible impact evaluations are needed to ensure that the most effective programs are scaled up at the national or international levels, they design randomized control trials (RCTs) or social experiments in which some units are randomly assigned an intervention while the rest form the control group and then compare the average outcomes of the two. Proponents of that method see it as the only incontestable way of identifying impact, because it appears to avoid assumptions based on economic theory or other sources. They assert that it can be used to leverage the benefits of knowing which programs work and which do not.

Yet the RCT approach also is fraught with methodological issues that make it unsuitable for generalizing about development strategies and policies. Although RCTs can be useful for understanding the effectiveness of some specific micro projects, they often do not start from a clear strategic assessment of how a particular method would fit the knowledge gaps of highest priority. Moreover, as Martin Ravallion, a renowned poverty expert and my colleague at the World Bank, has pointed out, randomization is feasible only for a nonrandom subset of the interventions and settings relevant to development. For example, it is rarely feasible to randomize the location of infrastructure projects and related programs, which are core activities in any poor country's development strategy. As Ravallion writes, "The very idea of randomized assignment is antithetical to most development programs, which typically aim to reach certain types of people or places."[66] Even assuming that RCTs can actually transfer lessons from localized development experiences to different geographic or cultural areas, they still fall short in providing useful overall guidance to policymakers who have to design development strategies.

The Need for New Strategic Thinking

Looking back at the difficulties of growth research and development economics thinking since Adam Smith and David Hume, I can make three perplexing observations. First, all these various approaches to growth research have shed light on interesting questions, but they hardly explain the failure and success of different countries in the process of industrial upgrading and structural change. This is evidenced by the fact that differences in output per worker and national income across countries are still puzzling to economists and policymakers. It is well known that sustainable economic development entails structural transformation from resource-based to industrial economies and then to a postindustrial stage. Yet few developing countries have completed this transformation since World War II.

On the one hand, many developing countries still depend on agriculture and primary product exports or have failed to diversify their manufacturing base beyond a narrow range of traditional goods. Economic analysis has so far not explained systematically why some countries have been able to move from a low-income agrarian economy to a middle-income and even high-income industrial status while most others remain seemingly trapped in dire poverty or stuck at the middle-income stage. It appears that countries' experience with import substitution led to overburdened budgets, rent seeking, and low productivity growth in protected sectors. Yet import substitution seems to be a necessary step for every new industry that a low-income, agrarian economy wants to move on its way to becoming competitive in international markets. Because of innate coordination and externality problems in the development of new industries, just leveling the playing field for private firms and improving the investment climate are clearly not enough to ignite sustained dynamic growth. The big questions addressed by Adam

Smith and others remain (largely unanswered) on the agenda today: How can a country accelerate its growth and wealth creation to move from a low-income agrarian economy to an industrializing middle-income economy and proceed to a postindustrializing high-income economy? What are the respective roles of the public and private sectors in this transformation?

On the other hand, middle- and high-income countries that have converted their economies from agriculture to manufacturing and services and raised their per capita income substantially still face daunting issues of continuous industrial and technological upgrading. Some of them have fallen into the middle-income trap of low growth, and others are struggling with high unemployment and economic insecurity.

Our second observation is that development policy has constantly evolved in parallel with development thinking. In fact, the policy recommendations of the international development institutions have closely followed changes in the dominant development paradigm and at times have been the main proponents of such changes. Starting in the 1950s, when the global political environment was dominated by Europe's reconstruction, the World Bank focused on rebuilding infrastructure. In the 1960s and 1970s, when the emergence of independent nations and the Cold War dominated the agenda, the headline motto shifted to developing heavy industries and infrastructure, with investment operations the main business lines.

The emergence in the 1980s of major macroeconomic imbalances in some emerging countries and the Latin American debt crisis led to the adoption of the Washington Consensus. Structural adjustment programs became the main vehicle for interaction between the World Bank and its low-income clients. With the fall of the Berlin Wall and the search for a new consensus on public policies, the World Bank shifted to a holistic approach to development. It adopted comprehensive development frameworks focusing on social development and poverty reduction in all client countries. It also sought to involve more partners (parliamentarians, civil-society organizations, and private-sector leaders) in its dialogue with government officials. In recent years, with globalization concerns dominating the world agenda, World Bank policies have focused on achieving the Millennium Development Goals, improving governance, and ensuring results on the ground through rigorous impact evaluation.

Our third observation is that the countries moving up the industrial and technological ladders have rarely followed the policy prescriptions of the dominant development paradigm of the time. Most successful developing countries, including many of the 13 identified in the 2008 Growth Commission Report, have expanded their manufacturing bases and moved into more sophisticated industrial products—by defying conventional wisdom. In their development process, they pursued an export-promotion strategy instead of an import substitution strategy as advocated by the old structuralist doctrine. And they each had a proactive government helping the private sector enter new industries instead of relying on market competition alone as advocated by the Washington Consensus. Their people's health and education improved greatly without their governments' carrying out the RCTs or social experiments on health and education programs first. This success raises a serious question about the pertinence and relevance of the generic policy advice given by economists.

Despite undeniable intellectual progress, some key questions on the growth and development agenda today remain the same as those confronting previous generations of researchers: If growth is driven largely by innovation, why are some countries successful at innovating and adapting to change, while others are not? What forces drive convergence, and what factors stifle material progress? What are the conditions for the kinds of structural change that allow low-income countries to become middle-income and then high-income economies? What are the most important determinants (initial conditions, institutions, policies) of growth? What is the appropriate role for governments and for markets in growth dynamics?

The time has come to complement existing knowledge with a broader theoretical framework that provides structural analyses of the determinants of continuous growth—specifically the identification of factors that would allow poor economies to move from one level of development to another and more advanced economies to continue creating opportunities and wealth. There is a need to conceptualize what works and what does not so that bold policy actions—such as Li Bing's more than 2,000 years ago when he decided to build the Dujiangyan Dam—no longer appear to be tales of unpredictable success. Economists might never be able to reach his high bar. But they can surely learn much from history and even economic theory—if they always exercise good judgment. Laozi, the ancient Chinese philosopher, warned: "Previous cognition is a flower of *dao* [the way, in the sense of a path] and a beginning of stupidity." Translated into modern language, the phrase means: "An existing theory is both a demonstration of the eternal *dao*'s function (under a specific condition) and the beginning of stupidity (because conditions change constantly)."[67] It is better for policymakers to systematically start their decisionmaking from a clear understanding of the nature of the problem that policy intends to address rather than from reliance on existing theories available on their shelves. The next chapter discusses examples of failures to do so—and draws lessons from the many mistakes of development policy.

THREE

Economic Development: Lessons from Failures

AS BACKGROUND READING FOR A WORLD BANK MISSION to Ghana in August 2008, I got a copy of the audio recording of the six-minute speech by President Kwame Nkrumah on the occasion of the independence of Ghana (the former Gold Coast and the first of the European colonies in Africa to gain independence) in 1957. The sound is scratchy and sometimes mildly distorted, and there are intermittent glitches. But it does not really matter. Listening to the recording today, more than half a century later, one can feel the sense of joy, excitement, and optimism that must have led the man that some call "the Nelson Mandela of the 1950s and 1960s" when he took the podium in front of one of the largest crowds ever assembled in the capital, Accra, to proclaim that the former British colony had regained its freedom and would be a sovereign nation.[1]

A gifted speaker trained in sociology and education, Nkrumah—Osagyefo, or "the Redeemer," as he was affectionately called by his fellow countrymen—spoke boldly and with a sense of purpose about his ambition for his people:

> At long last, the battle has ended! And thus Ghana, your beloved country is free forever. . . . [The] new African is ready to fight his own battles and show that after all, the black man is capable of managing his own affairs. We are going to demonstrate to the world, to the other nations, that we are prepared to lay our own foundation. . . . Ghana is

49

free forever and here I will ask the band to play the Ghana national anthem. . . . I am depending upon the people to help me to reshape the destiny of this country. We are prepared to pick it up and make it a nation that will be respected by every nation in the world. . . . It doesn't matter how far my eye goes, I can see that you are here in your millions, and my last warning to you is that you are to stand firm behind us so that we can prove to the world that when the African is given a chance he can show the world that he is somebody! We have awakened. We will not sleep anymore. Today, from now on, there is a new African in the world![2]

One can only imagine the excited atmosphere in which such words were pronounced. The audio reveals a rare sense of collective pride. The crowd erupts in applause and cheers at almost each sentence, confident in the future and excited by the unlimited economic possibilities that independence may bring. That sense of optimism was widely shared across Africa and throughout the developing world. As historian Frederick Cooper explains, "There [was] a particular poignancy to the history of Ghana because it was the pioneer. Kwame Nkrumah was more than a political leader; he was a prophet of independence, of anti-imperialism, of Pan-Africanism. His oft-quoted phrase 'Seek ye first the political kingdom' was not just a call for Ghanaians to demand a voice in the affairs of state, but a plea for leaders and ordinary citizens to use power for a purpose—to transform a colonized society into a dynamic and prosperous land of opportunity."[3] That same vision had been on display years before in Nehru's India, in Mao Zedong's and Sun Yat-sen's China, in Sukarno's Indonesia, and elsewhere in formerly dominated societies where political and economic modernization was the motto of development.

Soon after becoming Ghana's first leader, Nkrumah pledged to promote industrial development. Like many political leaders of the postwar period, he viewed the Soviet Union's industrialization as evidence that the central planning system was the way for a less developed country to achieve rapid industrialization and modernization. The economic strategy underpinning Ghana's Second Development Plan, launched in 1959, aimed at modernizing the country through the development of advanced high capital-intensity industries in record time.

In an address on July 4, 1960, Nkrumah announced that his government would embark on an intensified program of industrialization, which, with the diversification and mechanization of agriculture, would provide the main basis for the transformation of the economic and social life of the country. "The momentum of this development will increase so that in a relatively short period Ghana will become a modern industrial nation providing opportunities for all and a standard of living comparable with any in the world," he promised while advocating the establishment of factories ranging from steel mills and aluminum smelters to sugar refineries.[4] At that time, Ghana was a low-income country, and the major players in the world steel market were France, Japan, and West Germany. As it turns out, good intentions and great ambitions without appropriate consideration of economic reality would lead to failures in industrialization and development.

What caused such disappointments? This chapter explores reasons for the failures in economic development. It argues that much current knowledge about the root causes of development failures focuses on the symptoms or consequences of problems, not their true origins. It highlights the fact that capital-intensive projects built with the laudable goal of controlling the commanding heights so as to overtake or catch up with the industries in developed countries often ended up as costly mistakes. And it explains why.

Despite the good intentions of modernization that animated political leaders like Nkrumah, the projects selected to reach the goal were too capital-intensive for an economy characterized by relatively scarce capital. They were thus inconsistent with the economy's comparative advantages as determined by the distribution and structure of its factor endowments. As a result, firms in priority sectors were not viable in an open, competitive market. Their initial investments and continuous operations relied on the government's ability and willingness to mobilize a massive amount of resources for investment, on continuous protection of all sorts, and on subsidies through various distortions and direct interventions. The consequences were catastrophic, eventually ruining their dreams and reputations.

The mistakes were not in the design or implementation of the strategies followed by many developing countries but in the very development goals set by policymakers—goals inconsistent with the level of development of their countries and the structure of their endowments at that time. Deriving lessons from such unrealistic development goals, this chapter sketches an economic analysis of why strategies inconsistent with comparative advantage are bound to fail and stresses the need to go beyond conventional economic wisdom.

Viability as the Hidden Ingredient to Economic Success

Nkrumah was not alone. When reading world history, I frequently lamented the fact that many political leaders pursued goals with genuine and noble intentions but caused disastrous consequences for their nations, their people, and sometimes themselves as well. They took signs of a nation's development as the cause of its development and mobilized domestic and sometimes also international resources to construct grandiose projects to prove to the world that some nations had settled their pasts and reached new heights in development. Their dreams were of grandeur, but their pursuits were doomed to be costly failures because they were built on sand instead of solid foundations.

The motivation for Ghana to target modern, advanced capital-intensive industries such as steel or aluminum smelters in Nkrumah's time was clear and understandable. "Imperialism–colonialism left Ghana without the accumulation of capital in private hands which assisted the Western world to make its industrial revolution," Nkrumah's Convention People's Party wrote in its 1962 "Program for Work and Happiness."[5] Therefore, only government can find the means to promote "[the] basic services and industries which are essential prerequisites to intensive, diversified agriculture, speedy industrialization, and increased economic productivity."[6] Unfortunately, Ghana's bold plan for developing the type of ambitious new industries that were prevailing in advanced European countries was not rooted in any analysis of economic fundamentals. A visionary and charismatic political leader,

Nkrumah had developed strong personal relations with many great think-ers, including economist and future Nobel Prize winner W. Arthur Lewis, who served as advisor to his team in the early 1960s. Yet even Lewis later confessed that Nkrumah's noble ambition was not attainable in view of the country's reality.

Ghana's Development Plan included the creation of a state-owned com-pany called the Industrial Development Corporation and a quantitative tar-get for industrial development—600 factories were to be established in a "big push" along the lines of the old structuralist approach to economic development.[7] Ghana did not have the technical capability, the competitive cost structure, or the financing to achieve its ambitious goals. Despite the optimism of its assumptions, the Plan estimated that domestic resources would be sufficient to meet only about 25 percent of the projected financial requirements. So foreign borrowing by the public sector would have to be a large part of the financial framework.[8]

Pressing ahead with its bold capital-intensive projects, Ghana achieved high investment rates, on average 22 percent of real income during the Second Development Plan (1959–64). The scale of its production capacity in heavy industries was large, and its newly created capital-intensive industries had large economies of scale. But their products faced insufficient demand in the domestic market and were not competitive in international markets. As a result, they quickly ended up with excess capacity and severe losses.

To survive, these industries needed continuous protection and subsi-dies from the government, which created distortions and other macro-economic problems: the cumulated financial losses by public enterprises aggravated the country's savings deficit and contributed to balance-of-payments disequilibria, high inflation, and a severe macroeconomic crisis. The country recorded three consecutive years of negative growth in per capita GDP between 1964 and 1966, and inflation increased from 1.0 percent in 1957 to 22.7 percent in 1965.[9] With the country facing eco-nomic ruin, Nkrumah, the Osagyefo, was deposed in a military coup in 1966. Ghana entered a very long period of economic misery and political and social turbulence. The country's real GDP per capita, estimated at

$1,354 the year Nkrumah was overthrown, declined to $988 within 20 years and was only $1,650 in 2008.[10]

Ghana was not alone in its noble but disastrous pursuit of modernization. After World War II, Mao's China, Nasser's Egypt, Nehru's India, Sukarno's Indonesia, and almost every developing country in Africa, Asia, and Latin America adopted a similar strategy to industrialize their nations, only to encounter a similar fate.[11] In many Eastern European and Latin American countries, industrialization had started much before the mid-1960s. Regardless of historical circumstances and initial conditions, the results of early structuralist policies were either disappointing or unsustainable.

In trying to understand the reasons behind Ghana's and other developing countries' poor development performance in the postwar period, many neoclassical economists have focused on the obvious distortions that crippled the economy: the existence of state-owned enterprises with monopolies; the provision of large subsidies to certain industries; the high frequency of political capture and rent seeking; the pervasiveness of financial repression, often accompanied by the overvaluation of domestic currency and the rationing of capital and foreign exchange; and so on.

Not surprisingly, many researchers looked for political economy–type explanations, focusing on the power and dynamics of interest groups. Some argued that the magnitude of the economic, social, or political benefits to particular interest groups often lead them to garner enough political influence to force a government to adopt distortionary arrangements that are favorable to them.[12] The logical consequence of such an argument has been to recommend changes in the incentive system in developing countries as ways of getting rid of distortions: privatization, stronger property rights, and more intrasectoral and intersectoral competition.

Economists have thus often relied on political-economy analyses, with explanations varying from the suggestion that politicians tend to discount the future too much to the idea that they are mostly interested in redistributive taxation, in the impact of investment on the future political equilibrium, or simply in the low implementation capacity.[13] Because many developing countries like Ghana seem to be plagued not simply by underinvestment but by investment in the wrong industries, more recent analyses have argued that the construction of "white elephants" should be seen as redistribution aimed at influencing the outcomes of elections.[14] Robinson and Torvik (2005), for instance, offer a political-economy model showing that white elephants are a particular type of inefficient redistribution that is politically attractive when politicians find it difficult to make credible promises to supporters. They suggest that it is the very inefficiency of such projects that makes them politically appealing. Why? Because it allows only some politicians to credibly promise to build them and thus enter into credible redistribution. The fact that not all politicians can credibly undertake such projects gives those who can a strategic advantage.[15]

At face value, these political-economy conjectures seem plausible. After all, powerful interest groups in developing countries are often associated with advanced capital-intensive sectors, which tend to gain the most from government protection. But historical evidence suggests that when the protectionist policy measures that created distortions were first introduced in many developing countries, the most powerful interest group—that is, the landowners—would paradoxically lose the most from them. And although the powerful urban industrialists often gained from protectionist policies, they also lost from the many other distortions necessary to make the economic system work. For instance, they often suffered from the dominance of pervasive state ownership in advanced industries. In addition, the political leaders who initiated the strategy, such as Nkrumah and Sukarno, often lost popular support and political power due to the economy's poor performance.

Other development theorists have offered an alternative explanation for the origins of distortions in low-income countries, suggesting that weak governments had to find creative ways of alleviating their tax collection problems. Such a "public finance" argument is presented as follows: the existence of a large untaxable underground economy in developing countries makes it almost unavoidable for governments to find some quick fixes; to ensure a stable stream of fiscal revenues, governments must support the development of sectors that are easier to tax![16] But such an argument does not hold up to scrutiny. It does not explain why the amount of taxes collected from advanced modern sectors is often smaller than the subsidies provided to them. Nor does it explain how tax revenues in general are used in developing countries. Further, the "public finance" argument ignores the existence of other types of regulations and distortions in factor markets and the broader economic complications created by state ownership of large modern enterprises.

Looking carefully at the apparent causes of economic failure in Ghana and elsewhere, as described by much of the economic development literature, one can see that they were in reality the consequences of bad strategic choices in industry selection—and the necessity of keeping afloat public and private firms that were inherently not viable given the prevailing country circumstances. They were endogenous to the strategic choices made with a noble development goal. But most economists failed to capture the true causes of this development failure. It is no surprise, then, that their subsequent policy recommendations—and their hope that changes in the incentive system would suffice to spur sustainable growth—were either inaccurate or insufficient to help policymakers in poor countries get out of the poverty trap.

It is therefore necessary to discover the true reasons for the creation and persistence of the many distortions that have long plagued developing economies such as Ghana's. The quest should start with the acknowledgment that development strategists could not get to the bottom of the problem because they paid too little attention to the single most important determinant of a country's long-term performance: firm viability. The dictionary defines the notion of viability at its most basic level as "the capacity for living after birth" or "the capacity of normal growth and development." In the world of business and economics it can be defined with respect to the expected rate of profit of a firm in a free, open, and competitive market. A broadly well-managed firm is deemed viable if it is expected to earn a socially acceptable normal profit in a free, open, and competitive market, without any external subsidies or protection.

Go back for a moment to the historical and intellectual context of the post–World War II era. After the global tragedy of the war, many developing countries' leaders who emerged on the international scene believed in the development of state-of-the-art industries as a means for modernization and nation building. They designed and implemented overly ambitious plans for establishing the "commanding heights" given their level of development. And they attempted to accelerate the growth of advanced capital-intensive industries, which they perceived as a recipe for their nations' rapid industrialization and modernization.

There were also changes in the intellectual landscape, with respected economists in the newly established field of development economics providing a strong rationale for such policies. In parallel with political aspirations for modern heavy-industry development, there was almost an obsession with "market failure" in academic circles—especially in Latin American countries. Many influential economists and policymakers there (Albert Hirschman, Raul Prebisch, Roberto Campos, and Celso Furtado among them) argued that industrialization and growth could not take place spontaneously in developing countries because of structural rigidities and coordination problems.[17]

However, because developing countries are relatively rich in labor and natural resources but not in capital, advanced capital-intensive industries were not adapted to the endowment structures of these poor countries at the time—or aligned with their comparative advantage. Firms created in those industries could not compete with firms in capital-abundant developed countries. Therefore, they were nonviable in open competitive markets and could not survive without government subsidies or protection. Historical examples of such mistakes actually go back to Hungary or Russia, which tried to catch up with the modern industries in Britain in the late nineteenth century.[18] Although GDP statistics are scarce for individual countries, purchasing power parity estimates by Maddison (2006) indicate that their per capita GDPs were 25–30 percent of Britain's in 1900. Any attempt to overcome such a large gap in modern industrial development on the basis of these countries' agrarian economies would depend on state protection and subsidies through measures ranging from monopoly to distortions in all kinds of input prices.

The Soviet Union under Stalin was able to establish advanced heavy industries and became a military superpower for more than half a century because it was the most resource-rich country in the world and could use the large resource rents to subsidize uncompetitive industries. That was not the case for most developing countries in Asia, Africa, or even Latin America, where political leaders fell into the same trap. Their targeting of sophisticated modern capital-intensive industries in advanced economies at a time when their per capita incomes represented only a very small fraction of that of high-income countries could not be sustained.

Eastern Europe grew fast until the mid-1970s (as the Soviet Union did until the 1960s, during some periods at remarkable rates). Latin America's growth in 1945–80 was 5.5 percent a year (6.0 percent if the Southern Cone countries are excluded) in comparison to 3.2 percent per year on average since 1990. Brazil and Mexico grew very fast for about four decades before 1980 and very slowly after market reforms. Africa's performance did not look bad until the mid-1970s: excluding South Africa, the region grew 5.2 percent a year in 1950–74. These numbers have prompted some analysts to conclude that the former period can hardly be called a failure. But these numbers could be misinterpreted: the high growth in the initial period under the structuralist policies was a result of investment-led growth, a model that could not be sustained because the industries targeted by policymakers and private firms were often inconsistent with comparative advantage and required protection or subsidies. Not surprisingly, economic growth slowed down once domestic resources and the possibility of borrowing abroad were exhausted. With the slowdown in growth performance, the economic crisis was inevitable.

The truth is therefore unpleasant: most economists who have studied the many cases of failure of industrial policies that eventually led to poor or even disastrous economic performances have struggled to come up with convincing explanations. Although their political-economy theories are fairly well elaborated, their fundamental assumptions are often at odds with the incentive framework that seems to determine the way political leaders all over the world make decisions and behave. It is hard to believe that first-generation revolution leaders such as Nkrumah, Suharto, Nyerere, and

Nasser, who risked their lives to lead their nations to independence and freedom, intentionally developed large, inefficient industrial projects with ruinous consequences for their countries' economies and their own political survival and reputations in history.

Moreover, contrary to the argument by many political-economy theorists, for many years after independence (or revolution), the industrial elites in developing countries did not really represent a dominant class. These countries were generally agrarian or resource based. The ruling parties typically relied on farmers and the rural landed class for political support before gaining power. But usually after winning political independence they squeezed their rural political base to support industrial development. The elites in large industries did not exist or were too small to be politically powerful. Therefore, it is unconvincing to argue that the propensity to create and maintain "white elephants"—even when they were understood up front as failed experiments—was a *deliberate* public-policy decision.

The problem that impeded many of the ambitious industrial ventures initiated by developing countries' leaders and eventually made them unsustainable and bankrupt was apparently the quality of their managerial teams or their redistributive arrangements. But the actual problem was the viability of these development projects in the first place. Even if they had been entrusted with the best managerial capacities, the most effective institutional arrangements, and the optimal incentive systems for good performance, they could not have competed with firms from advanced countries in an open market and generated acceptable rates of return.

Why? Because they were created and operated in particular sectors and industries in which they had no chance of survival without protections and subsidies. In other words, compared with their global competitors, they were intrinsically misfits. No matter what they could achieve in terms of strategic significance, the Ghanaian firms launched in modern, capital-intensive industries after the country's independence were doomed to fail in open, unprotected, competitive environments. Their sectoral positioning did not match the requirements for economic success at the global level, which tend to reflect particular endowment structures.

A developing country is by nature endowed with relatively abundant labor or natural resources but has relatively scarce capital. The price of labor or natural resources will be relatively low and the price of capital relatively high. Therefore, a developing country will have a natural disadvantage in a heavy manufacturing industry, which requires large capital inputs and small labor inputs, because its costs of production will be inherently higher than in an advanced country. This is the notion of comparative advantage, which prescribes that countries produce goods and services requiring their relatively abundant factors as inputs, thus incurring lower costs than any other country.[19] President Nkrumah and many of his developing-country peers who chose to defy their economies' comparative advantage by attempting to launch heavy industrial projects in their capital-scarce environments should have reflected on an old Chinese proverb that warns: "One cannot pull up the seedlings to help them grow."

Why was the crucial issue of firm viability overlooked by development economists? Perhaps because they were trained in or influenced by neoclassical economics, which, in addition to embracing the well-known rationality assumption, implicitly assumes that any firm that exists in an economy is viable. Neoclassical theories, originating in developed countries, try mainly to explain what happens in developed countries. It is reasonable to assume that firms in those economies are viable because the governments in advanced countries generally do not provide subsidies to businesses, except for those in a few well-known small sectors such as agriculture (for jobs and political-economy reasons) or defense (for national security) or very new and highly risky technological industries (for public goods). In such contexts, it is reasonable to assume that business ventures in other sectors will be fully vetted by private investors and funded with private capital only if they are viable. That is, they can be expected to earn socially acceptable normal profits with normal management. Moreover, when private investors mistakenly bet on firms in industries that are not consistent with a country's comparative advantage and thus not viable, they will lose money and be quickly weeded out in the market, the essence of market competition.

Again, neoclassical economics implicitly assumes that all firms are viable. When the earlier development economists, unconsciously influenced by this assumption, saw developing countries' inability to develop the modern, capital-intensive industries spontaneously in open competitive markets, they attributed this inability to market failures arising from various structural rigidities instead of looking at the viability of firms in those industries.[20] Similarly, when economists in the 1980s observed the pervasive distortions in poorly performing transitional and developing countries, they failed to see that those distortions were second-best arrangements induced by the need to protect nonviable firms in the government's priority sectors and recommended that those distortions be eliminated quickly and decisively without first addressing the viability of those firms.[21]

The Political Economy of Dreams and Ignorance

Ghana's early development story illustrates a widespread phenomenon. Impressed by the power of modern industries in the former colonial countries and the apparent success of the Soviet Union's industrialization during the Great Depression in the 1930s, political leaders in developing countries across the world pursued similar big dreams in the 1950s and 1960s. As almost a stylized fact of political sociology and economic history, poor countries' leaders who came to power at crucial times in the histories of their nations (such as the end of colonialism or the beginning of a revolution) tended to be motivated by one great, holy aspiration for their countries: modernization through industrialization à la the Stalinist model in the Soviet Union, which appeared at the time to be a shining example of economic and military success. That aspiration was based on a belief in human progress and the idea that poor countries—including those at the lowest income levels—should use the administrative means of the state to mobilize resources for launching large projects and programs that symbolize the collective quest for prosperity.

The push for advanced heavy industries by political leaders across Africa, South Asia, and Latin America reflected primarily a lack of understanding of the relationship between the economic structure and the development levels of their countries. Had these leaders understood the trade-off between the pursuit of overly ambitious goals and the cost to their nations, their historical legacies, their political survival, and even their lives, most of them would probably have looked for alternative development strategies.[22] After all, politicians also are rational agents with perfectly sensible objective functions and preferences. They are never unnecessarily masochistic! Their quest for large capital-intensive projects and programs inconsistent with the comparative advantages determined by their countries' endowment structures essentially revealed a fundamental flaw in economic thinking—not just an identity affirmation or a political-economy calculation.

Throughout human history, the main motive for most leaders has been to stay in power and, if their staying in power is not under threat, to establish a good historical reputation for themselves.[23] Bringing economic prosperity to their nations has been crucial to achieving their objectives. But in the more than 200 years that have passed since the publication of Adam Smith's *The Wealth of Nations,* economists have yet to find the sure path to economic prosperity in a nation, and few political leaders understand the mechanism of economic success. They saw the power that advanced capital-intensive industries bestowed on the advanced Western countries. And most political leaders in newly independent developing countries simply chose to launch industries similar to those in the advanced Western economies, honestly believing such industries were necessary for their countries' modernization. They adopted policy instruments, means of intervention, and institutions that were required for their nations to develop those industries. And their goals and actions were in fact rationalized by the dominant structuralist development thinking that appeared after World War II.

The economic nationalism of these leaders was thus rooted in their lack of understanding of what could be called the endogeneity of economic structure. Because they did not perceive that the structural differences between developed and developing countries were endogenous to the differences in their endowment structures, they tended to follow policy prescriptions from various development theories of their time, which explained differences in economic structure between the industrial powers and the low-income countries mainly by the prevalence of market failures arising from structural rigidities in the low-income countries. Those theories recommended that developing countries use massive government interventions to overcome the market failures so as to alter the production structure of their economies with the hope of achieving the same level of development as advanced countries. Few developing countries' leaders realized that their vision for their nations could be achieved only step by step, not by leapfrogging development strategies.[24]

Nkrumah's Ghana was an example of such erroneous development strategies inspired by noble intentions. Political leaders in Cameroon, Kenya, Nigeria, Senegal, Tanzania, Zambia, and many low-income countries on other continents also saw the development of advanced industries as integral to achieving their long-pursued goal of catching up with developed countries, building equitable societies, and reducing their dependence on the old colonial powers. Not only were the academics promoting this approach, but there were also strong political ideologies intrinsically linked to self-sufficiency and import substitution industrialization. To justify their faith in the "macroeconomics of nationalism," many economists argued at the time that underdevelopment must be thought to be primarily about lack of investment.[25] Yet there actually was considerable investment in African countries. The problem was that investment growth did not lead to sustainable output growth. It was thus necessary to focus on the misallocation of investment.[26]

Other developing countries' leaders had a similar pursuit. My home country, China, was the world's largest and most prosperous for millennia before the eighteenth century. Defeated by Britain in the 1839–42 Opium War and repeatedly by other Western powers thereafter, it was reduced to a quasi-colony, with its territory surrendered to Britain, Russia, and Japan and its customs revenue controlled by foreigners. Industrial backwardness—especially a lack of the large heavy industries that were the basis of military strength and economic power—was perceived by social and political elites as the root cause of the country's political vulnerability and economic backwardness. Thus it was natural for Mao Zedong and other revolutionary leaders in China to give priority to the development of large advanced heavy industries after they won the revolution and started building the nation. Unfortunately, the wrong strategic choices and policy mistakes made in pursuit of a Great Leap Forward in industrialization led to a great famine in 1959–61, causing the deaths of more than 30 million people.[27]

Likewise, Jawaharlal Nehru, India's first prime minister (1947–64), launched an industrialization program to modernize his country soon after independence. At the heart of his plan was a fast-growing "heavy goods" sector of machine-building complexes with large capacity for the manufacture of machinery to produce steel, chemicals, fertilizer, electricity, transport equipment, and so on.[28] The government strategy for bringing about a fast-growing heavy goods sector was to invest disproportionately in these complexes. The underlying growth model was from Indian economist and Nehru advisor P. C. Mahalanobis—a model that critics saw as inspired by the Soviet planning literature. It estimated growth prospects based on current investment allocations and basically chose the allocation that maximized the rate of growth for any given investment outlay.[29]

Sukarno, the leader of Indonesia's struggle for independence and its first president (1945–67), also embarked on an ambitious modernization path. To support building a capital-intensive industrial base, the government took almost complete control of the economy, including foreign trade and bank credit. Because public expenditures in industry could not be funded by taxes, the government turned to central bank credit and large budget deficits, which quickly led to high inflation and a stagnant economy. As a result, real per capita income stagnated or declined for much of Sukarno's time in office.[30]

Under the New Order of his successor, President Suharto, the government also pursued ambitious investments in advanced technologies such as aeronautics—in which Indonesia could not compete and which offered few employment opportunities to the rapidly growing labor force. Protective trade policies were used to change the composition of industry away from light manufacturing such as food processing and toward heavy industries such as petroleum refining, steel, and cement—often owned privately but mostly owned by foreign investors with close connections to the president. It took the collapse of the oil market in the mid-1980s for the Indonesian government to change its economic policies, but the damage had already been done.

Egypt went through the same economic ordeal, starting with Gamal Abdel Nasser. Fascinated by the success of the United States despite his own inclination toward socialism, he engaged in a frantic search for a good development strategy. Yet he advocated "Arab socialism" and nationalized the banks and utilities to finance a program of industrialization that favored heavy industries such as iron, fertilizer, paper, and minerals in his First Five-Year Plan (1960–61 to 1964–65).

Critics of the plan noted the lack of coordination with the private sector in the design process and the absence of studies on the feasibility of targets and on the consistency of forecasts. They also noted the weakness of the investment criteria and methods of project appraisal—and the absence of explicit macroeconomic policies or policy guidelines for implementation.[31] The real issue was not the lack of coordination with the private sector but its lack of viability. Because of the inconsistency with Egypt's comparative advantage and the lack of profitability in an open, competitive market, private firms had no incentives to make the investments spontaneously. When the investments were made with supports from the government, if these firms were owned privately, they had even higher incentives to seek more subsidies and protection from the government.[32]

The economic outcomes and impact of Nasser's industrialization strategy were disappointing: while GDP per capita grew by 38 percent during the 14 years of his presidency (1956–70), the performance of the Egyptian economy was hurt by government interventions in the wrong industries.[33] This was reflected in the emergence of uncompetitive and inefficient public enterprises and in lower saving rates that eventually led to lower investment rates.[34]

Senegal's first Four-Year Development Plan (1961–64), adopted by the government only a few months after the country's independence, clearly stated that, although the government expected important private capital in industrial sectors, it "would not remain passive and would play the main role in the design of the industrialization program." It also stated that "the state will engage more directly in action to promote and encourage new industries, and participate and finance those in which the private sector may not have interest."[35] Such a policy stance led the Senegalese government in the early 1960s to create state-owned enterprises in sophisticated capital-intensive industries such as fertilizer production, as well as a very expensive truck assembly plant. Thinking rationally about the situation, it is not too surprising that private entrepreneurs were reluctant to invest in those heavy industries, which they knew were not viable in an open competitive market and would be profitable only if steadily subsidized or protected by the state. Indeed, despite being funded occasionally through credit from state-owned banks, they were never competitive.[36]

No encyclopedia of economic history would be sufficiently comprehensive to list all the examples of such misguided economic strategies around the developing world, many of them designed and implemented in good faith. But as Albert Einstein once said, "Anyone who has never made a mistake has never tried anything new." He was echoing Irish novelist James Joyce, who observed, "A man's mistakes are his portals of discovery."

Truly worrisome today is the fact that many economists and developing countries' leaders do not seem to have drawn the right lessons from experience. Many economists—faced with the sad fact that governments in almost all developing countries have attempted, at some point in their development process, to play that facilitating role and failed—conclude that active government policy is a mistake. The disastrous industrialization attempts after World War II are therefore treated as evidence that active government involvement in industrial development is bound to fail. Yet there is virtually no example in history of any successful catch-up economy in which the government did not play an active role in facilitating its industrial upgrading and diversification.

A close look at the history of capitalism reveals that even Britain and the United States, conventionally believed to have succeeded by adopting laissez-faire policies when other countries were stuck with outdated mercantilist strategies, actually promoted their national industries through various forms of active government interventions that included tariffs, subsidies, and other measures.[37] Many of today's other rich countries also used extensive government intervention to jumpstart their process of modern economic growth. In the nineteenth century, Germany and Japan kick-started their industrialization with state-owned enterprises in textiles, steel, and shipbuilding. After World War II, Austria, Finland, France, the Republic of Korea, Norway, and Singapore also used state-owned enterprises to modernize their economies.[38] But few systematic analyses have been devoted to these successful-country cases in which government intervention led to sustained growth, job creation, and structural transformation. It is therefore necessary to go beyond anecdotal evidence of failure or success and understand the economic dynamics of development.

"Do Not Look Where You Fell but Where You Slipped"

With his typical dark humor Oscar Wilde once observed, "Nothing that is worth knowing can be taught." That is probably an exaggeration: economic history has shown that smart political leaders can gain valuable knowledge by learning from the good and bad experiences of others. Still, Wilde's basic point was probably correct: although learning from one's own mistakes is never an easy endeavor, it is often necessary for gaining knowledge and achieving success. For developing countries' policymakers, failing to do so can have costly consequences.

In August 2008 I visited Accra and gave a lecture at the University of Ghana on rethinking economic development. Reminding the audience of some of the failures of the past, I made the point that the problem with past experiments was not the intention of the ambitions but their unrealistic nature and their inconsistency with a low level of development. An old and respected former minister who had participated in the country's early industrialization drive commented on what I had said. Despite the evidence accumulated over more than five decades, he still argued that Ghana needed to develop capital-intensive industries that can produce machinery and equip-ment for the development of other industries in Ghana. He was not just try-ing to defend the failed policies of the Nkrumah era; he genuinely still believed that the nation's leaders had acted in good faith and made the right decisions for their country and their continent, but that they had simply run into problems in implementing their "good" development strategy.

Economists and policymakers must understand why many other well-intended economic development strategies failed to achieve their stated objectives. "Give me a fruitful error any time, full of seeds, bursting with its own corrections. You can keep your sterile truth for yourself." That was the advice Vilfredo Pareto, the renowned Italian economist, engineer, sociolo-gist, and philosopher often gave to policymakers and researchers. Under-standing the economics of mistakes of the past is indeed a key prerequisite for moving forward more confidently in the quest for prosperity. In doing so, one might keep in mind a saying that I learned in my visits in Africa: "Do not look where you fell but where you slipped." Deciphering the economics of failure is also important because, despite the generally poor record of gov-ernment interventions, every country in the world, intentionally or not, still pursues interventionist industrial policy. That may actually be the best-kept secret of economic policy. This is true not only for the usual suspects such as Brazil, China, France, and Singapore but also for Chile, Germany, the United Kingdom, and the United States. This is surprising only if one forgets that industrial policy broadly refers to any government decision, regulation, or law that encourages ongoing activity or investment in a particular industry. After all, economic development and sustained growth are simply the results of continued industrial and technological upgrading, which requires public–private collaboration.

The real explanation for the failures of Nkrumah, Sukarno, Nasser, and other leaders of the world lies in the honest mistakes they made in their choices of development goals, looking not where they fell but where they slipped. Their noble intentions and nationalistic drive were not enough to save them from the economic disaster created by the vicious circle of un-sustainable industrial pursuit. They failed because they were *too* ambitious, which created distortions benefiting certain social groups that subsequently became politically entrenched. Understanding the negative economic dynamics of such failures is important for moving forward.

The greatest mistake of many developing and former socialist countries was their attempt to defy the comparative advantage determined by their endowment structures: in countries where factor endowments were characterized by the abundance of labor and scarcity of capital, government policy aimed at building modern advanced capital-intensive heavy industries.[39] Because of their high capital needs and their structurally high production costs in a developing country, the enterprises in these priority industries were not viable in open competitive markets. Even when they were well managed, they could not earn a socially acceptable profit in an undistorted and competitive market.

In order to mobilize resources to make investments and maintain operations in advanced capital-intensive sectors, it was necessary for developing countries' governments to subsidize and protect the firms in those priority industries. Due to limited tax-collection capacities, large-scale subsidies could not be sustained. So to reduce the costs of investment and continue the operation of their nonviable enterprises, governments resorted to administrative measures—granting market monopolies to firms in the priority sectors, suppressing interest rates, overvaluing domestic currencies, and controlling the prices of raw materials.[40] Such distortions enabled some poor countries to set up advanced capital-intensive industries in the early stage of their development, at least temporarily. But they also led to the suppression of incentives, the misallocation of resources, and economic inefficiencies.[41]

Nkrumah rightly believed that industrialization should be the main driver for economic growth and prosperity in Ghana and that it was important to add value to the production and export of commodities through local processing of finished goods. But he also believed, mistakenly, that his country was ready in the late 1950s to compete with developed economies in all types of advanced industries. For that purpose he built the industrial township of Tema (in southeastern Ghana, along the Gulf of Guinea) and even ensured that industries were set up in most districts and all regions in Ghana—regardless of their economic viability. He envisaged a wide array of manufactures, including aluminum, steel, refined petroleum, cement, and chemicals. But his labor-abundant, still capital-scarce economy was not ready to develop those capital-intensive industries without subsidies and protection. Despite his noble motivation, such ventures were bound either to fail or to burden public finance considerably.

Egypt's failed industrialization program in the 1950s, which featured such heavy industries as iron, steel, and chemical manufacturing, also illustrates a vicious circle. The country's per capita income was about 5 percent that of the United States, the world's largest steel producer at the time. Steel was considered particularly important because it is a strategic material for other industries (machines, cars, ships, railways). But it exhibits large economies of scale and requires sizable capital, which Egyptian private companies could not afford.

With government efforts, a single company was set up, eventually controlling more than 60 percent of the local market but still having unused excess capacity.[42] High tariffs were imposed to protect it from foreign competition, but at high costs to consumers. Although the government eventually maintained a local steel industry, it came at great cost to public finances. In addition, Egypt's ambitious development plan required large investments and equipment imports, at least at the initial stage, causing widespread shortages of financial resources and foreign exchange. Like many other developing countries' governments that fell into the same trap, the Egyptian authorities had to allocate their limited resources and foreign exchange directly to enterprises in the priority sectors through administrative measures including national planning, credit rationing, and entry and investment licensing.[43]

Once such distortions were introduced into the economy, it became politically hard to eliminate them—for three reasons. First, development strategies that defied comparative advantage created industrial elites who generally were rich and politically well connected, especially in the nonsocialist countries. Second, the industries were considered the backbone of the countries' modernization programs. Eliminating subsidies and protection would have led to their collapse, a result not acceptable to society. Third, their collapse would create high unemployment and social and political instability. That is why governments continued to subsidize large old industries in Eastern Europe and in countries of the former Soviet Union, even after their privatization.[44]

By shielding unsustainable industries from import competition, developing countries inevitably imposed various types of other costs on their economies. Protection typically led to an increase in the price of imports and import-substituting goods relative to the world price, as well as distortions in incentives, pushing the economy to consume the wrong mix of goods from the point of view of economic efficiency. It fragmented markets, with the economy producing too many small-scale goods, again resulting in losses of efficiency. It lessened competition from foreign firms and encouraged the monopoly power of domestic firms whose owners were politically well connected. And it created opportunities for rents and corruption, raising input and transaction costs.[45]

The initial distortions due to misguided economic development strategies were subsequently compounded with "white elephants" and the politics that accompanied them. Development strategies inconsistent with comparative advantage also led to a bureaucratic establishment that itself became an impediment to progress in some low- and middle-income countries.[46]

Not Throwing the Baby Out with the Bathwater

By the 1970s, after several decades of unsuccessful attempts in many countries to catch up with advanced economies through extensive government interventions, most economists had to acknowledge the heavy costs of government failures. But instead of carefully reviewing the specific reasons for the failures, they hastily concluded that almost any government intervention in the economy was harmful. The pendulum of development thinking swung to the other extreme. The unfortunate consequence was a general reluctance to engage the state apparatus in proactive economic policies toward structural change—a move ridiculed in the development literature as "picking winners." The neoliberal Washington Consensus policies that dominated development thinking after the Latin American debt crisis of the 1980s and the subsequent structural adjustment package of policy reforms from Bretton Woods institutions encouraged governments to remove market distortions, radically reform social programs, and stay away from industrial policy.

Although the canons of the Washington Consensus were commonsensical and embodied the broad principles of macroeconomic stabilization, they mostly reflected disappointment with the economic development strategies of the previous decades. Moreover, they ignored the key policy issues facing developing countries: how to ensure the viability of a large number of firms in former priority sectors that were a legacy of the development strategy previously adopted by the government and how to promote entry into industries with an actual or latent comparative advantage. Yet the Washington Consensus became the new blueprint for economic development strategies in the 1980s and was promoted by almost all major international development institutions.

As a result, many developing countries started doing too little to prevent the high unemployment and other dire consequences related to the collapse of old priority sectors or to create the conditions for competitive private sector development and economic growth. Even wide-ranging reforms were meant to ensure fiscal discipline, "competitive" exchange rates, trade and financial liberalization, privatization, and deregulation—that is, to ensure minimal state involvement in economic development. The new prescription did not always yield satisfactory results. El Salvador undertook an extraordinary amount of reform after the early 1990s without being able to identify clear dividends from its efforts. It achieved macroeconomic stability, the economy opened to foreign trade and investment, the privatization and deregulation of key industries were completed, the quality of public institutions improved, and democratic governance, as captured by various statistical measures, was established. Yet per capita GDP was slow to recover even to the levels of the late 1970s. Ricardo Hausmann, former Venezuelan minister and former chief economist of the Inter-American Development Bank, now a professor of development economics at Harvard University, often tells the story of one high-level Salvadorian government official who once asked him why his country did everything that Chile did but never experienced the same growth dynamics!

The same is true for Peru. Although it has recently enjoyed high rates of economic growth, its good performance is actually a recovery from a significant and sustained collapse that began in the 1970s. Transformation of the export sector has been surprisingly small: the same activities that declined—mining and energy—are the ones leading the current recovery in exports to levels in terms of real per capita similar to those of several decades ago. According to Hausmann and Klinger, "The lack of structural transformation is associated with Peru's position in a poorly connected part of the product space, and this accentuates coordination failures in the movement to new activities. In addition, Peru's current export package is very capital intensive and generates few jobs, especially in urban areas where the bulk of the labor force is now located. This limits the welfare benefits of the current growth path."[47]

The overall picture has been even worse in many African countries, including those long considered the successful models of free-market principles and reforms. In Côte d'Ivoire, where the implementation of stabilization and structural adjustment policies started in the early 1980s, progress has been slow to materialize despite the efforts to abandon old structuralist policies. According to Maddison (2006), per capita GDP there declined by 46 percent during 1981–2008, from $2,034 to $1,095. Surprisingly, despite Côte d'Ivoire's long track record as a reformer, some researchers have conjectured that the country's performance was in fact one of "partial adjustment," with several factors fettering the adjustment process: the severity and recurrence of economic shocks, as evidenced by the decline in the terms of trade; the persistence of rigidities and distortions, including pegging the CFA franc to the French franc and subsequently the euro, the movements of which may have undermined the country's competitiveness; and the limited political commitment from the authorities.[48] Such explanations are not fully convincing, because they could justify almost any policy failure anywhere. By advocating a total and rapid swing of the pendulum from all types of government interventions to complete free-market policies, the reformers threw away the baby with the bathwater.

Even Ghana, another early reformer regularly championed as the "front-runner in adjustment" since it embraced the Washington Consensus in 1983, has not done well when compared with good performers from Asia or Latin America with similar endowment structures (distributions of land, labor, and capital) or even with its own potential. Commenting on its performance, in the early 1990s the World Bank's Chad Leechor enthusiastically concluded that "Ghana's adjustment program has been a success. Policy reform has been extensive, despite opposition and institutional constraints. The benefits of adjustment have been large, visible, and widely shared."[49] Although Ghana increased its per capita GDP by nearly 77 percent in 25 years after the structural adjustment started (from $933 in 1983 to $1,650 in 2008), the increase was only 33 percent above the level in 1957, the year of its independence.[50] As a result, Ghana's economic and social progress has been painfully slow, with 29 percent of the population still below the poverty line in 2009. Moreover, Ghana has not achieved the type of structural transformation that the radical free-market revolution was supposed to bring to the country.

The former communist countries of Eastern Europe and the former Soviet Union also had disappointing performances, with serious inflation and economic decline. Russia's inflation rate reached 163 percent a year in 1991–2000, while Ukraine's hit 244 percent a year. The cumulative output decline in Central and Southeastern Europe and the Baltics reached 22.6 percent; in countries of the Commonwealth of Independent States, output fell 50.5 percent. In 2000 Russia's GDP was only 64 percent of what it had been in 1990, while in Poland, the best-performing economy among the former Soviet Union and Eastern European countries, GDP rose only 44 percent from the level in 1990.

Meanwhile, the Gini coefficient of income per capita, a measure of income disparity, rose from 0.23 in 1987–90 to 0.33 in 1996–98 in Central and Southeastern Europe and the Baltic and from 0.28 to 0.46 in countries of the Commonwealth of Independent States (a value of zero denotes perfect equality, and a value of one denotes perfect inequality).[51] Even after privatization, the needed restructuring did not always take place.[52] The subsidies to the large privatized, formerly state-owned companies in many cases did not decline—and even increased.[53] This contributed to a much slower macroeconomic performance during the transition from communism. Instead of conforming to a "J" curve—a small decline followed by quick robust growth of GDP—per capita incomes in the Eastern European economies did not recover to the levels achieved before the transition in 1990 until 2000, and in the economies in the former Soviet Union incomes did not recover until almost 20 years after the transition started.

Many other developing countries found themselves in situations comparable to that of Côte d'Ivoire, El Salvador, Peru, or Russia. Mindful of the disappointment of the old structuralism, their leaders chose to reform the economy aggressively. But misinformed about the true reason for the failures, they adopted new development strategies that were limited to ineffective Washington Consensus–type reforms.[54] They moved from one extreme of the development paradigm to another, throwing the baby out with the bathwater and setting themselves up for economic anemia and social instability.

Nihilist German philosopher Arthur Schopenhauer once wrote, "Opinion is like a pendulum and obeys the same law. If it goes past the center of gravity on one side, it must go a like distance on the other; and it is only after a certain time that it finds the true point at which it can remain at rest."[55] That time may have come. The urgency of today's global economic and social problems is such that policymakers around the world seem increasingly willing to learn not only from their own mistakes but also from the examples of successful countries. Analyzing the many cases that marked modern economic growth, from that of eighteenth-century Western Europe to those of the most recent success stories in countries such as Chile, China, Korea, Mauritius, Slovenia, and Vietnam, it pays great dividends to learn how competitive industries with a latent comparative advantage were targeted, encouraged, built, and developed.

FOUR

Lessons from Successful Catch-up Countries

"THE QUEST FOR THE GRAIL IS NOT ARCHAEOLOGY," Indiana Jones's father tells him in the 1989 movie *Indiana Jones and the Last Crusade.* "It is a race against evil. . . . And in this sort of race, there is no silver medal for finishing second." After some two hours of high suspense, frightening chaos, unexpected encounters, and charmingly improbable chase scenes, Indiana and his father eventually find the Holy Grail, the cup that Jesus Christ is said to have used at the Last Supper, at the Khaznat al-Faroun temple in the ancient rose-red city of Petra, Jordan. In a climactic scene that made *Indiana Jones and the Last Crusade* one of the great action adventures of all time, Jones comes tearing in through a small corridor in a mountain of rock and faces a high sandstone structure with very large pillars and a massive door carved into the face of the cliff. It is the treasury, the site of the Holy Grail.

Movie director Steven Spielberg manages to convey a complex atmosphere of hope, fear, frustration, and randomness in an epic search that culminates with a sense of fulfillment and excitement when the sacred goal is near reach. Still, even at this point, mistakes could be deadly. Choosing among all the many cups in the temple requires careful thinking, for selecting the wrong object would mean instant death. Facing a vast array of options, Jones is warned about the high risk involved in his decision: "You must choose. . . . But choose wisely. For as the true Grail will bring you life, the false Grail will take it from you."

Economists who have engaged in the chase for growth and prosperity in the past couple of centuries have not had to survive gunfights with other treasure hunters or Nazi villains. But they have sometimes been through the same kinds of emotions as if they had, experiencing excitement, frustration, and disillusionment. They are now in a situation in which they realize that choosing wisely the recipe for economic growth could also be a matter of life or death, perhaps not for themselves but for billions of anonymous, ordinary citizens whose lives are directly affected by public policies.

True, development researchers have gathered many of the ingredients of their Holy Grail. Yet "a list of ingredients is not a recipe."[1] Despite all the intellectual progress, some key questions on the agenda today remain the same as those confronting previous generations of researchers: "If growth is driven by continuous structural change," as was reconfirmed recently by Michael Spence, why are some countries successful at promoting continuous and sustained change, while others are not?[2] What forces drive convergence, and what factors stifle material progress? What are the conditions for the kind of structural change that allows low-income countries to become middle-income and then high-income economies? What are the most important determinants of growth (initial conditions, institutions, policies)? What is the appropriate role for governments and for markets in the growth dynamics?

Perhaps because economists have become much better at integrating lessons from the past into their analyses, they are making progress in their quest. There may be hope on the horizon for reaching some sort of Holy Grail after all. In recent years, important empirical studies have provided new insights and a good basis for optimism. Among them, the 2008 Growth Commission Report focusing on successful economies in the post–World War II era deserves special consideration.

This chapter presents that report's main findings and highlights the need for a framework to make them consistent. Looking more broadly at the experiences of successful economies in the past four centuries, it then derives lessons that could be useful to developing countries engaged in the catch-up process. One important clue emerges from the analysis: the need to design economic development strategies consistent with a country's comparative advantage. This requires that the state play a crucial role in creating conditions for private-sector development in the context of well-functioning market systems. That lesson also justifies a new framework for understanding the process of sustained economic growth.

Squaring the Circle:
The Contribution of *The Growth Report*

One of the oldest problems in mathematics, very influential in the development of geometry, was that of squaring a circle—that is, given a circle, geometrically constructing a square equal in area to that of the circle. The ancient Greeks developed a wide variety of methods in their attempt to find a solution, often using curves and other nonlinear instruments. They eventually came to the conclusion that the task could be carried out not using a ruler and a compass but only with some fairly general approximate geometrical constructions.[3]

Just like the Greek mathematicians, economists struggling to come up with prescriptions for economic growth have finally chosen a similar strategy. Faced with the difficulty of providing clear answers to the pressing questions involved and the impossibility of deriving actionable policy recommendations from growth analyses, some growth researchers have found it useful to avoid searching for robust determinants of growth and to look instead for stylized facts that can guide economic policy in developing countries.

That approach goes back several decades, most notably to Nicholas Kaldor's six characteristics of twentieth-century growth, derived from U.K. and U.S. macroeconomic data: a sustained rate of increase in labor productivity, a sustained rate of increase in capital per worker, a stable real interest rate or return on capital, a stable ratio of capital to output, stable shares of capital and labor as fractions of national income, and a wide variation in the rate of growth of fast-growing economies, on the order of 2–5 percent.[4] The stylized facts approach has had its critics—most prominently Robert Solow, who once said, "There is no doubt they are stylized, though it is possible to question whether they are facts."[5] But it has motivated decades of theoretical research trying to explore the underlying causes and mechanisms of these facts.

More recently, economists Charles Jones and Paul Romer have identified a different set of stylized facts using empirical findings from a much larger sample of countries: increases in the extent of the market through globalization and urbanization; acceleration of the pace of growth over time, from virtually zero to relatively rapid rates; variation in the rate of growth of GDP per capita, which increases with the distance from the technology frontier; large income and total factor productivity differences; increases in human capital per worker; and the long-run stability of relative wages.[6]

The Growth Report: Strategies for Sustained Growth and Inclusive Development, a landmark study published by the Commission on Growth and Development in 2008, just as I was starting my term as the chief economist of the World Bank, followed a similar approach but took it to a new level. It built on the findings of several other empirical studies initiated by the World Bank during the previous two decades to reassess the past theories of economic growth and poverty reduction and rethink its policy advice to developing countries.[7] Launched in April 2006, the Commission brought together 22 leading practitioners from government, business, and policymaking arenas, mostly from the developing world. It was chaired by Nobel laureate Michael Spence and Danny Leipziger, a World Bank vice president. Over two years the Commission sought to "gather the best understanding there is about the policies and strategies that underlie rapid and sustained economic growth and poverty reduction."[8]

The Commission was established to take stock of the state of theoretical and empirical knowledge on economic growth with a view to drawing implications for policy and avoiding the trap of purely theoretical exercises. Its work was motivated by the following:

- The sense that poverty cannot be reduced in isolation from economic growth and that the link has been missing in many development strategies.

- Increasing evidence that the economic and social forces underlying rapid and sustained growth are much less well understood
than generally thought; economic advice to developing countries
has been given with more confidence than justified by the state of
knowledge.

- The realization that the accumulation of highly relevant (both
successful and unsuccessful) growth experiences over the past
20 years provides a unique source of learning.

- A growing awareness that, except for China, India, and other
rapidly growing economies in East Asia, developing countries
need to accelerate their rates of growth significantly for their
incomes to catch up with those in industrialized countries and for
the world to achieve a better balance in the distribution of wealth
and opportunity.

The uniqueness of the Commission lies not only in its very diverse composition but also in the way it has reexamined growth analysis. Its approach
has been to "try to assimilate and digest the cumulative experience of growth
and development as well as careful and thoughtful policy analysis in a wide
spectrum of fields. We then seek to share this understanding with political
leaders and policymakers in developing countries, including the next generation of leaders; with an international community of advisors; and with
investors, policymakers, and leaders in advanced countries and international institutions who share the same goals."[9]

The Report starts with the observation that "fast, sustained growth does
not happen spontaneously. It requires long-term commitment by a country's
political leaders, a commitment pursued with patience, perseverance, and
pragmatism."[10] It is indeed useful to put to rest the myth that sustained
growth is a random phenomenon, something due mostly to luck. As Roman
philosopher Seneca once said, "Luck is what happens when preparation
meets opportunity."

The Report then identifies some of the distinctive characteristics of 13
high-growth economies that have been able to grow at more than 7 percent

for periods of more than 25 years since World War II.[11] At that pace of expansion, an economy almost doubles in size every decade.[12] The Report also asks the most pertinent question of all: how can other developing countries emulate the 13 successful economies? Observing that each country has specific characteristics and historical experiences that must be reflected in its growth strategy, the Report does not attempt to provide a generic formula for policymakers to apply. But it offers a framework that can help policymakers design a growth strategy. Although it does not lay out a full set of answers, it suggests the right questions to be addressed.

The Report's conclusion is optimistic: rapid, sustained growth is not a miracle confined to certain parts of the world; all developing countries can achieve it. More important than the list of "growth ingredients," a wide range of policy prescriptions whose validity depends on specific contexts and conditions, is the Report's list of five stylized facts or "striking points of resemblance" among all highly successful countries.

The first point of resemblance among these countries is their savvy and total exploitation of the world economy. In his famous *Letters to a Young Poet*, Rainer Maria Rilke wrote, "Only someone who is ready for everything, who doesn't exclude any experience, even the most incomprehensible, will live the relationship with another person as something alive and will himself sound the depths of his own being."[13] That wise thought has proven useful for countries, too. During their periods of fast growth, all the successful economies made the most of globalization. They did so in several ways: They imported ideas, technology, and know-how from the rest of the world—a world that has become more open and more tightly integrated since the end of World War II. They also exploited global demand, which provided an almost infinite market for their goods. In sum, successful economies "imported what the rest of the world knew, and exported what it wanted."[14] Perhaps not too surprisingly, the unsuccessful countries did the opposite.

The second stylized fact about the best-performing countries is their maintenance of stable macroeconomic environments. During their most successful periods, all 13 countries avoided the unpredictability in fiscal and monetary policies that damages private-sector investment. Growth was sometimes accompanied by moderate inflation in some of them (the Republic of

Korea in the 1970s, China in the mid-1990s), by budget deficits, or even by high ratios of debt to GDP, but the situation never got out of control.

A third characteristic of high-growth countries is their high saving and investment rates, which reflect their willingness to forgo current consumption in pursuit of higher incomes in the future. Excuse a slight digression on the causes of saving. Some may argue that this stylized fact has philosophical and cultural foundations. Since Max Weber suggested that a set of values and attitudes associated with the Protestant ethic (such as thrift, austerity, hard work, or rationality) constitute the basis for economic and material progress, many authors have enunciated culture-based theories of development.[15]

I disagree. It is ironic that cultural determinism is used these days to explain some features of economic success in Asia, for instance, whereas only a few decades ago the same cultural arguments were invoked as the main obstacles to modernization there.[16] Attitudes toward work, wealth, or thrift have been debated everywhere throughout human history. Seventeenth-century French poet Jean de la Fontaine, a master of comedy in Western literature, devoted one of his most famous satirical works, *The Grasshopper and the Ant,* to chastising his fellow citizens' propensity to overconsume and overspend.[17] Moreover, the concept of culture is difficult to define rigorously and to assess through experiment or experience, especially since anthropologists A. L. Kroeber and Clyde Kluckhohn surveyed 164 different definitions that appeared in the social science literature and the humanities during 1871–1951.[18] Almost three decades later, Ian Jamieson listed no fewer than 160 different definitions.[19] Culture—however defined—is never a static concept. Its contribution to saving and growth patterns is always likely to evolve dynamically.

That some of the most successful countries, such as Malaysia and Singapore, adopted mandatory saving schemes has led some researchers to stress the importance of deliberate saving policies as the main reason for these high saving and investment rates.[20] The Growth Commission Report suggests that the main explanation has been the ability of these countries to produce large economic surpluses and to generate rates of return on investment that were high enough to provide strong incentives to save. Before the 1960s, Korea's saving rate was low, stagnating at around 10 percent of GDP. After the 1970s it increased to more than 30 percent. Southeast Asia and Latin America had similarly low saving rates in the 1970s. Twenty years later, the Asian average rate was about 20 percentage points higher.

The fourth point of resemblance among successful economies is their adherence to a market system to allocate resources. The Growth Commission Report notes that the twentieth century saw many experiments with alternatives to a market system, all of which failed to help developing countries achieve sustained growth. Although successful countries may differ in the intensity and strength of their property rights systems, each of them adopted a well-functioning market mechanism that provided adequate price signals, transparent decisionmaking, and good incentives. Their governments did not resist the market forces in the reallocation of capital and labor from sector to sector, industry to industry. As a result, the process of "creative destruction," defined by Joseph Schumpeter as a "process of industrial mutation that incessantly revolutionizes the economic structure from within, incessantly destroying the old one, incessantly creating a new one," led to structural transformation: market forces and government action pulled people into the urban areas, destroying some jobs while creating others.[21]

The fifth characteristic of the high-performing countries in the sample is committed, credible, and capable governments. In some economies, such as Hong Kong, a Special Administrative Region of China, the administration chose a laissez-faire approach—though it also had quite a number of sectoral policies during the colonial and postcolonial periods. In others, the state was more hands-on, intervening with various tools (tax breaks, subsidized credit, directed lending) in the world of business to help private firms enter industries that they might not have otherwise considered.

Sustained growth that can help overcome poverty is typically a multi-decade process that takes place only in a stable and functional investment environment. It requires political leadership and effective, pragmatic, and sometimes activist governments. This point was echoed by Benjamin Mkapa, former president of Tanzania and a member of the Commission on Growth and Development, who commented, "In the long run it does not pay to build an economic mansion on a foundation of political sand."[22] A good illustration is Singapore, where political leaders often observe that the pursuit of growth has been an organizing principle of their country's politics for the past 40 years. Few people have expressed better the importance of leadership and governance as ingredients of political and sustained economic performance than did eighteenth-century political genius Charles Maurice, Prince de Talleyrand, who once said, "I am more afraid of an army of one hundred sheep led by a lion than an army of one hundred lions led by a sheep."

The Growth Commission Report also identifies a series of "bad ideas" to be avoided by policymakers in their search for growth. The nonexhaustive list includes subsidizing energy, relying on the civil service to deal with joblessness, reducing fiscal deficits by cutting expenditures on infrastructure investment, providing open-ended protection to domestic firms, imposing price controls to stem inflation, banning exports for long periods, resisting urbanization and measuring educational progress through infrastructure, ignoring environmental issues as an "unaffordable luxury," adopting regulation of the banking system, and allowing the exchange rate to appreciate excessively. Although the Report prudently offers the caveat that some situations and circumstances may justify limited or temporary resort to some of the policies listed, it notes that "the overwhelming weight of evidence suggests that such policies involve large costs and their stated objectives—which are often admirable—are usually much better served through other means."[23]

The Report clearly represents a major step forward in growth analysis. It provides a strong basis for the creation of the appropriate infrastructures, incentive systems, and institutions to sustain the evolving process of generating national wealth. But because its five stylized facts can be either preconditions for or results of the growth process, it may still be insufficient as a practical guide to policymakers, who must think carefully about the causes and consequences of various economic policies before engaging in the dynamics of catching up. To disentangle causes and effects and set priorities for public policies, it is useful to go beyond the mere association that these stylized facts suggest and reflect on the causal relationships among them. This requires some generally acceptable economic theory.[24] Therefore, the Report offers a new challenge to growth researchers, who must come up with a conceptual framework for making sense of its main findings.

Recognizing That Some Countries
May Have Found the Holy Grail

By identifying the points of resemblance among these high-performing economies of recent times, the Commission on Growth and Development paved the way for intellectual progress in the quest for prosperity. Summarizing the Report's findings, Chairman Michael Spence and coauthor David Brady concluded that it may be scientifically possible to identify "the ingredients of growth" but not a specific recipe that developing countries could follow to launch their economies on the path of prosperity. They observe that the work of the Commission on Growth and Development

> tended to confirm that political leaders play pivotal roles in the success
> —and the failure—of economic development. . . . Although these
> high-growth countries used different economic models and political
> structures and had different resources and histories, their governments
> followed broadly similar paths. Often ushered in by a crisis, new
> leadership chose a promising economic model and then stabilized the
> nation long enough to let the economic model take root. The leadership
> also began to create reliable and accountable institutions that kept
> politicians focused on citizens' long-term well-being. As growth caused
> change and created new tensions, the leadership corrected the course of
> the nation by honing the economic model and tuning institutions to
> emerging needs while maintaining stability.[25]

However, they conclude, "Rather than suggesting a single recipe for economic growth, our research reveals that there are different paths to development."[26]

Just like the ancient Greeks, who struggled with the idea of squaring a circle and eventually concluded that it was impossible to do so, Brady and Spence suggest implicitly that the Holy Grail of a general formula for success that development economists have been chasing for centuries is fundamentally an elusive prospect. Although development of the list of "ingredients of growth" is an important step in acquiring knowledge, it may not be a sufficient prescription for developing countries' policymakers, who still have to figure out specific strategies and measures to achieve each one of them simultaneously—and therefore run the risk of missing complementarities. It is therefore necessary to focus on the various elements, understand how to make sense of them, and put them into a consistent framework for action.

Let's go back to the five stylized facts highlighted by the Commission on Growth and Development and try to understand the root cause of success by distinguishing preconditions from consequences among them. I would submit that these stylized facts are simply the preconditions and the consequences of what happens when a country chooses to launch its economic development (industrial upgrading and diversification) along the lines of comparative advantages determined by its endowment structure. In other words, the Holy Grail of successful economic development is embodied in one not-so-hidden key idea: comparative advantage. Before explaining how the framework of comparative advantage helps explain consistently the main findings of the Growth Commission Report, I briefly discuss what it entails.

Nobel laureate Paul Samuelson was once challenged by a friend, the mathematician Stanislaw Ulam, to "name me one proposition in all of the social sciences which is both true and nontrivial."[27] After thinking about it for a few years, Samuelson responded that comparative advantage was the answer. With his distinctive sense of humor he explained: "That it is logically true need not be argued before a mathematician; that it is not trivial is attested by the thousands of important and intelligent men who have never been able to grasp the doctrine for themselves or to believe it after it was explained to them."[28] He went on to suggest that what distinguishes an economist from a noneconomist is whether one believes in the principle of comparative advantage.

Comparative advantage is indeed one of the most insightful ideas of economics. It started with Adam Smith's observation that free trade could be advantageous for countries: "If a foreign country can supply us with a commodity cheaper than we ourselves can make it, better buy it of them with some part of the produce of our own industry, employed in a way in which we have some advantage."[29] But that was just a comment on absolute advantages in production. The more refined idea of comparative advantage dates to the early part of the nineteenth century. Robert Torrens was the first to flesh it out, but much credit goes to David Ricardo, who formalized it in his famous 1817 book *On the Principles of Political Economy and Taxation*.[30]

The main principle of comparative advantage is straightforward: all countries would prosper if they chose to concentrate on what they can produce best and then traded those products for products that other countries produce best. But that powerful idea is counterintuitive, often requiring step-by-step explanation. Smith's framework of absolute advantage led to the conclusion that trade between two countries producing two different goods, using labor as the sole factor of production and with different levels of productivity of labor (the quantity of output produced per worker) would not be profitable—at least to the less productive one. Using a basic numerical example, Ricardo showed that, to the contrary, specialization of each country in the production line in which it has comparative advantage would actually raise total production and be profitable for both countries.

Economists sometimes have difficulty explaining such a counterintuitive idea to noneconomists.[31] One popular metaphor often used in classrooms is simply to suggest that an economics professor who can type his own papers and books at a faster pace than can his very able assistant, who might not teach as well as he, should focus on teaching while the assistant concentrates on typing—both would be more productive in the activities they perform relatively well and better off in their interaction. Likewise, a country like Switzerland that excels in capital-intensive industries such as watch production and labor-intensive industries such as garments should specialize in watches and trade for garments with, say, Bangladesh, where such goods are produced better than are watches.

Why do some countries produce some goods more cheaply than other countries do, especially in this era of information, with technological know-how often freely accessible or available for purchase to those who want to use it? Why are there differences among countries' production baskets when almost all countries could adopt the same technology? The answer lies in differences in the endowments of production factors that each country possesses. Regardless of their income levels, all countries have a given set of factor endowments—labor, capital, natural resources—that they can use to produce goods and services for their domestic markets or to compete overseas at any specific time.[32]

In general, lower-income countries are better endowed in labor or natural resources, and higher-income countries are better endowed in capital. The production of various goods requires different levels of particular factors of production: some goods, such as garments, are more labor intensive; others, such as grains, are more land or resource intensive; and yet others, such as cars, are capital intensive. A country that is better endowed with abundant labor or resources can produce labor- or resource-intensive goods and services more cheaply than capital-intensive goods, especially when compared with a country that is better endowed with capital. So it makes sense for a country with a relative abundance of labor or resources to produce more labor- or resource-intensive goods and trade for capital-intensive products with a country that has a relative abundance of capital. The obvious implication is that trade between the two nations normally raises the real incomes of both.

That is true despite the facts that labor and capital can move across borders, that world trade is constantly undergoing rapid changes in style, and that there are fewer stable products and industries to be targeted by any economy today than several decades ago.[33] In fact, changes in style and product customization have not altered the division of labor among countries at different levels of development determined by the relative abundance of their factor endowments. For example television evolved from black and white to color and to flat panel today. The main producing countries have changed from the United States before the 1960s, when TVs were a high-tech product, to Japan in the 1960s through the 1980s, to Korea in the 1980s through the 2000s, and to China today. A latecomer entering the market today could go into the labor-intensive assembly of flat-panel TVs first, just as forerunners such as Japan did in the 1960s, Korea in the 1970s, and China in the 1980s when they successfully decided to compete in the black-and-white and color TV markets.

It is useful to clarify the relationship between comparative advantage and competitive advantage. In an influential book, Michael Porter made the term *competitive advantage* popular.[34] According to Porter, a nation should pursue policies to enhance its competitive advantage instead of following the comparative advantage. More specifically, a nation enhances its competitive advantage in the global economy if its industries fulfill the following four conditions: first, their industries intensively use the nation's abundant and relatively inexpensive factors of production; second, their products have large domestic markets; third, each industry forms a cluster; and fourth, the domestic market for each industry is competitive.

The first condition in effect means that the industries should be aligned with the economy's comparative advantage determined by the nation's factor endowments. The third and fourth conditions will hold only if the industries are consistent with the nation's comparative advantage. Otherwise, as discussed in the previous chapter, investment in those industries must rely on government subsidies and protection. The domestic market for their products will not be competitive, and they will not form clusters—because only a small number of firms will be able to enter them. So the four conditions can be reduced to two independent conditions: comparative advantage and domestic market size. Between these two, comparative advantage is the most important because if an industry corresponds to a country's comparative advantage, the industry's product will have a global market. That is why many of the world's richest countries are also very small.[35]

That reasoning helps explain why the Growth Commission Report's stylized fact 1 about successful countries ("they fully exploited the global economy" and "they imported what the rest of the world knew, and exported what it wanted"[36]) simply results from the decision by these nations to develop their industries according to their comparative advantages in the globalized world. Indeed, if any country develops its industries according to its comparative advantages in the global economy, it can export what the world needs competitively and profitably. It will also not produce domestically the goods and services in which it has no comparative advantage but will choose instead to import them. In that process, as I will show later when discussing stylized fact 3, its endowment structure and comparative advantages in the global economy will change swiftly. As any country goes through the process of industrial upgrading according to the change in its comparative advantage, it can exploit the latecomer advantage by importing ideas, technology, and know-how from more advanced countries and reduce costs and risks. Its economy will be open, especially compared with those of countries that may have attempted to develop advanced industries in which they do not have comparative advantages.

Nikita Khrushchev, the former first secretary of the Communist Party of the Soviet Union, once complained, "Economics is a subject that does not greatly respect one's wishes." He might have been surprised to learn that in fact the "dismal science" (as economics is often called) actually yields satisfactory outcomes—when policymakers make the right decisions. That is most notably the case with macroeconomic stability (stylized fact 2), which is also a consequence of a country's following its comparative advantage in its development strategy. If a country develops industries with comparative advantages, its economy will be competitive in domestic and international markets. Overall, its domestic firms will be viable. Their profitability will depend on their management instead of the government's subsidies and protection. The government will have a strong fiscal position as well, for three reasons: first, its fiscal revenues will reap the benefits of dynamic growth; second, there will be no need to subsidize nonviable, inefficient firms; and third, the economy will generate more job opportunities and have less unemployment.

A country that develops industries in line with its comparative advantages will be much less exposed to homegrown crises caused by uncompetitive industries, currency mismatches, or fiscal shocks. Because of its external competitiveness, the country will also likely have strong external accounts. That will put the government in a strong position to adopt countercyclical measures if there are shocks to the economy from global crises like the recent one.

"Money is like a sixth sense—and you can't make use of the other five without it," English writer William Somerset Maugham once said. That also holds for any economy. Generating financial resources is a prerequisite to successful development. And recording high rates of saving and investment (stylized fact 3) is another logical result of following comparative advantage in economic development. Such a strategy allows a developing economy to be most competitive and produce the largest possible amount of economic surplus (profits), which can be saved. Competitive industries also imply a high return on investment, providing incentives to save and invest. Because the surplus that can be saved is large and the incentives for saving and investment are high when a country follows its comparative advantage in its development strategy, it will have high rates of saving and investment. The country's comparative advantages in the global economy will also change step by step, from relatively labor- or resource-intensive industries to relatively capital-intensive industries. That will swiftly close its structural gap with the advanced countries.

We must acknowledge, however, that *comparative advantage* is a term mostly relevant to economists. Entrepreneurs are typically concerned with profits, determined by the prices of their outputs and inputs. Most firms are indeed set up to pursue profits. They will follow the economy's comparative advantage, determined by the country's relative abundances of factor endowments, in their decisions to adopt technology and enter industries only if relative prices reflect the relative scarcity of each factor in the endowment structure. This will happen only in an economy with well-functioning markets.[37] So allowing a market system to allocate resources (stylized fact 4) is a precondition for an economy to follow its comparative advantage in its development.

A question: if the market is the institutional foundation for a country's successful development, why is a committed, credible, and capable government also required (stylized fact 5)? Why is a minimal state that maintains law and order insufficient for economic development? The answer lies in the fact that modern economic development is a process of continuous structural change, a process beset with inherent market failures. Structural change will not happen spontaneously or will be very costly and sluggish if the government is not proactive in assisting the private sector to overcome those market failures.

As factor endowments are accumulated and the country's comparative advantage is upgraded to more capital-intensive industries, the technology its firms use becomes more sophisticated and capital requirements increase, as do the scale of production and the sizes of markets. Market transactions tend to involve agents who interact directly with each other and increasingly take place at arm's length. A flexible and smooth industrial and technological upgrading process therefore requires simultaneous improvements in both "soft" infrastructure such as educational, financial, and legal institutions and "hard" infrastructure such as power supplies, telecommunications networks, and roads and transportation facilities, so that firms in the newly upgraded industries can reduce their transaction costs and reach the production-possibility frontier (the possible combinations of output that can be attained for a given set of inputs).[38] Clearly, individual firms cannot internalize all these changes cost-effectively, and spontaneous coordination among many firms to meet these new challenges is often impossible. Changes in infrastructure require collective action or at least coordination between the providers of infrastructure services and industrial firms. So it falls to the government either to introduce such changes or to coordinate them proactively.

Moreover, industrial upgrading in response to change in an economy's structure of factor endowments entails additional costs for the pioneer firms: it requires that they overcome issues of limited information about which new industries are consistent with the economy's latent comparative advantage as determined by the changing endowment structure. General

Colin Powell, the former chairman of the U.S. Joint Chiefs of Staff, once said, "There are no secrets to success. It is the result of preparation, hard work, and learning from failure." True. Valuable information externalities arise from the knowledge that pioneer firms gain from both success and failure. If the first mover fails, it bears all costs of failure and sends signals to others about avoiding the same move. If the first mover succeeds, signaling that the new industry is in line with the country's new comparative advantage, other firms will follow, competition will arise, and the first mover will not have a monopoly rent. There is an asymmetry between the costs of failure and the gains of success for the first mover. Therefore, in addition to playing a proactive role in improving soft and hard infrastructures, the government in a developing country, like that in a developed country, needs to compensate for the information externalities generated by pioneer firms.[39]

Finally, to be competitive in the global economy, firms in all industries also need to have good logistics, equipment maintenance capabilities, continuous supplies of skilled workers, and so on. The costs of obtaining all those services are greatly reduced by clustering many firms in the same industry in a given location. This is especially true for countries in their early stage of development: the prices of outputs are not high, and reducing transaction costs is crucial for their competitiveness. If industrial upgrading and diversification are left to random spontaneity, firms may enter too many different industries. As a result, only a few sufficiently large clusters may emerge, and evolution via "survival of the fittest" will typically be a very long and costly process. It is therefore better for the government to encourage the entry of firms into some industries aligned with the country's comparative advantage. That can reduce the time and cost of cluster formation.

Consequently, it is important for a country to have a committed, credible, and capable government to perform the information, coordination, and externality compensation functions discussed earlier. By playing such a role, the state can overcome market failures and facilitate industrial upgrading and structural transformation. The government must adopt a comparative advantage–following strategy, identify industries consistent with the country's latent comparative advantage,[40] improve the soft and hard infrastructure for efficient operations in those industries, and encourage firms to enter those selected industries and form clusters quickly.[41]

The 13 successful economies discussed in the Growth Commission Report did just those things.[42] Looking closely at the winning catch-up strategies, it appears that policy interventions depended on countries' circumstances and the specific binding constraints for new industries. Still, although the interventions often differed, the patterns of industrial development were similar. They all started from resource-intensive industries or labor-intensive industries such as mining, agriculture, garments, textiles, toys, and electronics in the early stage of development and moved up the industrial ladder step by step to more capital-intensive industries.[43] The newly industrializing East Asian economies, for instance, exploited endowment structures similar to Japan's to follow that country's development in a flying-geese pattern.[44]

Korea illustrates that strategy well. The government there took a proactive approach to industrial upgrading. It adjusted its strategy to enter industries consistent with the country's latent (and evolving) comparative advantage. Early in its growth, domestic manufacturers in the automotive sector concentrated mostly on assembling imported parts—which was labor intensive and in line with its comparative advantage at the time. Similarly, in electronics the initial focus was on household appliances such as TVs, washing machines, and refrigerators. Later Korean firms moved to memory chips, the least technologically complex segment of the information industry. Korea's technological ascent has been rapid, as has its accumulation of physical and human capital due to the conformity of the country's main industrial sectors to its comparative advantage and its changing dynamics.[45]

As a result, Korea—once a poor agricultural country with GDP per capita lower than that of Egypt, Senegal, and República Bolivariana de Venezuela—has enjoyed remarkable GDP growth for the past 50 years and has performed remarkably in upgrading to such industries as automobiles and semiconductors. Again, the secret of its success has been the consistency of the country's strategy with its comparative advantage in the development of textiles and light industries before moving gradually to heavy machinery, chemicals, and sophisticated electronics. Korea initiated its drive for basic metals and chemicals only in the 1970s to steer the composition of its industrial output toward more capital- and technology-intensive industries.[46] By contrast, labor-intensive and capital-scarce developing countries that failed in their attempt to industrialize often started the process by immediately targeting capital-intensive heavy industries in which they could not be competitive.[47]

Building committed, credible, and capable governments (stylized fact 5) —that is, creating a facilitating state—is therefore a precondition for an economy to adopt a comparative advantage–following strategy in its development process. The fact that many countries in the Growth Commission Report sample did not have Western-style democratic rulers seems to indicate that leadership has little to do with any particular form of government.[48] What seems to matter most is the ability of political leaders to "walk a fine line between accommodating evolving economic and political interests and maintaining some degree of stability, coherence, and persistence in the policy space. . . . As societies grow and change, leaders must continuously adapt political, economic, and institutional structures and interactions without disrupting growth dynamics."[49] A well-functioning government is required to maintain a competitive market and to overcome failures—situations in which a lack of certain economically ideal factors leads to disequilibrium, with the quantity of a product demanded by consumers not matching the quantity provided by suppliers. If the government's goal is to facilitate a development process that is consistent with its comparative advantage, its interventions will be implemented more easily and more successfully, strengthening its credibility. So a committed, credible, and capable state can also be viewed as the outcome of the country's following its comparative advantage. It can thus be said that the first three stylized facts from the Growth Commission Report were the consequences of following the comparative advantages in economic development and the last two were the preconditions for doing so.

In the recent action and science fiction movie *Inception*, which describes a world where technology exists to enter the human mind, actor Leonardo DiCaprio, who plays the main character, a highly skilled thief stealing valuable secrets from deep within the subconscious of his victims when they are in the dream state—when the mind is at its most vulnerable—ponders: "What's the most resilient parasite? A bacterium? A virus? An intestinal worm?" He then gives his own response: "An *idea*. Resilient, highly contagious. . . . Once an idea's taken hold in the brain it's almost impossible to eradicate. A person can cover it up, ignore it—but it stays there." Hollywood movies may not necessarily be a good source of wisdom. This one is. Former U.S. president John Kennedy said the same thing when he acknowledged the extraordinary power of ideas: "A man may die, nations may rise and fall, but an idea lives on. Ideas have endurance without death." That is why it is essential to avoid bad ideas in economic policymaking.

Policy recommendations derived from the comparative advantage principles would help developing countries' governments avoid the "bad ideas" identified by the Commission on Growth and Development. Most countries adopt energy subsidies to support nonviable firms for two reasons: to satisfy politically powerful constituencies (a political-economy rationale) or to help the poor (an equity rationale). A wide variety of measures keep prices for consumers below market levels or those for producers above market levels, with the goal of reducing costs for consumers and producers (through direct cash transfers to producers or consumers and indirect support mechanisms such as tax exemptions and rebates, price controls, trade restrictions, and so on).

These large, costly, and unsustainable government subsidies arise from development strategies that deviate substantially from the optimal industrial structure. If a country follows its comparative advantage in its development strategy, few of its state-owned or private enterprises will be nonviable, and there will be no need to subsidize firms. Its labor-intensive industries will create many jobs and achieve dynamic growth, reducing poverty rapidly. There will be little need to subsidize the poor through price distortions. And viable private firms offer the best insurance against joblessness. So there is no need to use public employment as a tool to deal with joblessness. Moreover, the government will not have to use open-ended protection to support or subsidize nonviable firms.

Thanks to the country's good economic performance, the government's fiscal position is likely to be strong, and there will be no justification for the erratic budget policies (expenditure cuts, public investment delays, payment arrears, salary freezes) caused by large fiscal deficits. Likewise, a government that implements a development strategy consistent with its comparative advantage will not need to have recourse to an overvalued exchange rate to subsidize nonviable firms created in the framework of ill-conceived import substitution policies.

Given the conclusion that comparative advantage helps conceptualize the good performance of the 13 countries in the Growth Commission Report sample, an important validation question is whether other successful countries that emerged from previous waves of economic growth followed a similar strategy. The historical and contemporary experiences of industrial upgrading and diversification help us understand the role of the state and the market in their development processes.

Modern Economic Growth:
The Secret of Advanced Countries

If a comparative advantage–following strategy is the Holy Grail for structural change and sustained growth, the next logical question is how to actually put it into practice. Our review of early historical experiences in today's advanced countries provides an important clue to the recipe for success by showing the role of the state in economic development. Historical evidence abounds that today's most advanced economies relied heavily on government intervention to ignite and facilitate their take-off and catch-up processes, allowing them to build strong industrial bases and sustain their growth momentum over long periods. List (1841), in his well-known survey of trade and industrial policies that led to early economic transformations in the Western world, documented various policy instruments that governments used to support the development of specific industries—many of which became successful and provided the bedrock for national industrial development.[50]

Likewise, Ha-Joon Chang has reviewed economic developments during the period when most of today's advanced economies went through their industrial revolutions (between the end of the Napoleonic Wars in 1815 and the beginning of World War I in 1914).[51] He has documented various patterns of state interventions that allowed these countries to implement their catch-up strategies. The industrial success of Western economies was also due to the use of industrial, trade, and technology policies. Government interventions ranged from the frequent use of import duties and even import bans for the protection of infant industries to industrial promotion through monopoly grants and cheap supplies from government factories, various subsidies, public–private partnerships, and direct state investment, especially in Britain when it attempted to catch up with the Netherlands and in the United States when it attempted to catch up with Britain.[52]

Then the state appeared heavier handed than in the 13 countries of the Growth Commission Report, but the global context was quite different. Globalization was at an early stage. The exchange of ideas and technology was not as free as in the post–World War II era. And the division of labor among countries was based on products rather than production activities, as in today's global production network, thanks to dramatically reduced costs of telecommunications and transportation. Moreover, latecomers were catching up with the most advanced countries, which had more protection for their technology and industries. However, the successful countries generally maintained free markets and targeted industries in more advanced countries where per capita income levels were close to theirs and thus comparative advantages were similar to theirs.[53]

Developed countries' governments continue to adopt various measures to support technological innovation, industrial upgrading, and diversification, even though these policies may not be announced under the formal label of "industrial policy." Besides patent systems, other such measures typically include support to basic research, mandates, defense contract allocations, and large public procurements. Of these, only patents are industry neutral; the others are industry specific. Because of budget constraints, even support to basic research requires that governments pick among all possible projects based on their likelihood of success and contribution to technological progress and industrial upgrading. Local governments also provide incentives to private firms to attract them to particular geographic areas and induce new investments. Implementing all these policy measures necessarily involves identifying specific industries or products, which amounts to picking winners.

A prime example is the United States, where the government has consistently offered strong incentives to private businesses and academic institutions for discovering new ideas valuable for sustaining growth—and making those ideas nonrival, available to all. It has also built infrastructure in key economic sectors such as transportation and provided financing for education and training to build the country's skill base in many industries. And it routinely provides subsidies for R&D and grants, patents, and copyrights. The Advanced Technology Program, launched in 1990, has been instrumental in the R&D of promising high-risk technologies. U.S. government subsidies also support defense and energy industries.

The same is true in Europe, where active industrial policy has been discussed since the end of World War II.[54] In fact, many of Europe's most remarkable industrial successes (space program Ariane, aircraft manufacturer Airbus) were the result of intergovernmental cooperation, with decisive political support from the EU. Since the early 1990s, the European Commission has issued several policy papers on the subject, including the 1994 report *An Industrial Competitiveness Policy for the European Union,* which set the stage for more determined government interventions.[55] Other official strategy documents cover the risk of deindustrialization, the regulatory burden, and the impact of enlargement of the EU on the competitiveness of European companies and their location. In a review of the Lisbon Strategy in March 2005, EU member states set the objective of "creating a solid industrial base" and restated the increasing importance attached to R&D and innovation in all forms and to information and communication technologies.[56]

France has always favored government-sponsored economic programs for the public and private sectors to coordinate their efforts to develop new technologies and industries. The government there often provides financial support and capital to the private sector through direct subsidies, tax credits, or government-run developmental banks.[57] In Great Britain the government, which defines itself as "a market shaper," recently released a new industrial policy aimed at supporting enterprise and entrepreneurial activity, including the access to finance required to start and grow firms; fostering knowledge creation and its application; helping people develop the skills and capabilities to find work and build the businesses and industries of the future; investing in the infrastructure required to support a modern low-carbon economy; ensuring open and competitive markets to drive innovation and rising productivity; and building on industrial strengths where Great Britain has particular expertise or might gain a comparative advantage and where government action can have an impact.[58]

Another interesting case is that of Finland, a late but successful state-led industrializer, thanks to a mix of heavy government intervention and private incentives.[59] Government intervention was aimed at a fast buildup of industrial capital to ensure a solid manufacturing base. One feature of the country's growth regime was a high rate of capital accumulation, which often required administrative rationing of credit through interest-rate controls and selective loan approvals for capital equipment investment. Another was a high rate of investment in targeted areas of manufacturing, particularly in pulp, paper, and metalworking. State enterprises were established in basic metals, chemical fertilizers, and energy. As late as the 1980s, state-owned enterprises accounted for 18 percent of the country's industry value added.[60]

Summing up the research findings on how to achieve sustained growth through structural transformation, the diffusion of ideas, and the accumulation of knowledge, Romer notes that "the challenge is to find better forms of government intervention, ones that have better economic effects and pose fewer political and institutional risks."[61] He also points out that "the temptation for economists, however, has always been to duck the complicated political and institutional issues that this kind of analysis raises and instead to work backward from a desired policy conclusion to a simple economic model that supports it."[62]

The real challenge for economists and policymakers looking for the Holy Grail of prosperity may instead be to help the private sector identify the new industries that are consistent with the economy's comparative advantage, which evolves as the endowment structure changes, and to facilitate the entry of firms into industries in which they can prosper. The next chapters take up that challenge.

FIVE

A Framework for Rethinking Development: A New Structural Economics

W HEN I DID MY ARMY TRAINING AS A YOUNG CADET in Taiwan, China, in the mid-1970s, one of the first and most intriguing exercises was to take an entire gun completely apart, identify the different pieces, understand their function and importance and the way they all fit together, and then reassemble them to immediately fire a shot. The task was both challenging and exhilarating, especially for someone who had never touched a gun before. It provoked my imagination and gave me some learning and teaching skills. Its main purpose was to help young minds gain the confidence to solve apparent mysteries and to overcome fear.

After some 250 years of hard work confronting issues of economic development, economists and policymakers have reached the point at which they may be in the same position as young army recruits. They basically have at their disposal almost all the pieces of the puzzle, as discussed in Chapters 3 and 4. But they still have to overcome the fear of failure, disentangle the mechanics of sustained growth, and try to put together a consistent and credible contraption.

Elhanan Helpman, who coined the expression "the mystery of economic growth," correctly identifies the pieces of the puzzle. He tells the story of growth economics as organized around a number of themes: the importance of the accumulation of physical and human capital, the effect of technological factors on the rate of this accumulation, the process of knowledge creation and its influence on productivity, the interdependence of the growth rates of different countries, and finally, the role of economic and political institutions in encouraging capital accumulation, innovation, and change.[1]

The questions before us are what to do with all these elements and how to organize them in a convincing new theory and a practical framework to help policymakers in poor countries solve the mystery of growth and sustain the dynamics of structural transformation. The task cannot be underestimated, nor can its potential rewards to people everywhere. As historian Robert Skidelsky reminds us, "The question of what causes economies to grow is theoretically interesting and practically important. If we could discover the secrets of economic growth—what causes income per person to increase over time—we might be able to make growth happen at will, abolishing poverty and creating a world of universal abundance."[2]

Lessons from development failures and successes and from economic analysis can be used to elaborate a new approach to economic transformation—one that could apply to all countries engaged in continual industrial and technological upgrading and from which policymakers from low-, middle-, and high-income countries could derive practical policy decisions.

This chapter puts together the pieces of the sustained growth puzzle. It reexamines the state of development economics and offers a new framework for growth analysis. The proposed framework—a neoclassical approach to structures and changes in the process of economic development, or new structural economics—builds on some of the insights from the old school of structural economics.[3] It emphasizes that structural features need to be considered in the analysis of the economic development process and that the state, as a facilitator in a market economy, helps a developing country convert its backward structure into a modern one. But contrary to the static and restrictive view put forward by "old" structural economics, this new framework proposes to start the analysis from what a country has now, that is, from its factor endowments (labor, capital, natural resources), and to identify market opportunities for competitive industries and growth niches according to what it can do well based on what it has now, that is, its comparative advantages.

The new approach to development considers structural differences between developed and developing countries to be largely endogenous to their endowment structures and determined by market forces rather than resulting from the distribution of power or other rigidities, as the old structural approach assumed. It therefore argues that acknowledging the importance of structures in economic development, understanding the market as the fundamental institution for resource allocation, and accepting the state as a strategic facilitator are the secrets to economic success everywhere. It also offers an analytically consistent explanation for the stories of success and failure discussed in the previous two chapters. Throughout history, developing countries that relied on their comparative advantages to guide their choices of industry and technology have become competitive in domestic and international markets, produced the largest possible economic surpluses, accumulated the greatest possible capital, and upgraded their human capital, technology, and industry in the fastest possible way. By contrast, developing countries that violated their comparative advantage have encountered stagnation and various crises.

Why Burundi Is Not Switzerland

Students of economic development often start their quest for explanation by simply examining the puzzling differences in prevailing industries and technologies in high- and low-income countries. In many cases the contrast is indeed perplexing. Consider Burundi and Switzerland, two landlocked countries of roughly the same population size at different levels of economic development. With a gross national income (GNI) per capita of about $400, Burundi is a resource-poor country where agriculture accounts for more than one-third of GDP and employs more than 90 percent of the population.[4] Since it achieved independence in 1962, Burundi's main exports have remained coffee and tea, which generate 90 percent of its foreign exchange earnings, though exports are a small share of GDP. Like many other poor economies that have undergone limited structural transformation over decades, Burundi's export earnings—and its ability to pay for imports—thus depend primarily on the weather and on international coffee and tea prices. Its industrial base is limited to light consumer goods such as blankets, shoes, and soap; assembly of imported components; public works; and some small-scale food processing. As a result, firms in Burundi make very little use of technology, as shown by very low information and technology indicators: in 2009 the country had only 31,500 main telephone lines and ranked 177th in the world on the Doing Business Indicators.[5]

Burundi illustrates quite well a general pattern observed by development economists in the 1950s: poor countries exhibit some general economic characteristics that make them different from rich ones and determine the types of industries and technology they use. They tend to have a very high proportion of their low-skill labor force in agriculture, evidence of disguised underemployment or unemployment, and a lack of opportunities outside agriculture. They also have little capital per person and make little use of technology. As a result, their productivity is low, and they export foodstuffs and raw materials, with low value added.[6]

By contrast, Switzerland has a highly skilled labor force and a per capita GDP more than 120 times that of Burundi—among the highest in the world. Although its labor force is about the same as Burundi's, agriculture there represents less than 2 percent of GDP, services more than 70 percent. Switzerland's economy is led by financial services and a manufacturing industry that specializes in high-technology, knowledge-based production. Its most successful industries include machinery, chemicals, watches, textiles, precision instruments, tourism, banking, and insurance. Not surprisingly, Switzerland is one of the leading countries in the use of sophisticated technology, often embedded in the top products or services of the country's main industries (banks, insurance, telecommunications, power, chemistry, watches, transportation, tourism). In all such industries, interdisciplinary R&D ranks high and is heavily based on information technology.

An interesting picture emerges from these basic observations. Differences in per capita incomes are related to differences in industries and technologies, which determine labor's marginal productivity (the increase in the output of an economy that results from using one additional worker, other factors remaining constant). Countries at different levels of development tend to have different economic structures and endowments. Burundi, with a GDP per capita of only about $200, cannot be expected to have land, capital, a labor force, highways, social institutions, and an economic structure that are similar to those of Switzerland, another landlocked country of even smaller size but with a GDP per capita well over $40,000.

A country's factor endowments tend to determine its relative factor prices and optimal industrial structure, which in turn determine the distribution of firm sizes and the level and nature of risks for firms.[7] Factor endowments for countries at the early stages of development are typically characterized by relative scarcity in capital and relative abundance in labor or natural resources. The production activities of these countries tend to be labor or resource intensive (mostly in subsistence agriculture, animal husbandry, fishing, and mining) and usually rely on conventional mature technologies to produce well-established "mature" products. Except for mining and plantations, their production has limited economies of scale and is engaged in by small households. Their firm sizes are usually small, with market transactions often informal and limited to local markets among people who know each other. The infrastructures and institutions to facilitate such production and market transactions are limited and rudimentary.

Burundi, at its current level of development, could not credibly create a sophisticated Swiss-type service sector led by financial services or a manufacturing industry that specializes in high-tech, knowledge-based production. To be competitive in the modern world, industries anywhere must be aligned with the comparative advantage of their country. And that comparative advantage is determined by the country's factor endowments. So the main force driving a structural change from labor- or resource-intensive industries to capital-intensive industries is the change in endowment structure from a low capital–labor ratio to a high capital–labor ratio.[8] In Burundi and other developing countries with abundant unskilled labor and resources but scarce human and physical capital, only labor- and resource-intensive industries will have comparative advantages in open competitive markets and be profitable to domestic firms.[9]

At the high end of the development spectrum, advanced economies such as that of Switzerland display a completely different endowment structure. Because they have accumulated capital for generations and reached a high level of income, the relatively abundant factor in their endowments typically is capital, not natural resources or labor. These economies tend to have a comparative advantage in capital-intensive industries with economies of scale in production. It is not surprising that Switzerland's economy relies more on high-tech industries than on traditional agriculture, which would require a large unskilled labor force. Rich economies, situated on the global technology and industrial frontier, rely on creative destruction or the invention of new technologies and products for technological innovation and industrial upgrading.[10] Individual firms engaged in this upgrading need to undertake risky R&D activities that generate nonrival public knowledge (the type that can be used or possessed by multiple users and therefore benefit other firms in the economy).[11]

For this reason, governments in the developed countries subsidize the R&D activities of individual firms by funding basic research in universities, granting patents for new inventions, and offering preferential taxes and defense and other forms of government procurement to subsidize the new producers. The soft and hard infrastructure needed in these countries—and visible in buoyant cities such as Zurich—is therefore likely to be quite different from that in low-income countries. Their financial arrangements are managed by large banks and sophisticated equity markets, which can mobilize a large amount of capital and diversify risks. The various types of hard infrastructure (such as highways, telecommunications networks, port facilities, and power supplies) and soft infrastructure (institutions, regulations, social capital, value systems, and other social and economic arrangements) must comply with the necessities of national and global markets. Business transactions are long in distance, large in quantity and value, and no longer informal but based on rigorously crafted and implemented contracts.

The endowments of a developing country such as Burundi can change from relatively abundant labor to relatively abundant capital, as in Switzerland, but only through the accumulation of capital from the economic surplus it produces in each subsequent production cycle. Therefore, for the country to embark on sustained economic growth, it must upgrade its industrial base step by step toward the level in high-income countries such as Switzerland.

How can this be done in a consistent, credible, and sustainable manner? That is perhaps the greatest challenge in development economics. A useful theory of development must explain the pattern of industry and technology selection and strategic choices, as well as the dynamic process of endowment upgrading that led firms in Switzerland—once the size of those in Burundi today—to become global leaders and to sustain one of the most successful economies in human history. This chapter proposes a framework called "new structural economics" to do just that. It explains the differences in industries and technologies for countries at different levels of development and lays out a path for closing the gap between poor and rich countries.

Understanding Economic Development:
A Conceptual Framework

Start with the observation that production in all countries is organized and operated within individual firms that need to hire labor, buy inputs, and sell outputs outside their boundaries. Infrastructure, critical to the profitability of domestic firms, affects an individual firm's transaction costs and its marginal rate of return on investment. Hard infrastructure determines the transaction costs of obtaining inputs and selling outputs, as well as the range and size of the market (which, in turn, determine the extent of the division of labor in production, as noted by Adam Smith). Soft infrastructure has a similar effect. Financial regulation, for example, affects the ability of a firm to get external funding. The legal framework determines the costs of writing and implementing a contract. And social networks determine the firm's ease of access to information, finance, and markets.

Infrastructure endowments determine firm transaction costs and how close the economy is, with its given factor endowments, to its production-possibility frontier. Although firms generally can control some of their production costs, they have little latitude over most of their transaction costs, which are largely determined by the quality of their soft and hard infrastructure, mostly provided by the state. Therefore, a crucial observation in the analysis of development dynamics is the fact that most hard infrastructure and almost all soft infrastructure are exogenously provided to individual firms and cannot be internalized in their production decisions.[12]

For policymakers in Burundi, economic development requires continually introducing new and better technology to existing industries and upgrading existing industries from labor- and resource-intensive industries to more capital-intensive industries. Otherwise, per capita income will stagnate, as Robert Solow's neoclassical growth model predicts.[13] How quickly can a country move from the lower end of the global industrial spectrum to the higher end? Factor endowments, while changeable over time, must be taken as a given at any specific time. True, the government and the private sector in Bujumbura, Burundi's capital, could theoretically import large amounts of capital and labor from abroad to suit their needs, but things are not so easy in practice even in a globalized world.[14] Developing countries have the advantage of backwardness and a whole spectrum of industries with different levels of capital intensity available to them. For them to upgrade from low to high capital-intensity industries, they must first upgrade their factor endowments, which requires that their stocks of capital grow faster than their labor forces.[15]

When a developing country like Burundi moves up the industrial ladder in the process of economic development, it also increases its scale of production due to the indivisibility of capital equipment. The upgrading moves its economy closer to the global industrial frontier. New opportunities also bring new challenges. With changes in the size of firms, the scope of the market, and the nature of risk during the upgrading of the industrial structure, the requirements for infrastructure services, both hard and soft, also change. Firms become large and need a larger market, which requires corresponding changes in infrastructure. For example, with the increase in the size and risk of capital, informal money lenders or small regional banks will no longer be able to serve firms' needs. To accompany the upgrading of a country's industrial structure, financial institutions must evolve in parallel—from small local informal or formal institutions to larger national banks or even equity markets. Similarly, the power supply, roads, telecommunications systems, port facilities, business regulations, and other soft and hard infrastructure need to be improved. For that, the government must either coordinate related private investments or provide those services directly.

Why is infrastructure that important? Labor productivity on the factory floor of a firm in a labor-intensive industry, such as garments, in a low-income African country is only slightly lower than or even the same as that in dynamic, growing countries like China and Vietnam. But despite having a much lower wage rate than Chinese or Vietnamese firms, African industrial firms are not competitive in global markets. The reasons are higher transaction costs arising from poor hard and soft infrastructure, such as frequent power blackouts; poor maintenance of equipment caused by the lack of parts and technicians; poor logistics; bad roads; ineffective port facilities; and bureaucratic red tape.[16]

We now have a much better understanding of industrial upgrading. In addition to increasing the need for more sophisticated hard and soft infrastructure, industrial upgrading also increases the risk that developing countries' firms face. As they move closer to the global technology frontier, it becomes increasingly difficult for them to succeed simply by borrowing mature technology from advanced countries. They need to invent their own new technologies and products, a challenging task that involves many risks.[17] At Burundi's early stage of development, firms there can use mature technologies available elsewhere to produce mature products for mature markets. At that level of development, the main source of risk for fund providers is the managerial ability of firms' owner-operators. But at a much higher level of development, Burundian firms will have to invent new technologies to produce new products for new markets. In addition to the risk arising from managerial capacity, such firms will eventually face risks arising from the maturity of technology and markets.[18] Firms in successful catch-up countries like Brazil, China, and the Republic of Korea now face that challenge.

Looking at economic development from this perspective yields an important lesson. For the analysis of economic development it helps to start from a parameter that is given, fundamental, and changeable. If the parameter is not given at a specific time, it cannot serve as a starting point for analysis. If it is not fundamental, the results of the analysis will be trivial. And if it is not changeable, the analysis will not provide useful knowledge to facilitate desirable changes in the economy. The one parameter that has those three properties is factor endowments, the starting point of the new structural economics framework proposed in this book.

Following the tradition of classical economics, economists tend to think of a country's endowments as consisting only of its land (or natural resources), labor, and capital (both physical and human). These are, in fact, factor endowments, which firms in an economy can use in production. Conceptually, it is useful to add infrastructure as one more component of an economy's endowments.[19] The total factor endowment in an economy determines the total budget in the economy at a given time, whereas its structure determines the relative factor prices of the economy at that time. The total budget and relative prices are two of the most important parameters in economic analysis.

The nature and structure of factor endowments in an economy can be changed through population growth and capital accumulation. Changes in endowment structure simultaneously increase the economy's total budget and change its relative factor prices, the two most important parameters for firms' production choices. This can be explained with a model in which the aggregate output in an economy comprises different goods, each produced using technologies that differ in capital intensity. As capital becomes more abundant and thus relatively cheaper, the optimal production shifts to more capital-intensive goods. At the same time, more labor-intensive goods are gradually displaced. Reflecting that evolution, the country will also increase the capital intensity of its exports.

This process generates an endless V-shaped industrial dynamic—the "flying geese" pattern of economic development in its structure of industry and trade.[20] In addition, the financial structure evolves endogenously as the demand for capital and the need for risk reallocation in production increase.[21] Other economic and social structures change accordingly. Successful countries have gone through that dynamic process. Because an economy's industrial structure is determined by its endowment structure, latecomers would benefit from learning and mastering their experiences when upgrading their industries due to changes in their endowment structures.

The Optimal Speed and Sequencing of Prosperity

How quickly can Burundi reach Switzerland's level of development? That is the one-million-dollar question that most policymakers in Bujumbura probably have in mind. The answer is sobering: it would take some time, because the dynamic of economic development should not be accelerated beyond its optimal pace. But if the government's strategy is right, it can be achieved in just one or two generations, as shown by some of the 13 successful economies in the Growth Commission Report. Nineteenth-century Danish philosopher Søren Kierkegaard once observed, "Most men pursue pleasure with such breathless haste that they hurry past it." The same can be said about policymakers in poor countries who often set economic objectives that are unrealistic given their countries' endowment structures.

Because the industrial structure in an economy at a specific time is endogenous to its relative abundance of given labor, capital, and natural resources, the speed of industrial upgrading and development depends on the speed of the upgrading of its factor endowments as well as the required corresponding improvements in infrastructure. At each level of development, the production structure will differ, as will the financial, legal, and other infrastructures. With capital accumulation or population growth, the economy's factor endowment will change, pushing its industrial structure to deviate from what was deemed optimal for its previous level. To stay optimal, the change will require industrial upgrading and new types of infrastructure services to facilitate production and market transactions and allow the economy to reach its new production-possibility frontier.

Developing a country's industries in line with its comparative advantages is not only the best way to make the country competitive but also the fastest way to develop the country's economy and to increase its income. Why? As competitive industries and firms grow, they claim larger market shares and create the greatest possible economic surpluses in profits and salaries. That is true in Burundi, Switzerland, and anywhere else in the world. Reinvested surpluses earn the highest possible returns as well, because the industrial structure is optimal for that endowment structure. Over time, this strategy allows the economy to accumulate physical and human capital, which upgrades the factor endowment structure as well as the industrial structure and makes domestic firms more competitive over time in more capital- and skill-intensive products.[22] Economic research has too often overlooked that basic truth about sustained growth and development.

American movie star Halle Berry once said, perhaps jokingly, "If you really want to be competitive in today's market, you have to be in movies that make money." Throughout history, businesspeople have held the same view of their activity. For firms to spontaneously enter industries and choose technologies consistent with the economy's comparative advantage, the price system must reflect the relative scarcity of factors in the country's endowment. This happens only in an economy with competitive markets.[23] So a competitive market should be the economy's fundamental mechanism for allocating resources at each level of its development.

A comparative advantage–following approach to economic development may seem slow and frustrating to many people in countries with major poverty challenges. But it is the fastest way to accumulate capital and upgrade the endowment structure, and the upgrading of the industrial structure can be accelerated by technologies and industries already developed by and available in more advanced countries. At each level of their development, firms in developing countries can acquire the technologies (and enter industries) appropriate to their endowment structures rather than having to reinvent the wheel.[24] This possibility of using off-the-shelf technology and entering existing industries is what has allowed some of the newly industrialized East Asian economies to sustain annual GDP growth rates of 8 percent, and even 10 percent, for several decades.

As a country climbs the industrial and technological ladders, many other changes take place. The technology used by its firms becomes more sophisticated. Capital requirements increase, as do the scale of production and the size of markets. More market transactions take place at arm's length. A flexible and smooth industrial and technological upgrading therefore requires simultaneous improvements in educational, financial, and legal institutions. It also requires hard infrastructure such as telecommunications networks, port facilities, and transportation networks so that firms in the newly upgraded industries can produce sufficient amounts to reach economies of scale and become the lowest-cost producers.[25]

Clearly, individual firms cannot internalize all these changes cost-effectively, and spontaneous coordination among many firms to meet these new challenges is often impossible. It is easy to imagine a group of business leaders anywhere in the world meeting secretly to collude on price gouging or to discuss a major investment project that would be a win-win for their firms. It is more difficult to imagine the same group discussing how they would jointly finance a highway, an international airport, or a major port facility. It is also impossible to imagine them meeting to design the country's legal or financial system. Changes in infrastructure require collective action or at least coordination between the providers of infrastructure services and industrial firms. For this reason, it falls to the government either to introduce such changes itself or to coordinate them.[26]

With the upgrading in factor endowment and industrial structure, infrastructure must be improved in parallel for an economy to reduce firms' transaction costs. This is not an easy process to design and implement. Governments often fail to play their role in the provision, coordination, and improvement of infrastructure. In such situations, infrastructure becomes a bottleneck to economic development. In fact, economic growth tends to make existing institutional arrangements obsolete because it induces constant shifts in the demand for institutional services, which by nature are public goods. Changes in institutions require collective action, which often fails because they run into the free-rider problem.[27]

Therefore, governments need to play an active role in the process of economic development—to facilitate timely improvements in hard and soft infrastructure to meet the changing needs arising from industrial upgrading. Former U.S. president George W. Bush, who often described himself as a proud conservative, once confessed, "I had to abandon free market principles in order to save the free market system." Although he was referring to heavy government interventions that he felt compelled to implement as a response to the 2008 global crisis, his statement acknowledged the indispensable role of states in allowing markets to function properly.[28]

Some skeptics may question whether a comparative advantage–following strategy can simply lead a developing country to lag behind the developed world forever. The answer is a definitive no. If developing and developed countries make industrial and technological decisions based on their respective comparative advantage, the rate of technological change in the developing countries will be higher than that in the developed, because developing countries rely mainly on technology imports, whose cost is much lower than the R&D costs in developed countries.

Rapid technological innovation yields higher returns on capital and more enthusiasm for accumulation. That is why the savings rate in successful developing countries is generally higher than in developed countries. With much faster capital accumulation in developing countries than in developed countries, the gaps in factor endowment structure and industrial structure between the two groups of countries will narrow. For that reason, developing countries that follow comparative advantage in their development can catch up with the advanced countries at the fastest possible pace. That is exactly what the successful economies in East Asia have achieved.

Summing up, the new structural economics is organized around four ideas. First, the economy's factor endowments and their structure (defined as the relative abundance of natural resources, labor, human capital, and physical capital), which reflect the level of the country's development, are given at any specific time but changeable over time. The optimal industrial structure of the economy will be different at different levels of development. In addition to differences in the capital intensity of industries, different industrial structures imply differences in the optimal firm size, scale of production, market range, transaction complexity, and nature of risks. As a result, each industrial structure requires corresponding soft and hard infrastructure to facilitate its operations and transactions.

Second, each level of economic development is a point on a wide spectrum from a low-income subsistence agrarian economy to a high-income industrialized economy. Thus the usual dichotomy between two economic development levels ("poor" versus "rich" or "developing countries" versus "developed countries") is not useful. Given the endogeneity of industrial structure at each level of development, the targets of industrial upgrading and infrastructure improvement in a developing country should not necessarily refer to the industries and infrastructure in high-income countries.

Third, at each given level of development, the market is the fundamental mechanism for effective resource allocation. In addition, economic development, as the dynamic process of moving from one level to the next, requires industrial diversification, upgrading, and corresponding improvements in hard and soft infrastructure. Industrial diversification and upgrading is a process of innovation. Pioneering firms in the diversification and upgrading process generate public knowledge for other firms in the economy: that is, consumption of the new knowledge by one firm does not reduce the availability of that knowledge to others (nonrival), and no one can be effectively excluded from using it (nonexcludable). In most cases, infrastructure improvements cannot be part of an individual firm's investment decisions. Yet they yield large externalities to other firms' transaction costs. So, in addition to an effective market mechanism, the government should facilitate industrial diversification and upgrading and the improvement of infrastructure.

Fourth, because specialization, agglomeration, and clustering are crucial to reducing transaction costs in any given industry and making it competitive in the global market,[29] the government should also provide incentives to induce private firms to enter sectors that meet the following criteria: they must be consistent with the country's comparative advantage, have a large international market, and provide great potential for further industrial upgrading and diversification. Such incentives will help private firms form clusters quickly and avoid the time and waste inherent in a merely spontaneous development process.

Putting New Wine in New Bottles

The Bible and other holy scriptures warn us about the danger of putting new wine into old bottles. In the King James Bible we read, "Neither do men put new wine into old bottles: else the bottles break, and the wine runneth out, and the bottles perish: but they put new wine into new bottles, and both are preserved."[30] The ideas outlined in the new structural economics approach to development have sometimes been initially perceived either as new wine in old bottles or as old wine in new bottles. I remember getting puzzled gazes and even some skeptical questions from various audiences after speaking about this new framework for the first time. It is therefore useful to sketch briefly what is "new" about it, and how it differs from other theories of development.

Like all learning ventures, economic development thinking is bound to be a continual process of amalgamation and discovery, continuity, and reinvention. The existing stock of knowledge, the result of many decades of work by thinkers from various backgrounds and disciplines, has come to light through several waves of theoretical and empirical research. It is therefore only natural that the proposed new structural economics has some similarities to and differences from previous strands in the development economics literature, most notably the "old" structuralism.

In terms of similarities, the new and the old structural economics are both founded on the structural differences between developed and developing countries and acknowledge the active role of the state in facilitating the movement of the economy from a lower to a higher level of development. But there are profound differences between the two approaches in the targets and methods of state intervention. The old structural economics advocates development policies that go against an economy's comparative advantage and advises governments in developing countries to develop advanced capital-intensive industries through direct administrative measures and price distortions. By contrast, the new structural economics stresses the central role of the market in resource allocation and advises the state to assist firms in industrial upgrading by addressing externalities and coordination issues.

The differences between the new and the old structural economics derive from their dissimilar views of the sources of structural rigidities. The old structural economics assumes that the market failures that make the development of advanced capital-intensive industries difficult in developing countries are exogenously determined by incorrect price signals, which are themselves distorted by the existence of monopolies, by labor's perverse response to price signals, or by the immobility of factors. In stark contrast, the new structural economics posits that the failure to develop advanced capital-intensive industries in developing countries is endogenously determined by their endowments. The relative scarcity in their capital endowments and their low level of soft and hard infrastructure make reallocations from the existing industries to advanced capital-intensive industries unprofitable for firms in the economy.

Moreover, the old structural economics assumes a dual and restrictive view of the world, with the binary classification of only two possible categories of countries: "low-income, periphery countries" versus "high-income, core countries." As a result, it views the differences in industrial structure between developed and developing countries as a dichotomy. Contrary to that vision, the new structural economics considers these differences as the reflection of a whole spectrum of many different levels of development.

The new structural economics challenges the dichotomy between developing and developed countries, which led old structuralist thinkers to miss the fact that economic development is a continuous process that gives each country following its comparative advantage the opportunity to improve and adjust its optimal economic structure at each development level. That process makes countries competitive and able to benefit from advantages of backwardness in technological, industrial, and institutional innovations—

and to upgrade their endowments and industrial structures in the fastest possible way. Although the old structuralists too often viewed developing countries as resource-dependent victims of external dominant political and economic forces that set a secular decline in commodity prices, the new structural economics rejects dependency theories. In an increasingly global-ized world, it sees opportunities for developing countries to counter nega-tive historical trends by diversifying their economies and absorbing available knowledge to build industries that are consistent with their comparative advantage to accelerate growth and converge with developed countries.

Another major difference between the new structural economics and the old is the rationale for using key instruments of economic management. The old structural economics sees systematic government intervention in eco-nomic activities as the essential ingredient in modernization. Among the key instruments to be used to move from "developing" countries to "indus-trialized" countries are generalized protectionism (such as government-imposed tariffs on imports to protect infant industries), rigid exchange-rate policies, repression of the financial system, and state-owned enterprises in most sectors.[31]

The new structural approach recognizes that import substitution is a nat-ural phenomenon for a developing country climbing the industrial ladder in its development process as long as it is consistent with the shift in compara-tive advantage that results from changes in the endowment structure. But it rejects conventional import substitution strategies that rely on the use of fiscal policy or other distortions in low-income labor- or resource-abundant economies to develop high-cost advanced capital-intensive industries that are not consistent with the country's comparative advantage. It also stresses the idea that the industrial upgrading in a developing country should be consistent with the change in the country's comparative advantage, which reflects the accumulation of human and physical capital and the changes in its factor endowment structure. This ensures the viability of firms in new industries.

The new structural economics concludes that the role of the state in industrial diversification and upgrading should be limited to providing information about new industries, coordinating related investments across different firms in the same industries, compensating for information externalities of the pioneer firms, and nurturing new industries through incubation, attracting foreign direct investment, and encouraging clustering. The state also needs to lead in improving hard and soft infrastructure to reduce transaction costs for individual firms and facilitate the economy's industrial development process.

Is this new theoretical framework too abstract? The main value added of any economic theory should be assessed for the new policy insights it provides and for the pertinence of the research agenda, which I will discuss in the next chapter.

SIX

What Would Be Done Differently under the New Structural Economics?

Henry Kissinger, a preeminent U.S. policymaker, once said, "No foreign policy—no matter how ingenious—has any chance of success if it is born in the minds of a few and carried in the hearts of none." His admonition applies to economic policy as well, especially when it involves a serious change in dominant thinking. Until change is widely shared by the largest group of committed policymakers, who can see its practical implications and benefits, there is little probability that it will be endorsed, let alone have a serious chance of implementation.

One of the first times I outlined the main ideas of the new structural economics framework to my World Bank colleagues in Washington, on the occasion of my first anniversary as the chief economist, not everyone immediately endorsed it. I did this at a small, intense brainstorming meeting with economists from diverse backgrounds, each with great expertise and experience in development. As always in these instances, questions and suggestions erupted, some fueled by skepticism.

One person in the audience was Martin Ravallion, the director of the Bank's research group and one of my closest advisors. A widely admired Australian economist known around the world for his path-breaking work on a wide range of issues—most notably measuring poverty—Martin holds strong views and relishes making his points with intimidating clarity. Yet he demonstrated that day that he has also mastered the art of holding back in tense meetings. With his laid-back attitude and serious gaze, he was disarmingly quiet. He listened intently to the back-and-forth of the discussion and occasionally took some notes. At first he seemed puzzled by the intensity of the exchange. And then, toward the end of the discussion, he simply asked me: "OK. Assuming that the new structural economics framework is a much better analytical tool for economic development, how would public policies change if a country actually followed that approach? How would governments carry out macroeconomic, sectoral, or institutional policies?"

The discussion quieted down as everyone at the meeting paused in response to those questions. Martin then suggested to me: "You may want to flesh out more explicitly what economic policy would look like under the new structural economics. Then we will all have a concrete basis to assess its novelty and pertinence." I thought this was good advice: beyond the obvious question of what was "new" about new structural economics, it was indeed quite logical to look into the policy implications of the theoretical approach I was advocating.

I started thinking about this issue in great detail. In the next brainstorming meeting on the subject, Shahrokh Fardoust, another of my colleagues, recommended doing just the opposite. Although he agreed on the importance of being practical, he also warned that it might be too early to offer definitive policy recommendations from a framework that still had to be complemented by further empirical testing. He argued that it would be desirable to refrain from policy conclusions before the ongoing research program I had launched on new structural economics yielded all its major results. As the director of operations and strategy in my department and an experienced World Bank staffer, Shahrokh showed great instincts in helping me navigate some complicated situations. A tough-minded Iranian economist with refined and elegant manners, he also knew how to operate as a shrewd political advisor.

American poet and playwright Edna St. Vincent Millay once said, "I am glad that I paid so little attention to good advice; had I abided by it I might have been saved from some of my most valuable mistakes." Although I understand and even appreciate the wisdom in her words, in some instances

I have thought that it is better to avoid making mistakes that could be too costly. After reflecting on the various pieces of advice from my trusted advisors, I came to the conclusion that they were both right, and I should try to follow their suggestions even if they appeared contradictory. Proposing a credible new approach to economic development could not be limited to the presentation of a theoretical explanation of past failures and successes—even a convincing one. But offering detailed policy prescriptions on a new brand of ideas with potential for controversy while country studies were still being carried out might seem like a rush to predetermined conclusions.

This chapter addresses both Martin's and Shahrokh's concerns. The ultimate goal of development thinking is to provide policy advice that facilitates the quest for sustainable and inclusive economic and social progress in poor countries. The new structural economics applies the neoclassical approach to the study of issues related to the nature and determinants of economic structures and their patterns of change in the process of economic development. In addition to reexamining the role of the state in facilitating industrial upgrading and diversification for economic development, discussed in the previous chapter, that framework brings structure to the core of development analysis. It can lead to many new policy insights that differ from those of the old structural economics and the conventional neoclassical theories.

Although specific policy measures to be derived from the new structural economics will require further research and depend very much on country contexts and circumstances, I can posit a few preliminary insights on various topics. Here I discuss some key policy differences and similarities among the old structural economics, neoclassical economics, and the new structural economics on fiscal issues, public revenue management in resource-rich countries, monetary issues, financial-sector development, trade, and human development.

Fiscal Policy: Free Airplanes, Railroads, and Bridges?

Fiscal policy, always an attractive topic for economists and politicians, is a good place to start thinking about what types of practical changes a new development framework would imply. As one of the main macroeconomic tools, it is basically about the government's changing levels of taxation, indebtedness, and public spending to influence aggregate demand (the total expenditure in an economy) and therefore the level of economic activity and the distribution of welfare among social groups. Its main goals are to stabilize economic growth, avoid the boom-and-bust economic cycle, stimulate economic growth in a recession, ensure that the most vulnerable groups have some basic income, and hold down inflation. Although almost everyone tends to agree with such laudable objectives, there is disagreement among economic theorists about how exactly to achieve them and about which instruments to use. Part of the disagreement has to do with ideological differences between conservatives and liberals and the faith that one has in the effectiveness of tax policy or the expectations about consumer or investor behavior.

Until Britain's very high unemployment of the 1920s and the Great Depression, economists generally held that the appropriate stance for fiscal policy was for governments to maintain balanced budgets. The severity of the early twentieth-century crises gave rise to the Keynesian idea of countercyclicality, which suggested that governments should use tax and expenditure policies to offset business cycles in the economy. In Keynes's theory, there is no strong automatic tendency for output and employment to move toward full employment. Indeed, macro trends are seen as overwhelming individual behavior. Contrary to classical economists such as Adam Smith, who focused on continuous improvements in potential output, Keynes was more concerned with the aggregate demand for goods and services, which he considered the driving economic factor—especially during downturns. From that perspective, he argued that government intervention should promote demand at a macro level and fight high unemployment and deflation.[1]

Proponents of the rational expectations theory (neoclassical economics) reject that premise. They suggest that in an economy in which money creation is restrained, a well-functioning price mechanism leads to a general tendency toward equilibrium. They also observe that for Keynesianism to work, one must assume that an increase of one unit in government purchases, and thereby in the aggregate demand for goods, would lead to an increase of at least one unit in real GDP (a multiplier of at least one).[2] They are quite skeptical about the implicit assumption behind the Keynesian model of a multiplier greater than one and its implication that governments are able to do something that the private sector has been unable to do: mobilize idle resources in the economy (unemployed labor and capital) at almost zero social cost—that is, with no corresponding decline in other parts of GDP (consumption, investment, and net exports).

Robert Barro calls active fiscal policy of the Keynesian type "the extreme demand-side view" or the "new voodoo economics."[3] He writes:

> [In that model,] the added public goods are essentially free to society. If the government buys another airplane or bridge, the economy's total output expands by enough to create the airplane or bridge without requiring a cut in anyone's consumption or investment. The explanation for this magic is that idle resources—unemployed labor and capital—are put to work to produce the added goods and services. If the multiplier is greater than 1.0, . . . the process is even more wonderful. In this case, real GDP rises by more than the increase in government purchases. Thus, in addition to the free airplane or bridge, we also have more goods and services left over to raise private consumption or investment. In this scenario, the added government spending is a good idea even if the bridge goes to nowhere, or if public employees are just filling useless holes. Of course, if this mechanism is genuine, one might ask why the government should stop with only $1 trillion of added purchases.[4]

Few neoclassical economists share the extreme (humoristic) view of conservative American columnist P. J. O'Rourke, who asserts, "Giving money and power to government is like giving whiskey and car keys to teenage boys."[5] But many of them share Barro's opinion that peacetime multipliers are essentially zero, which underpins their skepticism about the government's ability to create economic growth. They warn against the possibility of the Ricardian equivalence trap and point to the fact that households tend to adjust their behavior for consumption or saving on the basis of expectations about the future.[6] They suggest that expansionary fiscal policy (a stimulus package) is perceived as immediate spending or tax cuts that will need to be repaid in the future. They conclude that the multiplier could be less than one in situations in which the GDP is given and an increase in government spending does not lead to an equal rise in other parts of GDP. The rational expectations theory even suggests the possibility of some rare instances in which multipliers are negative, pointing to situations in which fiscal contractions become expansionary.[7]

Who is right? What is the true multiplier of fiscal policy? Is it largely positive, as Keynesians would say, or essentially nil or even negative, as proponents of the rational expectations revolution assert? The answers to these questions are not straightforward. They obviously depend on country contexts and circumstances and on the specific fiscal policy under consideration. "Democracy is an abuse of statistics," celebrated Argentinean writer Jorge Luis Borges once said, perhaps expressing the difficulty of sorting out the truth on such questions.

The new structural economics proposed in this book may help reconcile Keynesianism and rational expectations analyses. From its viewpoint, countercyclical policy is the appropriate fiscal strategy for developing countries.[8] Because their governments need to play a role in industrial upgrading by providing essential infrastructure, recessions are typically good times for making infrastructure investments, for three main reasons. First, such investments boost short-term demand and promote long-term growth. Second, their cost is lower than in normal times. And third, the Ricardian equivalence trap can be avoided because the increase in future growth rates and fiscal revenues can compensate for the cost of these investments.[9]

Moreover, if a developing country's government follows the new structural economics of facilitating the development of industries according to the country's comparative advantage, its economy will be competitive and its fiscal position and external accounts are likely to be sound, thanks to the likelihood of strong growth, good trade performance, and the lack of high unemployment and nonviable firms that the government has to subsidize.

Under this scenario, the country will face fewer homegrown economic crises. If the economy is hit by external shocks such as the recent global crisis, the government will be in a good position to implement a countercyclical fiscal stimulus and invest in infrastructure and social projects. Such public investments can enhance the economy's growth potential, reduce transaction costs for the private sector, increase the rate of return on private investment, and generate enough future tax revenues to liquidate the initial costs. Developing countries can actually get free airplanes and bridges, as Robert Barro joked, especially during a recession, if they invest wisely in productivity-enhancing, bottleneck-releasing infrastructures that meet the market test for profitability.

Money to Impoverish—or Money to Enrich

The old structural economics had little to say about monetary policy except to recommend that it be placed under government control (not that of independent central banks) and directed at influencing interest rates and even sector credit allocation. But it also acknowledged that many other factors that influence the investment demand schedule in developing countries are too powerful for monetary policy alone to achieve sufficient levels of investment, channel resources into strategic sectors, and combat unemployment.

Take a quick look at the website of the central bank of Cuba, perhaps the best source left for a modern version of such policies. One learns there that the Banco Central de Cuba is an institution "capable of coping with the needs which arise from the development of new ways to organize the internal and external economic relations of the country."[10] Its mission includes proposing and implementing "a monetary policy which allows the attainment of the economic goals established by the country." Among its functions, Banco Central de Cuba must undertake other challenges such as improving "the monetary system, in such way, that it can make feasible execution of the economic activity" and encouraging "the efficacy of the economy in general and, particularly, work productivity." The page on monetary policy starts with the clear statement that "it is necessary to take into account that it adopts particular characteristics in the case of Cuba, since there is not a market economy but a central planning, mainly, of a financial type."[11] It then goes on to highlight the instruments of monetary policy, mainly legal reserve ratios and controls over exchange rates and interest rates. Unfortunately, the use of monetary measures for purely planning purposes without ensuring that the financial system supports the development of competitive industries consistent with the economy's comparative advantage has mostly resulted in impoverishment.

Neoclassical economists doubt that monetary policy can support industrial development, as seems the case in Cuba and other countries where the old structural economics guided economic thinking. Building on lessons from the rational expectations revolution, they recommend that its main goal be price stability, which implies avoiding both prolonged inflation and deflation. This is the view of the European Central Bank, whose experts highlight the fact that price stability contributes to achieving high levels of economic activity and employment by improving the transparency of the price mechanism. Under price stability people can recognize changes in relative prices (prices between different goods) without being confused by changes in the overall price level. This allows them to make well-informed consumption and investment decisions and to allocate resources more efficiently, reducing inflation risk premiums in interest rates (the compensation creditors require for the risks associated with holding nominal assets). And this reduces real interest rates and increases incentives to invest. It avoids unproductive activities to hedge against the negative impact of inflation or deflation. It also reduces distortions of inflation or deflation, which can heighten the distortionary impact of tax and social security systems on economic behavior. And it prevents an arbitrary redistribution of wealth and income as a result of unexpected inflation or deflation.

The scope of monetary policy is similar to that of a central bank under the old structural economics. The monopoly supplier of the monetary base, the central bank is the sole issuer of banknotes and bank reserves. By virtue of this monopoly, it can set the conditions for banks to borrow from the central bank. So it can also influence the conditions for banks to trade with each other in the money market. The use of short-term interest rates by independent central banks serves to maintain the general level of prices (or control the growth of the money supply), not to stimulate economic activity and trigger inflation. In the short run, a change in money market interest rates induced by the central bank through a wide variety of direct and indirect instruments sets in motion a number of mechanisms and actions by economic agents.[12] Ultimately, the change will influence developments in such economic variables as output or prices. This process—also known as the monetary policy transmission mechanism—is much more complex than it is under the old structural economics.[13]

Until the recent global crisis, neoclassical economists and most central bankers in the Western world felt quite happy with the outcome of their approach to monetary policy. Commenting on the substantial decline in macroeconomic volatility around the world in recent decades—at least prior to the 2007 global crisis—Ben Bernanke, the chairman of the U.S. Federal Reserve Bank, called "the Great Moderation" "one of the most striking features of the economic landscape over the past 20 years."[14] He said, "Few disagree that monetary policy has played a large part in stabilizing inflation, and so the fact that output volatility has declined in parallel with inflation volatility, both in the United States and abroad, suggests that monetary policy may have helped moderate the variability of output as well."[15]

The Great Recession brought many new questions to the intellectual agenda of neoclassical monetary policy. David Blanchflower, a member of the Monetary Policy Committee of the Bank of England, said: "As a monetary policy-maker I have found the 'cutting edge' of current macroeconomic research totally inadequate in helping to resolve the problems we currently face."[16]

A few years earlier, Gregory Mankiw, a Harvard University economist who also served as chairman of former president George W. Bush's Council of Economic Advisors, had observed, "New classical and new Keynesian research has had little impact on practical macroeconomists who are charged with the messy task of conducting actual monetary and fiscal policy."[17] Paul de Grauwe, another highly respected monetary economist, offered similar warnings: "There is a danger that the macroeconomic models now in use in central banks operate like a Maginot line. They have been constructed in the past as part of the war against inflation. The central banks are prepared to fight the last war. But are they prepared to fight the new one against financial upheavals and recession? The macroeconomic models they have today certainly do not provide them with the right tools to be successful."[18]

The new structural economics acknowledges that monetary policy is often ineffective for stimulating private investment and consumption in recessions and excess capacity situations in developed countries, especially when nominal interest rates hit the zero bound in a context of limited profitable investment opportunities, pessimistic expectations, low confidence about the future, and the likelihood of liquidity traps caused by the large excess capacity in the existing manufacturing, construction, and housing sectors.[19] However, developing countries are less likely to encounter such liquidity traps. Even when faced with excess capacity in existing domestic industries, their scope for industrial upgrading is large. Their firms have incentives to undertake productivity-enhancing, industrial upgrading investments during recessions if interest rates are sufficiently low. Further, they tend to have many infrastructure bottlenecks. Lowering interest rates in such contexts would also encourage investments in infrastructure.

To address these issues, the new structural economics envisions the possibility of using interest-rate policy in developing countries as a countercyclical tool and as an instrument to encourage infrastructure and industrial upgrading investments during recessions—measures that may contribute to productivity growth in the future. Monetary policy can thus be used not only countercyclically to stabilize the economy but also strategically to foster structural transformation and contribute to the enrichment of developing countries.

Surviving Wealth:
Public Revenue Management in Resource-Rich Countries

One of the most pressing public revenue management issues—especially in developing countries—is handling and using revenue from natural resource wealth. The old structuralist analysis considers the world economy a system in which the center (rich, dominant economies) and the periphery (poor economies) are intrinsically linked, with many economic problems of the periphery deriving from that interaction.[20] So it views the management of revenue from natural resources as an important aspect of a developing country's strategy to address the center–periphery imbalances. In República Bolivariana de Venezuela, for instance, President Hugo Chavez has made energy nationalization the main pillar of his "revolution" and development strategy— just as leaders of many Latin American, African, and Asian countries did in the 1950s and 1960s.[21]

The creation of national marketing boards in many African countries extended such policies to agriculture. They often led to poor results. Palm oil in Nigeria, groundnuts in Senegal, cotton in Uganda, coffee in Cameroon, and even cocoa in Ghana were once the most prosperous industries in Africa. But because of excessive and misguided government intervention, farmers of these crops eventually produced less, exported less, and earned less in foreign markets.[22]

Those principles of resource management, even applied mainly to developing countries, led government skeptics such as former conservative U.S. president Ronald Reagan to joke, "Government's view of the economy could be summed up in a few short phrases: If it moves, tax it. If it keeps moving, regulate it. And if it stops moving, subsidize it." Neoclassical economics, which underpinned his economic philosophy, generally recommends that resource-rich countries adopt policies aimed at avoiding internal and external imbalances. In that regard, one of the main goals of resource management is to save a substantial portion of revenue from natural resources (often deposited in a separate central bank account or trust fund, normally held in foreign currency, for future generations) and use only a small fraction of it for current consumption. In the short and medium terms, that strategy smoothes public expenditure in the face of commodity price fluctuations. In the long term it raises total government savings and ensures that enough wealth from natural resources is accumulated for future generations.

The current neoclassical literature also highlights sound management of foreign reserves in resource-rich countries to increase resilience to shocks. Sound reserve management can maintain confidence in monetary and exchange-rate policies. It can mitigate external vulnerability by keeping foreign currency liquid to absorb shocks during crises, signal to markets that a country can meet its external obligations, and ensure the backing of domestic currency with external assets. It can also provide reserves for use in national disasters or emergencies.[23]

Because sound reserve management policies and practices can support, but not substitute for, sound macroeconomic management, neoclassical economics also recommends that portfolio management policies concerning the currency composition, choice of investment instruments, and acceptable duration of the reserves portfolio be consistent with a country's specific policy settings and circumstances and ensure that assets are safeguarded, are readily available, and support market confidence. It also stresses the need for a framework of transparency that ensures accountability and clarity of reserve management activities and results, sound institutional and governance structures, and prudent management of risks.

But saving money has never been enough to ensure continuing success and sustained growth. The neoclassical resource revenue management policy may not be sufficient to facilitate industrial diversification and upgrading in a resource-rich country, accelerate its growth rate, and enhance its inclusiveness and sustainability.[24] When asked about the secret of his phenomenal success as an investor and financier, American billionaire Warren Buffett once explained his two rules: "Rule number one: Never lose money. Rule number two: Never forget rule number one." He corroborates Henry Ford's admonition that success is really about making sound investment decisions: "Old men are always advising young men to save money. That is bad advice. Don't save every nickel. Invest in yourself. I never saved a dollar until I was 40 years old."

The new structural economics would recommend that an appropriate share of revenues from commodities be used to invest in human, infrastructure, and social capital and provide incentives for developing manufacturing industries consistent with their comparative advantages to facilitate industrial diversification and upgrading. Paul Collier rightly observes that in the coming decade, the poorest societies in the world, where the poorest (the "bottom billion") live, will need to manage the huge opportunities and risks posed by natural resources: "Central Asia and Africa are the last frontiers for resource extraction, and with high global commodity prices and new prospecting technologies, the natural assets hidden beneath their territories will be discovered. Whether this leads to environmental degradation and violent plunder or a meteoric ascent out of poverty depends on the choices that these societies make. Not only are the stakes high, but the choices involved are complex. Harnessing natural assets for environmentally responsible prosperity is not just a matter of 'good governance': the decisionmakers need to know the underlying economics along a whole chain of decisions."[25]

To accomplish this with the greatest effect, these resources should finance investment opportunities that remove binding constraints on sustainable and inclusive growth, especially in infrastructure and education, with the goal of incentivizing domestic entrepreneurs and attracting foreign direct investment (FDI) for diversification to manufacturing industries aligned with the country's comparative advantage. In Afghanistan, where new aerial prospecting technology has been used to scour the country for natural resources and find an estimated $1 trillion worth of minerals, it would be crucial for the authorities to quickly adopt a development strategy (and set up a corresponding institutional framework) that channels a fraction of the revenue into sustainable and inclusive growth. That could avoid the resource curse that other geologically rich countries, such as the Democratic Republic of Congo, have suffered.

The exploitation of natural resources can generate large revenues, but it is generally very capital intensive and provides limited job opportunities. Low-income, resource-abundant countries tend to have abundant labor and huge job needs. In a visit in 2009 to Papua New Guinea, I observed that the Ok Tedi copper and gold mine in Tabubil generates almost 80 percent of the country's exports and 40 percent of government revenues but provides only

2,000 jobs. A proposed liquefied natural gas project would double Papua New Guinea's national income after its completion in a few years but would provide only 8,000 employment opportunities. Most of Papua New Guinea's 6.5 million inhabitants still live on subsistence agriculture. Not surprisingly, the contrast between the lifestyle of a few elite workers in modern mining towns and that of subsistence farmers is becoming a source of social tensions.

Similar observations can be made about Botswana, an African country that has generally performed well since its independence in 1966 and is one of the 13 successful economies discussed in the Growth Commission Report. The failure to diversify the economy from diamond mining and to generate employment opportunities may explain widening income disparities and deteriorating human and social indicators despite the diamond industry's great success in sustaining Botswana's growth miracle in the past 40 years.

Still, one question deserves to be posed: does a resource-rich, labor-abundant economy like that of Papua New Guinea have comparative advantages in labor-intensive manufacturing industries? My answer is yes. The country's wage rate is low, and wages are the major cost of production for labor-intensive industries. Therefore, labor-intensive manufacturing industries can be competitive in such a country with improved infrastructure and reduced transaction costs. The labor-intensive industries in Indonesia and Thailand are good examples. Moreover, not only does labor-intensive manufacturing offer the potential to absorb surplus labor from the rural subsistence sector, but the development of such industries can also pave the way for continuous upgrading to higher-value-added industries. Finland's Nokia is a good example. Today most people see that country only as a dominant player in the sophisticated mobile phone business. Yet it started its economic development process with logging and diversified its operations to labor-intensive activities such as the production of rubber boots, and later to the production of household electronics under an "original equipment manufacturer" agreement for Philips, before venturing into mobile phones.

True, the exploitation and export of natural resources may be accompanied by the so-called Dutch disease as export receipts from, say, oil, natural gas, or minerals push up the value of the currency, reducing the competitiveness of manufacturing exports. And if the wealth from natural resources is captured by powerful groups, as in Nigeria, the resources can become a curse. Scandinavian countries have demonstrated good management of natural resource wealth. They have shown that transparent administration and investment in human capital and infrastructure can increase labor productivity, reduce production and transaction costs, and offset the adverse effects of the Dutch disease.

The Scandinavian experience holds valuable lessons for labor-abundant, resource-rich economies. As promoted by the World Bank's Extractive Industries Transparency Initiative Plus Plus (EITI++), countries that use their natural resource wealth to fight poverty, hunger, malnutrition, illiteracy, and disease—and to support structural transformation by facilitating the development of labor-intensive manufacturing industries—can turn their resources from a curse into a blessing. Such countries have opportunities to accumulate capital, upgrade endowments, improve infrastructure, transform industrial structure, and subsequently raise incomes faster than labor-abundant, resource-poor countries.

The need for economic development strategies that foster structural transformation is confirmed by the fact that microeconomic analyses show that even when factory floor costs are comparable, inefficiencies in infrastructure can make it impossible for poor countries to compete in international markets. Freight and insurance costs in African countries are 250 percent of the global average, with road freight delays two to three times longer than in Asian countries.[26] Lacking financial resources and the appropriate policy frameworks, many of these countries cannot sustain much-needed investment and maintenance.

Recent research suggests that *economic* returns on investment projects in developing countries average 30–40 percent for telecommunications, more than 40 percent for electricity generation, and more than 200 percent for roads. In Thailand production loss due to power outages represented more than 50 percent of the total indirect costs of doing business in 2006. Firms often rely on their own generators to supplement the unreliable public electricity supply. In Pakistan more than 60 percent of firms surveyed in 2002 owned a generator. The cost of maintaining a power generator is often high and burdensome, especially for small and medium firms, which tend to be large sources of employment. Yet although these costs must be privately borne, their benefits are felt across the economy.

In such contexts, the effective strategy of natural resource management derived from the new structural economics would be not to keep revenues in sovereign funds and invest in foreign equity markets or projects but to use a substantial portion of the revenues for financing domestic or regional projects that facilitate economic development and structural change. Such projects stimulate new manufacturing industries, diversify the economy, provide jobs, and offer the potential of continual upgrading.

Financial Development:
Those Bankers We Love to Hate

American poet Robert Frost is often quoted as saying, "A bank is a place where they lend you an umbrella in fair weather and ask for it when it begins to rain." There is ample consensus among economists that financial system development is essential to a well-functioning modern economy. There is, however, much less agreement on its specific role and on the direction of causality. Starting with the observation that one of the major constraints facing developing countries was limited capital accumulation, the old structural economics regarded the inability of the financial sector in underdeveloped economies to mobilize funding for investment as resulting from widespread market failures that could not be overcome by market forces alone.[27] They recommended that governments adopt a hands-on approach in that process, mobilize savings, and allocate credit to support the development of advanced capital-intensive industries. And yes, they did this in countries as different as Japan, Mexico, and Senegal.[28]

Analyzing the effects of such policies throughout the developing world, especially in the 1960s and 1970s, economists observed that price inflation combined with numerous government interventions to set interest rates and direct the flow of credit had shrunk the deposit base for domestic bank lending. This very often led to "financial repression"; excessive government intervention in the financial system through formal rules (regulations, laws), along with other informal norms and nonmarket restrictions, prevents the financial intermediaries of an economy from functioning at their full capacity. The policies that cause financial repression typically include low interest-rate ceilings, high liquidity ratio requirements, high bank reserve requirements, rigid capital controls, (arbitrary) restrictions on market entry into the financial sector, credit ceilings or restrictions on the directions of credit allocation, and government ownership or domination of banks.[29]

In some countries, especially in Eastern Europe, the former Soviet Union, and Africa, government-owned enterprises could overspend their budgets and lose money. They were not allowed to fail. Instead, the government always kept them afloat with large subsidies and capital investments financed by low-interest-rate loans from banks. Thus enterprises that should have been managed more efficiently, reformed, or liquidated continued to function at a high cost to taxpayers. That practice, termed the "soft budget constraint," led governments to accumulate deficits in state-owned financial institutions. It also created a pervasive business culture of self-repression, not only for banks but also for private enterprises. Credit became an enrichment tool for many elites in the ruling class because they knew they did not have to reimburse it.[30] American industrialist Jean Paul Getty half-jokingly summarized the conundrum facing financial institutions with large amounts of nonperforming loans: "If you owe the bank $100, that is your problem. If you owe the bank $100 million, that is the bank's problem."

Drawing consequences from such situations, neoclassical economists advocated financial liberalization. They contended that bureaucrats generally do not have the incentives or expertise to intervene effectively in credit allocation and pricing and that a well-defined system of property rights, good contractual institutions, and competition would create the conditions for the emergence of a sound financial system. Criticizing "bureaucrats as bankers," they contended that greater state ownership leads to less financial-sector development, lower growth and lower productivity, higher interest-rate spreads, less private credit and nonbank financial development, greater concentration of credit, and some tendency toward weaker monitoring and more crises. They recommended that government exit bank ownership and lift restrictions on allocating credit and determining interest rates.[31] They also advocated developing large modern banks and equity markets with separate financial authorities to implement the Basel regulations.

While agreeing with the need to address the deleterious effects of financial repression, the new structural economics posits that the appropriate financial structure at a given level of development should be determined by the prevailing industrial structure, the average size of firms, and the typical risk they face—all factors that are, in turn, endogenous to the economy's factor endowments at that level of development.

In the early stage of a country's development and because of the nature of its endowments, comparative advantage is typically found in resource-intensive and labor-intensive industries. Except for a few large mining companies or plantations, a large portion of its production and employment is organized in small farms or firms in agriculture, manufacturing, and services. The capital requirements of these enterprises are small. They use mature technologies to produce mature goods, mostly for local markets. They often lack the standard financial documents and do not exhibit a long financial history.

In providing credit to such firms or farms, financiers see the main risk as the managerial ability of the firm or farm operators. The financial arrangements that can best serve customer needs involve informal moneylenders and small local banks, which can provide small loans and have information advantages over their borrowers, with whom they maintain regular and even intimate contact.[32]

When the economy grows and its endowment structure changes, operations in industries and farms are upgraded to more capital-intensive ones, and their sizes increase. The funding requirements for their investments and operations also rise. The upgrading extends their market range and moves their technologies closer to the global frontier, which in turn elevates their risk. The appropriate financial institutions for serving such new needs are gradually changed to larger national banks or equity markets, which have the ability to mobilize large amounts of funds and spread risks.

Too often, financial-sector policy advice to developing countries includes the development of large banks and equity markets similar to those in the developed countries, regardless of the level of development and the structure of the economy. The new structural economics would suggest that low-income countries choose small, local banks as the backbones of their financial systems instead of trying to replicate the financial structures of advanced industrialized countries. This would allow small firms in agriculture, industry, and services to receive adequate financial services. As industrial upgrading takes place and the economy relies increasingly on more capital-intensive industries, the financial structure will change to give greater weight to large banks and sophisticated equity markets.[33]

The Need for Poor Countries to Choose Their Type of Foreign Capital

American scientist Howard Scott, famous for his attempts to apply thermodynamics and vector analysis to economic and other social phenomena, held highly suspicious views of capitalists. He once said, half-jokingly, "A criminal is a person with predatory instincts without sufficient capital to form a corporation." Some old structuralist thinkers shared that deep distrust of capital, especially in foreign hands. In a world that they thought was characterized by the core–periphery relationship, they tended to view foreign capital mainly as a tool in the hands of industrialized countries and their multinational firms that they used to maintain harmful control over developing countries. They rejected the idea that free capital movements among countries could deliver an efficient allocation of resources. They considered FDI (foreign investment that establishes a lasting interest across boundaries in or effective management control over an enterprise) flows to poor countries as an instrument for foreign ownership and domination. And they advocated tight restrictions on almost all forms of international financial flows.

Not surprisingly, neoclassical economists hold a radically different view. They argue that international capital mobility serves several purposes. It allows countries with limited savings to attract financing for productive domestic investment projects. It enables investors to diversify their portfolios. It spreads investment risks more broadly. And it promotes intertemporal trade—the trading of goods today for goods in the future.[34] So neoclassical theory generally favors open or liberalized capital markets, with the expectation of more efficient allocation of savings, increased possibilities for diversification of investment risk, faster growth, and the dampening of business cycles. Note, however, that some neoclassical economists also argue that liberalized financial markets in developing countries can be distorted by incomplete information, large and volatile movements in and out of the system, and many other problems leading to suboptimal consequences that damage general welfare.

The new structural economics considers FDI a more favorable source of foreign capital for developing countries than other capital flows because it is usually targeted toward industries consistent with a country's comparative advantage. It is also less prone to sudden reversals during panics than are bank loans, debt financing, and portfolio investment. And it does not generate the same acute problems of financial crises as do sharp reversals of debt and portfolio flows. In addition, it generally also brings technology, management, access to markets, and social networking, which are often lacking in developing countries and yet crucial for industrial upgrading.

An overview of empirical studies concludes that FDI contributes both to productivity and to income growth in host countries, beyond what domestic investment normally would trigger.[35] Although some of these benefits are difficult to measure, one study shows that FDI benefited Venezuelan manufacturing in marketing and after-sales service but, because of high dependence on imported inputs, failed to generate positive spillovers in backward linkages.[36] The ability to capture technological spillovers is often a function of absorptive capacity—that is, infrastructure and education. Among higher-income developing economies that have received large amounts of FDI—such as Hong Kong SAR, China; the Czech Republic; Mexico; and the

Philippines—labor market and technology spillovers have been substantial.[37] Thus liberalizing inward direct investment should generally be an attractive component of a broader development strategy.

By contrast, portfolio investment—purchases of stocks and bonds and money market instruments that, unlike direct investment, do not create a lasting interest in or effective management control over an enterprise—may move in and out of countries quickly in large quantities, targeting speculative activities (mostly in equity markets or housing) and creating bubbles and fluctuations. The unprecedented increases in short-term capital inflows financed housing bubbles in Greece, Ireland, Spain, and several other European countries, triggering the sovereign debt crisis in the euro zone. Large portfolio flows to emerging economies also caused equity and housing bubbles and currency appreciations, complicating macroeconomic management during the crisis.

One should always remember that a sudden large inflow of portfolio capital is most likely to be invested in speculative sectors rather than in productive sectors, for two reasons. First, a large increase in investment in existing industries may encounter diminishing returns to capital. Second, the potential for quick and extensive industrial upgrading is limited by infrastructure and human capital constraints. That is why portfolio investment should be carefully managed.[38] The new structural economics may also shed new light on the puzzle posed by Robert Lucas about the flow of capital from capital-scarce developing countries to capital-abundant developed countries.[39] Without improving infrastructure and upgrading to new comparative-advantage industries, a developing country may encounter diminishing returns in accumulating capital, causing lower returns to capital and justifying the outflow to developed countries.

Sorting Out the Paradoxes of Trade Policy

"There is no point in asking whether we should be for or against globalization," one of my predecessors at the World Bank and a former International Monetary Fund deputy managing director, Stanley Fischer, once said in a speech to African heads of state. He added: "The problem is summarized in one of the signs seen at last year's demonstrations against Bretton Woods institutions: *Worldwide coalition against globalization.* Globalization is here to stay: the reality is that we already live in a global economy—where flows of trade, capital and knowledge across national borders are not only large but also increasing every year. Countries unwilling to engage with other nations risk falling farther behind the rest of the world in terms of both income and human development. That way lies the very real threat of marginalization."[40]

On a different occasion, Fischer, who had clearly thought deeply about the issue, also observed: "The evidence strongly supports the conclusion that growth requires a policy framework that prominently includes an orientation toward integration into the global economy. This places obligations on three groups: those who are most responsible for the operation of the international economy, primarily the governments of the developed countries; those who determine the intellectual climate, which includes this audience but also government and nongovernment organizations and individuals; and the governments of the developing countries who bear the major responsibility for economic policy in their countries."[41]

The old structuralists have approached globalization—particularly external trade—in many ways. But one constant feature has been the belief that integration into the global economy is bound to maintain the world power structure, with Western countries and their multinational corporations dominating poorer countries and exploiting their economies. To break the dependency trap, old structuralist thinkers have suggested that priority be given to import substitution strategies, with developing economies closed and protected until they can compete with advanced industrialized countries in world markets.

Neoclassical economists—many of them former students or colleagues of Stanley Fischer—adopted the opposite view in the 1980s. Observing that macroeconomic crises in developing countries almost always have an external dimension, they considered that their immediate cause was the lack of foreign exchange with which to service debts and purchase imports. They recommended trade liberalization and export promotion to generate foreign exchange through export earnings. This was also consistent with the view that, in the long term, outward-oriented development strategies are more effective than inward-looking policies. This view was bolstered by the argument that such a strategy would increase demand for unskilled labor and hence unskilled wages, as happened in successful East Asian countries.[42]

The new structural economics is consistent with the neoclassical view that exports and imports are endogenous to the comparative advantage determined by a country's endowment structure (they are essential features of industrial upgrading and reflect changes in comparative advantage). Globalization offers a way for developing countries to exploit the advantages of backwardness and achieve a faster rate of innovation and structural transformation than is possible for countries already on the global technology frontier. Openness is therefore an essential channel for convergence.

The new structural economics recognizes, however, that many developing countries start climbing the industrial ladder with the legacy of distortions from old structural economics strategies of import substitution. That is why it suggests a gradualist approach to trade liberalization. During the transition, the state may consider providing some temporary protection to industries that are not consistent with a country's comparative advantage while liberalizing and facilitating the entry of firms into other more competitive sectors that previously were controlled and repressed. The dynamic growth in the newly liberalized sectors creates the conditions for reforming the old priority sectors. That pragmatic dual-track approach helps achieve growth objectives without incurring heavy losses in the transition.[43]

Deciphering the Mysteries of Human Development

Scottish writer Sir Arthur Conan Doyle, creator of the detective Sherlock Holmes, once wrote, "Skill is fine, genius is splendid, but the right contacts are more valuable than either." His intuition may have provided an answer to economist Lant Pritchett, who wondered in an influential article, "Where has all the education gone?"[44] It is indeed puzzling that cross-national data show no association between increases in human capital attributable to the rising educational attainment of the labor force and the rate of growth of output per worker. Observing that the development impact of education varied widely across countries, Pritchett conjectured that it had fallen short of expectations for three possible reasons. First, the institutional and governance environment could have been so perverse that the accumulation of educational capital lowered economic growth. Second, marginal returns to education could have fallen rapidly as the supply of educated labor expanded while demand remained stagnant. Third, educational quality could have been so low that years of schooling created no human capital.

The old structural economics generally said little about the role of human development in economic growth. By contrast, neoclassical economics has argued that the continuing growth in per capita incomes of many countries in the nineteenth and twentieth centuries was mainly due to the expansion of scientific and technical knowledge, which raised the productivity of labor and other inputs in production. Economic theory has suggested that growth is the result of synergies between new knowledge and human capital, which is why large increases in education and training have accompanied major advances in technological knowledge in all countries that have achieved significant economic growth. Investments in education, training, and health, the most important for human capital, are considered to be the most important driving force for economic development.[45]

If that is so, why are some empirical studies reaching conclusions similar to Pritchett's and giving credence to Conan Doyle's sarcastic comment? The new structural economics considers human capital as one component of a country's endowments. For economic agents, risks and uncertainty arise during the industrial upgrading and technological innovation that accompany economic development. As various firms move up the industrial ladder to new, higher capital-intensity industries and get closer to the global industrial frontier, they face more risks.

Human capital increases workers' ability to cope with risk and uncertainty, but its formation requires a long gestation.[46] A person who loses the opportunity to receive education at a young age may not be able to compensate for that loss at a later age. In a dynamic, growing economy it is important to plan ahead and make human capital investments before the economy requires the set of skills associated with new industries and technologies. But improvements in human capital should be commensurable with the accumulation of physical capital and the upgrading of industry in the economy. Otherwise, either the human capital will become a binding constraint for economic development if it is undersupplied because of insufficient investment or the country will have many frustrated, highly educated youth if the industrial upgrading of the economy is not progressing fast enough to provide skilled jobs. Just look at the Arab Spring in Egypt, Tunisia, and other countries.

A well-designed policy for human capital development should be integral to any country's overall development strategy. The new structural economics goes beyond the neoclassical generic prescription for education and suggests that development strategies include measures to invest in human capital that facilitate the upgrading of industries and prepare the economy to make full use of its resources. The key components of such strategies should follow Lucas's suggestion of allowing human capital to have both a quality and a quantity dimension.[47] They should also include alternative policies for promoting skill formation targeted to different parts of the life cycle, with the government and the private sector working closely together to anticipate or respond to the skill needs of the labor market.[48] Singapore, one of the 13 high-growth economies that were able to grow at more than 7 percent for more than 25 years after World War II, provides a good example of human capital development as a national strategy.[49] Its strategy went beyond the schooling decision and recognized that on-the-job training is important for aggregate human capital. Its human resources policies have been continually revised and adjusted in conjunction with other national strategic economic goals.

Summing up, the new structural economics proposed in this book builds on advances in economic understanding and lessons from history and suggests a rigorous analysis of social realities. But it is also a very pragmatic framework that policymakers from all countries could use to maximize the likelihood of success on their path to prosperity. To ensure that development practitioners can use it effectively, it must be accompanied by a sort of user's manual for implementation (see Chapter 7).

SEVEN

Putting the New
Structural Economics into Practice:
Two Tracks and Six Steps

FROM ANYWHERE IN THE WORLD and with a simple click of a mouse, one can instantly visit the jewelry zone in Thailand, the leather zone in Turkey, the single-commodity zone for tea in Zimbabwe, the single-factory export-oriented units in India, or the single-company zones in the Dominican Republic.[1] One can also order soft copies of the nice brochures that business promotion agencies issue, listing the many special incentives each country offers global investors. Skeptical businesspeople who might not want to confine themselves to virtual images or documents on a computer screen and are willing to travel can visit factories in many of these countries, where large tracts of land have been given special zone status. For instance, Mauritius offers interested investors a field visit to the potential fish-breeding sites around the island, where tropical-water seafood species can be farmed both in and outside the lagoon.

The policy incentive packages that governments of low-income countries offer today easily match the attractiveness of what the port cities like Hong Kong and Singapore offered half a century ago through special customs regimes for export processing and transshipments. The zones have a variety of names—from export processing zones to special economic zones.[2] They have extended the list of preferred industries well beyond the traditional textiles, clothing, and electronics to more sophisticated technology and even software, as in Bangalore, India. The signal is clear—even the poorest of the low-income countries in Sub-Saharan Africa no longer want to depend simply on cocoa, coffee, cotton, and other raw commodities that have been their traditional exports. Indeed, 22 African countries already have industrial zones and are willing to leverage more than just the zones, as evident from the Ghanaian President's Special Initiatives launched in six industries (garments and textiles, salt mining, cotton production, oil palm production, cassava starch production, and distance learning) and Uganda's very ambitious and comprehensive National Development Plan for 2011–15.

The same excitement can be perceived in middle-income countries, too. Russia is building the Skolkovo project, establishing a high-tech research hub near Moscow. It will focus on research in five priority sectors: energy, information technologies, communication, biomedical research, and nuclear technologies. The media dubbed the project "Russia's Silicon Valley" after the Northern California region that has served as a model for such centers in the United States and worldwide. On a recent visit to the "real" Silicon Valley, President Dmitry Medvedev explained that he seeks to diversify the Russian economy by reducing its dependence on oil and gas exports, developing high-tech sectors, and encouraging research.

By resorting to new tools of industrial policy, developing countries' governments are simply trying to replicate the facilitating role that the state has played successfully even in the richest countries throughout history.[3] As Ha-Joon Chang observes, "Industries such as computers, aerospace, and the Internet, where the United States still maintains an international edge despite the decline in its overall technological leadership, would not have existed without defense-related research and development (R&D) funding by the country's federal government."[4] The same has been true in Europe, where discussions of active industrial policy have been constant since the end of World War II.[5] In recent years, the official strategy documents of the EU have focused on new aspects of industrial policy: the risk of deindustrialization, the regulatory burden, and the impact of enlarging the EU on the competitiveness of European companies and their location. In the context of the review of the Lisbon Strategy in March 2005, EU member states clearly maintained the objective of "creating a solid industrial base" and reiterated the increasing importance attached to R&D and innovation in all forms, as well as information and communication technologies.[6]

Traveling constantly across the world in my capacity at the World Bank, I have always been impressed with the number of government officials at all levels of responsibility who ask me for help in designing and implementing strategies to identify sources of growth and facilitate the emergence of competitive industries that can create employment and help fight poverty. Although a few of them may have the intention of creating conditions for rent-seeking and personal enrichment, as the economic literature suggests, most political leaders and administrative elites I have met are motivated by the genuine desire to do something good for their people—and for the legacy that they can leave for their country. Unfortunately, many of them have no clear understanding of the conditions that make government intervention in the economy successful—or of the nuances in the types of strategies, policy measures, and tools appropriate to their levels of development.

This chapter offers a practical, easy-to-use guide for policymakers to apply the new structural economics. It focuses on two tracks: growth identification and growth facilitation. The challenge of moving from the "why" to the "how to" for government facilitation is obviously trickier than for growth identification. The reason is that countries at different levels of development and with different endowment structures have to choose different policy packages, with many possible outcomes and often some unintended consequences. Despite these difficulties, it is important for policymakers to grasp fully their country conditions and to identify and seize the economic opportunities available to them at any time in a globalized world. The growth identification and facilitation (GIF) framework presented here can help them do just that.[7]

To Identify or Not to Identify: That Is the Question

Before suggesting a strategy for getting the identification "right," it helps to recall that the objective is to discover industries that will allow a country to implement a comparative advantage–following approach to technological and industrial upgrading, the quintessence of rapid and sustainable growth. Less developed countries can start their industrialization by exploiting their latecomer advantages—by importing modern technology, industries, and institutions from more advanced countries. They do not have to reinvent the wheel. With the facilitating hand of government, they can become competitive in industries that have comparative advantages in domestic and international markets, reinvest the profits, and, over time, become more capital abundant. That strategy allows them to upgrade their industrial structures. Although the process sounds gradual and slow, it is actually the fastest, most sustainable way to close their gap with the developed countries.

In practice many developing countries are unable to do so. Their economists and policymakers often feel like Hamlet, Shakespeare's well-known character who wondered whether the unknown beyond death is any easier to bear than life: "To be or not to be: that is the question." His soliloquy, perhaps the most famous in the English language, expresses his uncertainty about the proper course of action and his frustration at his inability to assess the potential consequences of his actions.

Likewise, many of those who acknowledge the validity of the strong theoretical case for industrial policy (made by the likes of Adam Smith in the lesser-known Book V of *The Wealth of Nations* and Alfred Marshall, who outlined the analytical framework for externalities and coordination) still have doubts about its implementation, fearing the possibility of things going badly wrong. Pondering the uncertainty of an industrial policy and the potential costs of failure, they find it easier to accept the notion that the government should provide general incentives and an enabling environment to firms (through improvements in business environment) and leave the issue of which industry to develop to private entrepreneurs. Even though some of them agree with the desirability of setting up special economic zones or industrial parks to overcome the infrastructure constraints, they are still reluctant to endorse the idea of targeting specific industries for those zones or parks.

I submit that identifying industries with good potential for growth and competitiveness is a precondition for a successful industrial policy in developing countries. Why? The appropriate hard and soft infrastructure improvements for development are often industry specific. Look at the list of recent success stories in poor African countries: they include textiles in Mauritius, apparel in Lesotho, cotton in Burkina Faso, cut flowers in Ethiopia, cocoa in Ghana, gorilla tourism in Rwanda, and mangoes in Mali.[8] Clearly the successful development and dominance of these industries in global markets require more than a "general" laissez-faire development strategy. The refrigeration facilities at the airport and the regular flights to ship cut flowers from Ethiopia to auctions in Europe are obviously quite different from the improvements to the port facilities for textile exports in Mauritius. Similarly, the infrastructure for the garment industry in Lesotho is distinct from that for mango exports in Mali or for attracting gorilla tourism to Rwanda. Because of limited fiscal resources and implementation capacity, the government in each country must decide what infrastructure to improve and where to provide services to make those success stories happen.

Identification is also needed because clustering is key to turning an industry consistent with a country's comparative advantage into a competitive industry domestically and internationally. As Chapter 5 argued, specialization, agglomeration, and clustering are crucial for reducing transaction costs in any given industry.[9] If the government does not provide incentives for private firms to enter some specific industries consistent with the country's comparative advantage, firms may be spread thinly over too many different industries. As a consequence, none of them will form sufficiently large clusters to be competitive internationally. Some clusters may eventually emerge spontaneously but only at the cost of many failed industries and after a long process of trial, error, and elimination.

Ravi Menon, formerly permanent secretary of the Ministry of Trade and Industry and currently managing director of the Monetary Authority of Singapore, explained the issue well in a speech he made in October 2010. In the 1980s his country saw a coming global boom in petrochemicals and decided to upgrade its petroleum-refining industry. To overcome Singapore's cost disadvantage and foster a viable chemicals cluster, it was necessary to move "downstream" to the production of higher-value-added specialty chemicals. But an integrated development would require much land—which

Singapore was obviously short of. The government created an integrated "chemicals island" and prepared a who's who of the global chemical industry —listing Chevron, Sumitomo, Mitsui, Exxon, Shell, and others. By the time Jurong Island officially opened in October 2000, more than 60 leading petrochemical-related companies had invested more than $20 billion on the island. As Menon explained,

> The government's activist role in the petrochemical industry helped address several coordination failures in the market, something no single private company could have easily resolved. The key to Jurong Island's success was not infrastructure—it was *government-enabled industry integration*. Companies came together in one location, supported by common pipeline corridors and a fully integrated logistics hub. They could buy and sell their products and services from one another "across the fence." Upstream refineries could sell feedstock to downstream manufacturers. Horizontal linkages allowed different plants to outsource and share common services such as warehousing and waste treatment. Companies could reduce operating costs, enjoy economies of scale, and focus on their core operations.[10]

Ireland's contrasting performance before and after the late 1980s also provides convincing evidence in support of the idea that improving the business climate is insufficient for success and that the government must complement it with industry identification. Ireland started to adopt an industrial policy characterized by "a heavy state interventionist but hands-off approach" in the early 1950s, providing tax incentives (zero corporate income tax), grants, and subsidies to encourage any investment that targeted exports.[11] That policy did not produce many results, and Ireland remained one of the poorest countries in Western Europe, resulting in a large exodus of its talents and winning Irish people a nickname, "the beggars of Europe."

The situation began to change only when Ireland's Investment Development Authority started to pick winners—focusing only on electronics, pharmaceuticals, software, and chemicals. Its staff proactively courted FDI from the United States, the United Kingdom, and Germany in those four industries during the late 1980s.[12] The change in policy allowed the Association to persuade multinational information and communications technology (ICT) companies to invest in Ireland. It also helped attract 9 of the world's top 10 pharmaceutical companies and 12 of the world's top 15 medical products companies. Leading e-business firms such as Google, Yahoo, eBay, and Amazon set up their production facilities and European headquarters in Ireland. The strategy turned Ireland into the Celtic Tiger, making it one of Western Europe's richest countries and the destination of migration from Eastern Europe.[13]

"Aim first before you fire" is one of the first lessons that I learned as a military cadet. The government's facilitation is essential for industrial upgrading and diversification. Without industry identification by the policymakers working closely with the private sector, the chance of good government facilitation is low. Yet there is widespread skepticism in the mainstream economic profession and in Washington-based development institutions about the desirability of any industry-specific interventions, which people tend to relate to past government failures to pick winners. As Chapter 3 showed, those failures were mostly due to unrealistic ambitions by political leaders to develop industries that went against their countries' comparative advantages. Firms' investment and survival in those priority industries depended on the government's heavy protection and large subsidies through various distortions and direct resource allocations, such as monopoly rents, high tariffs, quota restrictions, and subsidized credits. The large rents embedded in those measures became easy targets for political capture and created governance problems.

For government facilitation to succeed, the precondition is clear: the identified industries must be aligned with the economy's latent comparative advantage. Based solely on factor costs of production, such industries will be competitive in domestic and international markets; they are typically not yet competitive simply because of the high transaction costs of firms in those industries due to poor infrastructure, inadequate logistics, lack of financial services, and other hard and soft constraints. Government facilitation should be limited to helping private firms overcome those constraints so that the country's latent comparative advantages can become its realized comparative advantages. Once one accepts that reasoning, the main question becomes this: if the latent comparative advantages are, by definition, not yet apparent, how is it possible to identify them? This is one area of development thinking in which we hope that the new structural economics can make a contribution.

How to Identify Industries with Latent Comparative Advantages: A Few Principles

In recent years the development community has taken up some of the old pervasive issues of how to identify industries on the research agenda. Before discussing growth identification and facilitation, I briefly present two of the newest and most promising methods in the recent economic literature.

The first is found in the work of Hausmann and Klinger (2006) and Hidalgo et al. (2007). Built on the idea of tacit knowledge and starting with the universe of products exported by all countries, the authors identify what they call "distances between products." If a country exports a particular product, it is possible to examine how close it is to all other products. The closer the distance between any two products, the more similar the required tacit knowledge for production of these two products, the easier it is for a country exporting one of them to expand to export the other. For instance, if a country exports blouses, it is likely that it can easily export T-shirts, and it may also upgrade to export more sophisticated business suits.

Start by accepting that such a suggestion makes good sense and that it even has some similarity to the approach that I would like to develop later in this chapter. Thinking about it carefully, one realizes that it has two limitations. First, most low-income countries today are exporters of natural resources and agricultural products. That type of "proximity" approach would not help them identify the manufacturing products they can develop. Yet the diversification from agriculture and resources to modern manufacturing industries is essential for a low-income country to start modern economic growth. If Finland had followed this approach, it would not have had Nokia—it would have continued to export lumber and probably also furniture. Second, this approach assumes that all products that a country exports are consistent with the country's comparative advantages. Yet that is not always the case. Then what? As Chapter 3 discussed, many developing countries were tempted to develop capital-intensive manufacturing of products such as automobiles. Some countries might have indeed become car exporters, but only in small quantities and with heavy (explicit and implicit) subsidies from their governments. Should their government further encourage these subsidized and protected firms to expand into truck production? Obviously not.

A second approach proposed by Harrison and Rodríguez-Clare (2010) explains that if market failures and externalities are associated with the size of the industry, it should be appropriate for a government to foster particular industries in the interest of enabling the economy to produce a larger variety of products, upgrade its industrial sector, and grow faster. Although this approach is built on solid ground for interventions—market failures or externalities—it, too, falls short of helping policymakers in developing countries link facilitation to identification, because it does not provide guidance on which new industries should be encouraged or supported.

Using the concepts of comparative advantage and the advantage of backwardness, I suggest that a good way of identifying a country's latent comparative advantages is simply to look at the dynamically growing mature tradable industries and services in the country, which have a similar endowment structure but with a somewhat higher income and have grown fast in recent decades.[14] The logic of the proposal is as follows.

First, it is impossible for a country to subsidize its dynamically growing tradable industries and maintain fast growth for several decades. Therefore, the dynamic tradable industries in a country that has been performing well for several decades must be consistent with the country's comparative advantages. With fast growth, the volume of capital in the country accumulates quickly, and the wage rate also increases rapidly. As a result, the country will gradually lose comparative advantage in those tradable industries.

Countries with a similar endowment structure will generally have similar comparative advantages. So those industries will become the latent comparative advantage for countries with a similar endowment structure but lower wage rates. If governments in those lower-wage, similarly endowed countries can facilitate the entry of private firms to those industries by overcoming coordination and externality issues, latecoming countries can outcompete incumbent firms through wage advantages.

Second, for resource-intensive industries like mining, agriculture, and fishing, a country could look to other higher-income countries with similar resource endowments and learn some recipes for success. Chile ventured into salmon farming because it has an oceanic environment similar to Norway's and Scotland's. It also started wine production because it has soils and a climate similar to Italy's.[15] Similarly, Ecuador developed cut flowers because it has natural conditions similar to Colombia's.[16] In modern manufacturing, a country's comparative advantages are determined mainly by its relative abundance of capital and labor, reflected in its level of income. A resource-scarce, labor-abundant developing country can develop a list of manufacturing industries that may be latent comparative advantages by analyzing the dynamic tradable industries in other higher-income, faster-growing countries. A resource-abundant country can follow the same approach to identify the manufacturing industries into which to diversify. Finland, resource rich, started Nokia as a household electronics firm by producing goods under "original equipment manufacturer" agreements for Philips of the Netherlands, a resource-scarce country, in the 1960s.

"A wise man proportions his belief to the evidence," said David Hume. So, let us look at the historical evidence. A quick review of various experiences indicates that countries catching up with more advanced ones targeted mature industries in economies that had per capita incomes, on average, about 100 percent higher than their own (measured in purchasing power parity).

When Britain applied industrial policies to help its wool textile industry catch up to that of the Netherlands in the sixteenth and seventeenth centuries, its per capita income was about 70 percent that of its target country.

When France, Germany, and the United States used industrial policies to help their steel, machinery, shipbuilding, and textile industries catch up with Britain's in the nineteenth century, their per capita incomes were about 60 to 75 percent that of Britain. Similarly, when Japan's industrial policy targeted the U.S. automobile industry in the 1960s, its per capita income was about 40 percent that of the United States.[17]

The same strategy was used by countries that successfully moved from low- to middle-income status. After the Meiji restoration, Japan took the German kingdom of Prussia as a model. According to estimates by Angus Maddison, Germany's per capita income in 1890 was $2,428 and Japan's $1,012, or 42 percent that of Germany, so Japan's strategy was realistic.[18] When Taiwan, China, and the Republic of Korea adopted industrial policies to facilitate their industrial upgrading in the 1960s and 1970s, they targeted the industries in Japan instead of the United States, and for a good reason: their per capita incomes were about 35 percent of Japan's and only about 10 percent that of the United States at that time.[19]

By contrast, when China started its industrialization drive in the 1950s under the leadership of Mao Zedong, its goal was to overtake Britain in 10 years and catch up to the United States in 15 years! The industrial targets in that ambitious plan were modern advanced industries in Britain and the United States, despite the fact that China's per capita income, measured by purchasing power parity, was only about 5 percent that of the United States and 7 percent that of Britain. Other developing countries in Africa, Asia, and Latin America made a similar mistake in the development plans they implemented after World War II under the stewardship of their visionary leaders. Such plans were rationalized and given intellectual justification by the ideas underpinning the old structural economics. This was a major mistake, because a common feature of the industrial upgrading and diversification strategies adopted by all successful economies (advanced countries and the East Asian newly industrializing economies of the postwar period) was the decision to target mature tradable industries in countries whose per capita incomes were *not too far in excess* of their own.

The principle articulated here is the single most important secret for successful catch-up strategies. Throughout human history it appears that pioneer countries always played (often unwillingly) the role of "economic compass" for latecomers. The Netherlands was imitated by Britain, and Britain was imitated by France, Germany, Japan, and the United States. Japan was, in turn, imitated by Hong Kong SAR, China; Taiwan, China; Korea; and Singapore in the 1960s and 1970s. Mauritius picked Hong Kong SAR, China, and Taiwan, China, to serve as its compasses in its catch-up strategy in the 1970s. China chose Korea; Taiwan, China; and Hong Kong SAR, China, in the 1980s.[20]

Having outlined the logic and basic principle for identification and gathered the historical evidence supporting it, it is now time to suggest a practical framework for operationalization, which could be of value to policymakers around the world who are confronted with the same issues that others were able to resolve successfully. The GIF framework, presented next, is built on the two pillars of an effective strategy for industrial and technological upgrading—identification and facilitation—and involves six essential steps.

A Practical Guide for Sequencing Structural Transformation
Step I: Choosing the Right Target

Lewis Carroll's classic children's story *Alice in Wonderland* is full of intriguing and colorful characters who sometimes offer useful wisdom through absurd quotes. For instance, the King gives this advice: "Begin at the beginning and go on till you come to the end: then stop." And when asked by the Caterpillar the simple question, "Who are *you*?" Alice responds: "This was not an encouraging opening for a conversation. I—I hardly know, sir, just at present—at least I know who I was when I got up this morning, but I think I must have been changed several times since then."[21]

A government that embarks on the path of industrial development and diversification may take away some insights from Carroll's dry humor. It must know exactly where to begin and where to stop, and it must think carefully about the question, "Who are you?"—and grasp precisely the country's economic identity and endowment structure. It should do so to avoid over-estimating its potential while knowing that things can change over time.

First, the government in a developing country can identify the list of dynamically growing tradable goods and services that have been produced for about 20 years in fast-growing countries with similar endowment structures and a per capita income that is about 100 percent higher than its own.[22] That first step in growth identification and facilitation is the most critical principle for a developing country to reap the advantage of backwardness in its industrial upgrading and diversification. The reason is simple. As explained in the previous section, whenever a country records high growth rates over a long period, it accumulates capital, its wages eventually rise, and it loses the comparative advantage in industries that it had in the past. As these industries become its sunset industries to move out of, they become the latent comparative advantages or sunrise industries of countries with similar endowment structures but lower wages. That window of opportunity for latecomers can be exploited until the possibilities for catching up are exhausted. Governments can use as forerunners countries whose per capita incomes are on average about 100 percent higher than their own, measured in purchasing power parity.

"Art begins in imitation and ends in innovation," American writer Mason Cooley said. The same can be said about industrial and technological up-grading. Low-income countries with per capita incomes at about $1,000 in terms of purchasing power parity and whose policymakers have a good understanding of their economic identity (defined as their endowment structure) have even more possibilities to exploit their backwardness. In addition to identifying mature tradable goods in countries whose per capita incomes are about $2,000 currently, they may also identify tradable goods produced in countries that had similar per capita incomes 20 or so years ago and have been growing dynamically since. China, India, Indonesia, and Vietnam 30 years ago had incomes similar to or even lower than most of today's poor Sub-Saharan countries. Therefore, the latter could start their identification strategies by focusing on the list of dynamically growing tradable goods and services produced in China, India, Indonesia, and Vietnam 20 years ago as references. To set their targets for industrial upgrading and diversification, they could also review their imports and identify the list of simple labor-intensive manufacturing goods that have limited economies of scale and require only small investments.

When a latecomer's income reaches about half the income of advanced countries, or about $20,000 in today's dollars, it finds it more difficult to identify industries likely to be consistent with its latent comparative advantage. Most of its industries are on or close to the global frontier, and its industrial upgrading and diversification rely increasingly on indigenous innovations—not simply on copying successful examples from abroad. In that situation, policies to support industrial upgrading and diversification begin to resemble those of the advanced countries and carry much higher risks of failure.

Step 2: Removing Binding Constraints

Among the industries on the list constructed in Step 1, the government may give priority to industries in which some domestic private firms have already entered spontaneously and identify either what is preventing them from upgrading the quality of their products or scaling up or the barriers limiting the entry of other private firms to form clusters. Why? Because in addition to such inputs as finance, land, and utilities, which are common to all industries, some industries have specific inputs, such as local raw materials, industry-specific knowledge, intermediate inputs, labor skills, and so on.[23] The existence of a few private firms in the industry has a signaling effect— indicating that the economy at least partly possesses those special inputs— and points to that industry's untapped potential. Because these firms have already borne the risk of entering the industry, the government should try to identify the obstacles preventing them from upgrading the quality of their products and extending their markets or the barriers that limit entry by other private firms.

"The devil is in the details," the old English idiom goes. Indeed, identifying and removing the true constraints to an industry's or country's growth potential is not easy. The literature focuses mostly on various ways of improving infrastructure and the business environment, which affect firms' operations and transaction costs. There is robust empirical knowledge based on quantitative data on firms' performance and perceptions-based data on the severity of potential constraints facing firms in the developing world. The literature points out that in most of Sub-Saharan Africa, firms tend to consider many areas of the investment climate major obstacles to the development of businesses and the adoption of more sophisticated technology. Finance and access to land seem to be particular concerns to smaller firms; larger firms tend to perceive labor regulations and the availability of skilled labor as the main constraints to their activity. Firms across the board are concerned about corruption and infrastructure—especially network utilities such as water, electricity, telecommunications, and transportation.[24]

"How many legs does a dog have, if you call the tail a leg? Four. Calling a tail a leg doesn't make it a leg."[25] That famous quote, often wrongly attributed to Abraham Lincoln, makes the point about investment-climate surveys, which try to capture the policy and institutional environment for firms. They are clearly very useful to policymakers and investors, but they can be misused or misinterpreted. Just as individual perceptions of well-being are subjective and do not always correlate with objective measures such as income or consumption, firms' perceptions of binding constraints to their development often differ from the actual determinants of their performance.

That limitation is due to the nature of investment-climate data and how they are often used. In a typical survey, the managers of a sample of firms rate each dimension of the investment climate (such as "infrastructure," "access to financing," or "corruption") on a scale of one to four corresponding to how great an obstacle it is to the firm's performance.[26] High mean reported values for particular dimensions of the investment climate are then interpreted as evidence of the severity of obstacles to growth.

This may not be the case, however. French historian and biologist Jean Rostand wrote, "Falsity cannot keep an idea from being beautiful; there are certain errors of such ingenuity that one could regret their not ranking among the achievements of the human mind." Perceptions of some investment-climate variables differ from the actual effect of these variables on firms' productivity, business performance, and growth. Despite intimate knowledge of their business processes and operating environment, firms may not fully recognize the true origin of their main problems and mistakenly identify as a constraint something that is in fact a symptom of another less obvious problem. Because of these shortcomings, investment-climate constraints are increasingly complemented by the World Bank's Doing Business Indicators, based on expert surveys (not just firm perceptions), and provide a more comparable cross-country perspective across a detailed range of regulation.

The problem remains, however, because survey results can vary depending on whether respondents are asked to rate their most important constraints or to rank them. Ranking, favored by researchers, may not be entirely reliable: firms or experts asked to rank constraints may not have a good basis for determining whether their top-ranked constraint is serious. Ranking, without a solid and meaningful benchmark for local firms in a country to rate the severity of a particular constraint, may not provide useful information.

In addition, picking any single quantitative criterion ("infrastructure," "taxes," "access to financing") could be misleading: all businessmen in Caracas, Lagos, or Delhi would confirm that firms face several constraints simultaneously. Ranking all of them as important may not be very helpful for policymaking. To account for the major role of firm heterogeneity in growth analysis, one must go beyond extracting the means of investment-climate variables from firm surveys. Careful econometric modeling of firm performance is therefore needed to identify which particular variable has the greatest effect on growth. In other words, the policy variables with the greatest economic impact can be quite different from the policy variables with the highest perceived values.[27]

Investment-climate surveys have two more limitations. First, they do not provide information about industries that do not yet exist but in which a country has a latent comparative advantage. If Costa Rica's current endowment structure allowed its economy to compete in, say, the production of flat-panel television screens, none of the existing expert surveys would reveal it. Moreover, the industries surveyed may not be consistent with the country's comparative advantage, either because they are too advanced (as a legacy of a development strategy that defied comparative advantage) or because they have become fundamentally uncompetitive (as a result of a general wage increase that accompanied the country's development). These two additional limitations make it highly desirable for investment-climate surveys to cover only a sample of firms that meet the criteria of viability and can represent the true economy's potential.

Second, many other constraints to business development are endogenous to the industries that might be targeted by a developing country. Good examples are specific types of human capital, financing instruments, or infrastructure that may be needed only by firms moving to specific industries. Identifying and removing them may require several complementary analytical tools.

Another widely used tool for identifying and removing constraints to industrial development and growth is the Growth Diagnostics framework suggested by Hausmann, Rodrik, and Velasco.[28] It is based on the observation that policymakers, when presented with a laundry list of needed reforms, either struggle to try to solve all the problems at once or start with reforms not critical to their country's growth potential. Because reforms in one area may create unanticipated distortions in another area, focusing on the one that represents the greatest hurdle to growth is the most promising avenue. So countries should figure out the one or two most binding constraints on their economies and then focus on lifting them.

The Growth Diagnostics approach provides a "decision tree" with which to identify the relevant binding constraints for any given country. It starts with a list of possible causes of low growth in developing countries, which generally suffer from either a high cost of finance (due either to low economic and social returns or to a large gap between social and private returns) or a low private return on investment. Policymakers must figure out which of these conditions more accurately characterizes the economy. In some countries the growth strategy should identify the reasons for the low returns on investment. In others it must explain why domestic savings do not rise to exploit large returns on investment.

Although the Growth Diagnostics framework attempts to take the policy discussion of growth forward, it is also beset with the same problems as the investment-climate survey approach, and its focus and model specification remain quite macroeconomic, which is understandable. After all, growth is a macroeconomic concept, and taking the analysis to a sectoral level would raise issues of sectoral interactions and trade-offs. Even more problematic is the imprecision of the Growth Diagnostics framework in its links to the institutions that facilitate the growth process.[29] Even where it leads to relative certainty about the binding constraints to growth in a country, a wide range of policy options is still available to choose from. The most critical constraint to growth in a country could be a concentration of economic activity in one or two industries, as is the case in natural resource–based countries like Zambia, where the predominance of copper is overwhelming. The framework that Hausmann, Rodrik, and Velasco suggest cannot assist policymakers in identifying new industries in which the country may have a latent comparative advantage. Nor can it indicate whether Zambia's current industries are consistent with its current comparative advantage.

Clearly, all these various methods of identifying and removing binding constraints to industrial upgrading bring some partial truths to the difficult art and science of policymaking. And they should be considered in turn, depending on specific country conditions. It is therefore necessary for policymakers not just to rely on one approach but to use several different macro and micro tools to identify binding constraints to the growth of industries identified in this step. Establishing a diagnostic of growth at the aggregate level requires good knowledge of what happens at the micro level. Microeconomic analyses show that differentiated firm dynamics drive a good part of aggregate productivity growth and capital accumulation. In particular, monitoring the entry and exit of firms and the policy variables that affect them is essential to understanding overall gains in productivity in economies subject to substantial structural changes. One must consider the heterogeneity in country circumstances and among micro agents. This can be done more effectively through country-specific analyses.

In addition to the methods discussed here, the investigation of business constraints could benefit from integrated value-chain analyses that compare the cost structure of the goods produced by domestic firms with those in reference countries and identify areas in which government interventions would produce the highest payoffs. Randomized controlled experiments can also test the effects of releasing those constraints and implementing appropriate interventions to ensure the effective scaling up of interventions at the national level.[30]

Even if one could identify the relevant binding constraints to industrial development in industries with a latent comparative advantage and induce improvements in a country's business environment, the crucial issues of externality encountered by first movers and coordination would remain unresolved. Even after removing the constraints, a country may find its industrial upgrading and diversification stalled. My recommendation that governments identify a list of industries with a latent comparative advantage and support industries that some domestic private firms have already entered spontaneously and successfully helps address that fundamental problem.

A good example is Chile's wine production industry. Chile produced wine for a long time but did not export much before the 1970s. The change from being a negligible wine exporter to the world's fifth-largest exporter in the 1970s benefited greatly from the government's programs to disseminate foreign technology to local farmers and vineyards through Grupos de Transferencia Tecnológica to improve quality—and to promote Chilean wine abroad through the Export Promotion Office, ProChile, to change foreign consumers' perception of Chilean wine.[31]

In India the private initiative of small grape growers in rural Maharashtra caught the eye of policymakers in the provincial government because of the grape sector's export potential and a severe paucity of foreign exchange. Maharashtra's grape farmers previously were unable to transport grapes over long distances within India because of poor domestic trade logistics. Then, once a domestic firm identified demand in the EU market, a grape producers' organization, in partnership with the government, conducted sector-specific diagnostics to identify binding constraints to exporting grapes to the EU. The main obstacles were the poor quality of grapes, outdated machinery, and poor infrastructure, especially cold chains.

Through a public–private partnership, the government removed constraints and helped in scaling up, enabling the sector to become a net exporter. Generous government support took the form of technological upgrading through study tours to educate farmers, grape-specific research institutes, and collaboration with international experts from major grape-producing countries to enable farmers to produce grapes of a size and shape that complied with EUREPGap's phytosanitary standards. State grants of up to 95 percent covered import cold-chain machinery and infrastructure development. In addition to joining the coveted club of summer suppliers to the EU—Chile, Israel, and South Africa—India gave other perishables a foothold in Europe with its grapes.[32]

Step 3: Seducing and Attracting Global Investors

France's Charles de Gaulle once said, "Greatness is a road leading toward the unknown." That corroborated the thought of his fellow countryman and famous writer Antoine de Saint-Exupéry, who wrote: "Once men are caught up in an event, they cease to be afraid. Only the unknown frightens men." The third step in growth identification and facilitation involves dealing with the unknown. Some industries on the list of potential targets may be unknown and thus completely new to domestic firms. In industries in which no domestic firms are present, policymakers should aim to attract FDI from the countries being emulated or organize programs for "incubating" new firms. Although this is not easy, there are several clear advantages in doing this.

Globalization and competition have added new pressure on firms producing tradable goods and services to search for new investment locations to remain competitive. And greater integration in the global market has made it easier for global producers to shop for investment locations with the cheapest inputs. Foreign firms in footloose industries such as garments, footwear, toys, and electronics usually shop around for the cheapest labor-cost locations, so it is not unusual for governments in low-income countries with abundant unskilled labor to attract such global producers.

The lack of information about the feasibility of a new industry makes foreign and local firms reluctant to bear the risk of investing in an unknown. To offset the risk of failure, developing countries' governments can adopt specific measures to encourage firms in the higher-income countries identified in Step 1 to invest in these industries. Firms in those higher-income countries will have incentives to reallocate their production to a lower-income country so as to take advantage of the lower labor costs. Governments may also set up incubation programs to catalyze the entry of private domestic firms into these industries.

Much theoretical and empirical work shows that it is worthwhile for a government to attract foreign firms to jumpstart a new industry, which can bestow abundant spillovers on domestic firms, starting with an opportunity to learn about, enter, and grow the new industry.[33] The entry of foreign firms into a new industry can increase the local availability of inputs previously not obtainable in the host country or raise the quality of existing inputs to global standards—which is also beneficial for domestic firms if inputs are available to them. Foreign firms also spur industrial development in the host country through spillovers of technologies, market channels, and managerial skills.[34] Both effects are evident in China's manufacturing sector, in which the technology transfers from foreign buyers to domestic input suppliers spurred the productivity of domestic firms.[35] Spillovers also arise with the availability of better-quality inputs at lower prices prompted by intense competition among domestic input suppliers. This, in turn, benefits emerging domestic buyers, such as the trading companies that purchase locally to directly supply overseas foreign buyers.

Lessons from successful Asia are relevant here. When local Asian firms had no knowledge of an industry of interest to the country, the state often attracted FDI or promoted joint ventures:

- After the transition to a market economy in the 1980s, China invited direct investment from Hong Kong SAR, China; Taiwan,

China; Japan; and Korea. This promotion policy helped the local economy to get started in various industries.

- Bangladesh's vibrant garment industry also started with direct investment from Daewoo, a Korean manufacturer, in the 1970s. After a few years, substantial knowledge transfers had taken place, and Daewoo's investment proved to have been a sort of "incubation." Local garment plants mushroomed in Bangladesh, with most of them traced back to that first Korean firm.[36]

- Vietnam's leading export industries for garments, footwear, and furniture were also launched following that strategy. The government offered foreign firms attractive incentives to locate in Vietnam, enabled economic diversification in manufacturing, and made these new footloose industries the country's key industries.

- High-income Singapore did the same. In the 1970s it started to lose competitiveness in labor-intensive activities like semiconductor assembly. The government convinced Seagate that the country could provide components at a much lower cost. The company began its disk-drive manufacturing in Singapore, which soon became the world's largest producer of Winchester hard–disk drives. In the 1980s and 1990s, as the hard–disk drive industry came under pressure, the government created the market conditions to woo computer manufacturers.[37]

Development success stories in Central and Latin America also confirm the effectiveness of such active government strategies. The booming cut-flower export business in Ecuador from the 1980s onward started with three companies founded by Colombia's flower growers.[38] Another example of a successful government incubation program is the commercial salmon farming initiated by the Fundación Chile.

According to the United Nations Conference on Trade and Development, the government undertook several trials to master fish-farming technologies, including attempts spanning several decades, to stock rivers and lakes:

"It solicited technical support from several international institutions with experience in fish breeding and farming and used its national institutions to acquire, assimilate, develop and diffuse fish farming technologies. Some of the early firms were created by public institutions and researchers that had accumulated some basic operational knowledge and skills in fish farming. Several prominent national players that promote the development of firms and technologies facilitated the diffusion of salmon farming technologies."[39] Fundación Chile demonstrated the commercial viability of large-scale farming, breeding, and producing of salmon through Salmones Antártica, a limited company. The firm also carried out research on farming procedures and provided technical assistance to small and emerging producers. Its success stimulated private interest and led to the industry's expansion.

Costa Rica's success in convincing Intel, the high-tech microchip producer, to locate a major plant within its borders is particularly impressive, because until the late 1990s, the main memory chip assembly and testing were done in Taiwan, China, and Malaysia. In comparison with their per capita incomes at the time of $13,354 and $7,199, respectively, Costa Rica's per capita income was only $5,242.[40] Intel considered six other countries: Argentina, Brazil, Chile, Indonesia, Mexico, and Thailand. Costa Rica also had an impressive investment climate but did not have a single information technology (IT) firm. Case studies of Intel's decisionmaking conclude that Costa Rica was chosen because it offered location-specific advantages—among them, tax exemptions for firms satisfying certain conditions under the free zone scheme, the high education level of the labor force, a low cost structure, a stable political system, a fairly corruption-free environment, and a committed government.[41]

Before Intel came in, Costa Rica was losing its advantage in apparel, its leading export, and the prices of coffee and bananas, its other main exports, were falling rapidly. The Costa Rican Investment Promotion Agency (CINDE) coordinated the rapid development of local suppliers and attracted top technology companies such as Intel that had previously turned down invitations to come. The president of the Central Bank, Eduardo Lizano, identified FDI as a key catalyst for revitalizing the economy. CINDE's promotional efforts in 1996–98 were targeted at electronics: establishing and consolidating Intel, developing the cluster by attracting more high-tech companies, and strengthening the support industry around them. Thanks to that strategy, Costa Rica's exports evolved from the "golden bean" (high-quality coffee) to the "golden chip."[42]

The country has enjoyed spillovers from Intel's presence in commercial links through exports to Germany, Japan, Malaysia, and the United Kingdom. Costa Rican executives found new opportunities to learn about doing business in markets otherwise closed. The economic structure changed in a few decades: in the 1970s traditional coffee and bananas made up 80 percent of exports, and today nontraditional exports make up 80 percent.

Step 4: Scaling Up Self-Discoveries

A fourth step in growth identification and facilitation consists of rewarding the successful self-discoveries of private enterprises by providing support to scale them up. Because technology changes rapidly, some business opportunities might not have existed 10 or 15 years ago and do not show up in the list of opportunities with latent comparative advantages based on the criterion in Step 1. Moreover, every country may have some unique endowments and comparative advantages that the comparator countries do not have. If domestic private firms have discovered new industries with great business potential, policymakers should also identify and remove the constraints to those firms' technological upgrading or to entry by other firms, even though they do not appear in the list from Step 1.

India's information industry is a good example. Indian professionals in Silicon Valley helped Indian companies take advantage of expanding opportunities for outsourced IT work in the 1980s. Early on they relied on expensive satellite data transmission. Once the potential for information service exports was demonstrated, the Indian government helped build a high-speed data communications infrastructure that allowed many Indians in the diaspora to return home and set up offshore sites for U.S. clients. The Indian information service industry has grown more than 30 percent annually for 20 years.[43]

The success of Ecuador's cut-flower exports in the 1980s is also a good example. That Ecuador had latent comparative advantages in producing and exporting cut flowers to the U.S. market was known to the flower farmers in the 1970s. But the industry did not expand and exports did not take off until the government helped arrange for regular flights and cooling facilities near the airport in the 1980s.[44]

Ethiopia's success in cut-flower exports is another example. Before the government decided to support these exports through industrial policy in the 1990s, a local private firm had exported cut flowers to the European market for over 10 years. Although the results of such policies are still being debated, exports of cut flowers have grown exponentially, creating several hundred thousand jobs, 70 percent for women. More than 100 private firms are now in cut-flower production and export operations, over half of them owned by foreign investors.[45]

Asparagus development in Peru is another example of successful government intervention in support of private initiative. The possibility of growing asparagus, a foreign crop, probably seemed counterintuitive to many people in Peru, yet it was discovered by some farmers there in the 1950s. However, the industry and exports did not take off until 1985, when the U.S. government through the U.S. Agency for International Development provided a grant for a farmers' association to obtain invaluable and critical knowledge. That technical advice came from a specialist from the University of California–Davis, who had recently invented the UC-157 variety of asparagus, which was suitable for the U.S. market—and from another expert who showed members of the association's experimental station how to set up seedbeds for large-scale production and to package the asparagus for export. The state supported cooperative institutions such as the Peruvian Asparagus Institute and Frio Aereo Associación Civil for research, technology transfer, market studies, export drives, and quality promotion. The state also invested in freezing and packing plants that handled 80 percent of fresh asparagus exports. With these interventions, Peru eventually overtook China to become the world's largest asparagus exporter.[46]

The Indonesian government pursued a similarly successful strategy to revive its profitable but uncompetitive pulp and paper industry. By the mid-1980s the government was keen to replace the declining oil industry, the main source of foreign exchange, with manufacturing. As Indonesia had developed a manufacturing capacity, the reduction in tariffs and other liberalization reforms improved the competitiveness of the pulp and paper industry, an industry consistent with its comparative advantage. However, the government wanted to elevate Indonesia to the list of the world's top 10 pulp and paper producers. This required lower costs of production and a large and renewable raw materials base, which private firms could not achieve. During the export-oriented industrialization phase (1984–97), the government leveraged industrial policy to transform primary wood exports into pulp and paper through the provision of large tracts of mixed tropical hardwood against very low concession costs for private industrial tree plantations. License holders were allowed to clear-cut their concession areas and use the obtained wood as a temporary "bridging supply" until the pulpwood plantations were fully online. This led to a 20–30 percent drop in Indonesian companies' raw material costs relative to those of American and European producers. Other support included plantation subsidies, discounted loans from state-owned banks, and tax deductions. Rapid growth in the sector placed Indonesia among the world's leading pulp and paper producers and exporters.[47]

Step 5: Recognizing the Power and Magic of Industrial Parks

A major question in economic development is how to overcome insufficient hard and soft infrastructure as a major barrier to productivity growth in developing countries. Any visitor who arrives in Ouagadougou, the capital of the landlocked West African country of Burkina Faso, is struck by the very busy airport in the middle of town. The same is true in many other developing countries, where poor roads, malfunctioning electricity grids, outdated and expensive telecommunications systems, and myriad forms of red tape burden production and business transactions and make it difficult for firms to compete in a global environment.

In a piece devoted to infrastructure in Africa, written in its typical color-ful and humoristic style, *The Economist* notes: "Today, getting a container to the heart of Africa—from Douala in Cameroon to Bangassou in the Central African Republic, say—still means a wait of up to three weeks at the port on arrival; roadblocks, bribes, potholes, and mud-drifts on the road along the way; malarial fevers, prostitutes, and monkey-meat stews in the lorry cabin; hyenas and soldiers on the road at night. The costs of fuel and repairs make even the few arterial routes (beyond southern Africa) uneconomic."[48] This is confirmed by empirical studies by the U.S. Department of Commerce, which found that it cost more to ship a ton of wheat from Mombasa in Kenya to Kampala in neighboring Uganda than it did to ship it from Chicago to Mombasa.

Not surprisingly, there is a wide consensus among economists: "Well-designed infrastructure facilitates economies of scale, reduces costs of trade, and is thus central to specialization and the efficient production and con-sumption of goods and services. It is a vital ingredient to economic growth and development, which is the key to raising living standards."[49] For poor economies, infrastructure raises productivity and reduces the cost of private production. It also has a (positive) disproportionate effect on the incomes and welfare of the poor: it reduces transaction costs and costs to access markets, raises returns on existing assets, facilitates human capital accumu-lation, and stimulates agglomeration economies and the dissemination of knowledge—all ingredients for sustained growth.

The 2009 Global Monitoring Report estimates that if Sub-Saharan Afri-ca's infrastructure level reaches that of Mauritius, its annual growth rate will increase 2.1 percentage points, 2.7 percentage points if its infrastructure level reaches that of Korea.[50] In addition, recent work by economists from various backgrounds, including my World Bank colleagues Cesar Calderon and Luis Servén, offers new estimates of returns to infrastructure. Defining infra-structure more broadly to include the physical stock of infrastructure and not simply infrastructure spending, they calculate that the output elasticity of infrastructure lies between 0.07 and 0.10—meaning that a 10 percent increase in infrastructure assets directly increases GDP per capita by 0.7 to 1.0 percent.[51]

To address such an important problem, I propose that developing countries with poor infrastructure and an unfriendly business environment rely on the power and magic of industrial parks and export-processing zones, which are more manageable and realistic alternatives to the dream of building excellent infrastructure rapidly across the entire country and improving the business environment for the entire economy. The parks and zones also have the benefits of encouraging industrial clustering. Several successful countries have followed such a path, even in Africa, where Mauritius provided good-quality infrastructure to domestic and foreign firms and overcame the constraint of rigid labor regulation by allowing labor employment to be flexible in the export-processing zone while maintaining existing regulations for the domestic economy.[52]

In India, as far back as 1976, the government of Karnataka attempted to encourage the electronics industry through the Karnataka State Electronics Development Corporation. Even today, with one of the worst infrastructure deficits, India's manufacturing business is conducted mostly in industrial parks across the country. In China the governments in the poorer inland provinces have leveraged industrial parks to provide "plug-and-play" sites to firms at an affordable price. To scale up manufacturing firms that can employ several thousand people at a time, the government has also constructed workers' hostels next to each factory shell. That strategy has reduced the cost and time for workers to travel to and from work, as well as the cost of housing, which the firms are happy to provide along with meals at a token charge. It has also reduced labor costs and improved efficiency.

In Vietnam much of the large-scale garment, footwear, and furniture production by foreign firms is done in industrial parks that provide factory shells and the basic infrastructure to firms. In Africa more than 22 countries have at least one special zone or park, usually for export purposes. Given the weak state of infrastructure in most of them, the zones seem to be the only solution, especially if they are sincere about attracting large firms.

Governments can also set up industrial parks to incubate new industries that have been identified following the growth identification and facilitation criteria. An example is Taiwan, China's, Hsinchu Science–based Industrial Park, a comprehensive industrial zone built in an area of more than 500 hectares for the electronics and IT industries. It was designed to accommodate the demands of rapid regional industrial development, prevent unauthorized establishments, discourage any improper use of agricultural lands that could lead to public disasters, and better use investments in public infrastructure (roads, water supply systems, wastewater and sewage treatment facilities, power grids, and telecom systems).[53]

Step 6: Providing Limited Incentives to the Right Industries

Governments may also provide limited incentives to domestic pioneer firms or foreign investors that work with firms from the list of industries identified in Step 1 to compensate for the nonrival public knowledge created by their investments. This proposal may sound controversial, but it is not. All countries in the world do this, but often in a way that creates distortions and opportunities for rent seeking.

To understand the rationale for such measures, remember that being a pioneer is risky and costly. Firms usually hesitate to be the first movers because nobody has complete confidence in the viability of their business. They know that if they fail they will have to bear all the costs of failure and provide useful warnings to other firms, but if they succeed, other firms will obtain free information about the viability of the industry, enter it, and partake of the profits. Their failure or success generates information externalities for other firms in the industry. A World Bank field study in Zambia in 2010 found that a local entrepreneur, advised by a visiting Indian relative in 2008, successfully started to produce corrugated roofing sheets. Within a year, more than 20 firms had entered the production of such materials. Stories like that occur every day all over the world. If there is no compensation for the information externalities that a pioneer firm creates, fewer firms will have incentives to spend resources to obtain production information and take risks to be the first movers, and thus the process of industrial upgrading and diversification as well as economic growth will be impeded.[54]

In advanced developed countries, pioneer firms are rewarded with patents ensuring that, for a limited time, they are the sole beneficiaries of the profits from successful innovation. In developing countries, patents may not be applicable because the industry could be new in those countries but is already old elsewhere in the world. Providing subsidies for a limited time can achieve the same result—that is, providing a financial reward to the pioneer firms for information externalities about the viability of a new industry. I therefore suggest that subsidies be used to redress the asymmetry between the losses associated with the failure and the gains associated with the success of a pioneer firm's activity.

Limited government support, in terms of both financing and time, should be sufficient to reward a pioneer firm for generating information externalities, because when success materializes, that firm (and any other new entrant into the newly discovered industry) can earn a normal profit. Such incentives will not become a burden on public finance. If firms discovered new industries by themselves in Step 4, the government may award them with special recognition for their contributions to the country's economic development.[55]

These incentives may be in the form of a corporate income tax holiday for a limited number of years, directed credits to cofinance investments, or priority access to foreign reserves to import key equipment. China's example is worth considering. To attract FDI the government has typically exempted foreign companies from corporate income tax for the first two years of operation and reduced the tax rate by half for an additional three years. This seems to have worked. An empirical study of industrial promotion policies in China during 1998–2007 shows that the government facilitated technology spillovers from foreign to domestic firms through the use of targeted tariff and tax breaks.[56] Similar arrangements could be considered in other developing countries as part of a holistic growth identification and facilitation strategy.

The obvious question raised by such a proposal is about the risk of rent seeking and political capture. Such problems are indeed serious for industrial policies advocated by the old structural economics because the targeted industries go against comparative advantages, firms in those industries are not viable, and their investment and continuing operations rely on monopoly rents, high tariffs, or other forms of subsidies or protections. The truth is that, in all political systems, the likelihood of capture and rent seeking of a program is proportional to the magnitude of protection and subsidies. The more money that is available for distribution, the more that political operatives, civil servants, and businesspeople will line up to get it.

The industries identified in Step 1 are consistent with a country's comparative advantages, and the government's incentives advocated here compensate pioneer firms for their positive information externalities, so the magnitude of the support required is limited. Therefore, the gains from corruption will be small, and the elites will not have incentives to use their precious political capital to capture the small amounts of rent. In addition, once the pioneering firms are successful, many new firms will enter, and the market in these industries will be competitive, further reducing the danger of capture by elites.[57]

The secret for success in implementing the GIF framework is straightforward. The industries identified by a government for provisional and limited support should be consistent with the country's latent comparative advantage. Once the pioneer firms enter, many other firms will enter as well. The government's facilitating role is mainly restricted to providing information, coordinating hard and soft infrastructure improvements, compensating for externalities, and offering incentives for FDI and cluster formation. Government facilitation through this approach is likely to help developing countries tap into the potential of the advantage of backwardness and realize dynamic and sustained growth.

For a very long time, mainstream economists were reluctant to engage any intellectual exercise that could be construed as facilitating industrial growth. The legacy of the failure of industrial policies based on development strategies inconsistent with comparative advantage has certainly led many economists to conclude that it may be impossible for any government to successfully pick winners. But things have changed lately, and a rich body of research now exists—and several approaches have recently been suggested by various authors to reopen the debate on the government's role in promoting growth.[58] Although many of the suggested approaches are likely to yield some useful results, none of them focuses specifically on the identification of industries in which a developing country may have latent comparative advantage. The GIF framework fills that gap and presents a practical tool that policymakers can use to elaborate and implement a realistic strategy for industrial upgrading and diversification.

The question now is whether the insights from the GIF framework could be extended to countries with a long legacy of distortions and central planning and to middle- and high-income economies—a question discussed in the next chapters.

EIGHT

The Peculiar Identities and Trajectories of Transition Economies

WALTER ISAACSON, IN HIS ELEGANT AND RICH BIOGRAPHY of Albert Einstein, offers a nice presentation of the two main strategic options from which scientific theorists must choose.[1] Some depend primarily on induction—analyzing a large number of experimental findings and then deriving theories that explain the observed empirical patterns. Others rely more on deduction—starting from some plausible principles and assumptions considered sacred and then deducing logical implications from them. Isaacson notes that these strategic choices are not mutually exclusive and that all scientists tend to blend both approaches to differing degrees. Einstein seemed to have a good feel for experimental findings and used his knowledge of and curiosity about the world around him to identify interesting facts and observations ("fixed points") on which to construct a theory. But he also emphasized the deductive approach.

Economists and other social scientists face a much more difficult challenge than experts in the "hard sciences" in their quest for testable theoretical frameworks susceptible to replicable experiments with consistent results across different environments. But they, too, face the broad strategic choices that Isaacson laid out. Perhaps more than others, they must try to reconcile both approaches to deal with the inherent epistemological challenges of their science.

So it is prudent to submit the new structural economics and its GIF framework to the rigorous logic of both induction and deduction, highlighting the design of the GIF framework as an industrial and technological upgrading strategy for a distortion-free environment. Yet in reality, many developing countries have a history of multiple and compounded distortions to acknowledge and address. This book would be incomplete without an analysis of the types of economic development strategies that would work best in such environments.

Submitting economic theories to the double test of induction and deduction also reveals some of the main shortcomings of the Washington Consensus policies widely recommended to many developing and transition economies in the 1980s and 1990s. These countries epitomized the problems of multiple and compounded distortions, which traditional neoclassical development prescriptions could not address.

This chapter focuses on the issues transition economies faced in their quest for sustained growth after decades of socialism. The discussion is also relevant for nonsocialist developing countries, which are also beset with serious distortions as a legacy of their previous structuralist comparative advantage–defying (CAD) import substitution strategies. One of the biggest yet least studied problems in economics is the compounding of bad decisions that created a complex web of distortions in developing countries. Such multilevel distortions emerged in many socialist countries throughout the twentieth century because their governments followed a development strategy of promoting advanced heavy industry—a strategy inconsistent with the countries' endowment structures at the time. In the end, their CAD strategies led to distortions and inefficiencies similar to, but likely more serious than, those in other regions of the world that implemented the old structuralist import substitution strategies.

It took a long time for almost anyone to observe and acknowledge these failures. Why? Because the mistakes of CAD strategies are not always immediately obvious. The countries that pursued them all had an initial period of successful investment-led growth, supported by massive resource mobilization, whose duration depended on the stocks of their natural resources, the sizes of their populations, and their opportunities for foreign borrowing. In the former Soviet Union, this investment-led growth lasted for about 50 years, averaging 5 percent a year over 1929–79.[2] In Africa, Latin America, and other regions, the success lasted a decade or two. Brazil, in the decades following World War II, grew at around 6–7 percent fairly consistently. A slowdown in the early 1960s prompted more export-oriented reforms, and Brazil experienced "miraculous" growth rates averaging about 11 percent over 1968–73. But growth slowed sharply thereafter, and heavy external indebtedness—a hangover from the import substitution period—resulted in decades of periodic macroeconomic crises.[3] After initial success, these economies were generally plagued with myriad distortions and a structure dominated by large nonviable firms in the "advanced" sector.

In the presence of distortions, policymakers face the dual challenge of designing and implementing a viable economic development strategy to resolve the coordination and externality issues discussed in previous chapters while engaging in difficult structural reforms that often carry great sociopolitical risks. That dual challenge raises questions about the pace and sequencing of reforms: they must ensure efficiency gains from distortion removal, but they must also be consistent with growth identification and facilitation policies for industrial upgrading in a sustainable and self-reinforcing manner. It was a particularly tall order for the centrally planned economies of China and the former Soviet Union, where inward-looking CAD strategies were more persistently and comprehensively pursued, and for a longer period, than in other developing countries.

This chapter reviews the different reform strategies adopted by the two former giants of communism (China and the former Soviet Union), examines the paths their leaders chose during their transitions, assesses the results, and reflects on the lessons from the various experiences—and how they inform, enrich, and complement the new structural economics and the GIF framework.

Imaginary Confessions in Heaven: The Politics of Reforms

Imagine that two former communist leaders meet Karl Marx in heaven—sharing thoughts and reflections about some of their important strategic choices at crucial times in the economic history of their countries.

One is Boris Yeltsin, the flamboyant character who presided over the dissolution of the Soviet Union and the demise of the Communist Party. Trained as an engineer, he initially worked in construction and later began a career in the Communist Party, eventually becoming first secretary of the Party in the city of Sverdlovsk. In 1985 Mikhail Gorbachev, the newly elected general secretary of the Soviet Union Communist Party, brought Yeltsin to Moscow to serve as secretary for the construction industry. Within a year Yeltsin was appointed head of the Communist Party of Moscow. Eventually he toppled Gorbachev, was instrumental in dismembering the Soviet Union, and allowed its former republics to make their way as independent states. He was also the Russian Federation's first elected president (1991–99).[4]

The other former communist leader is the subdued and unassuming Deng Xiaoping, the de facto leader of China from 1977 until he died in 1997. Mao Zedong, who at different times was his mentor, nemesis, and ally, once said about him: "Deng is a rare talent. He is known in both military and civilian circles for this. He is like a needle wrapped in cotton. He has ideas. He does not confront problems head-on. He can deal with difficult problems with responsibility. His mind is round and his actions are square."[5] After Deng gave up any formal responsibilities within China's Communist Party, he held no other title than "honorary chairman of the Bridge Society."

How would Yeltsin and Deng rate their own performance? How will history eventually judge their divergent performances at the critical junctures of their countries' histories? How would the two men who led the transition from a planned economy to a market economy in Russia and China defend their radically different decisions? The political and economic legacies of these two men will be the subjects of analysis and debate by many generations of researchers, but it can safely be said that they were both visionaries. They were clearly transformational figures in the history of communism. The events they initiated or witnessed in their countries also had profound implications for the world economy and for the evolution of parallel market-oriented reforms in developing countries. Yet Russia's and China's experiences reflect the different paths chosen by their leaders and can be seen as remarkable identities that help us in understanding the larger narratives of political and economic development in transition economies.[6]

Yeltsin's views of his actions and justification for key strategic decisions are aptly presented in his tell-all three-volume memoir.[7] By contrast, like many other great leaders in history, Deng left behind no book or memoir. But what we do have is a collection of his speeches that explain his actions and visions, published as a three-volume collection of the *Selected Works of Deng Xiaoping*.[8]

We also have the benefit of hindsight but lack the counterfactuals (what would have actually happened under different scenarios). We know that since Russia launched its market-oriented reforms in 1991, the country's GDP per capita declined sharply, stagnated for almost a decade, and recovered recently, thanks to the global commodity prices boom. Its GDP per capita now is only 14 percent higher than it was in 1991. In contrast, China maintained 32 years of uninterrupted dynamic growth at a 9.9 percent annual growth rate, unprecedented in human history. Its GDP per capita is now a staggering 14 times its 1978 level.[9] Initial conditions are certainly important determining factors in such diverging performances, but Yeltsin and Deng would probably agree that some of their main policy decisions at the outset of the transition played major roles, too.

Perhaps Yeltsin and Deng would start off their exchange by reminding each other what powerful ideological and economic forces communism and socialism were around the world well before they became involved in politics. Indeed, between 1917 and 1950, Eastern European and Asian countries (with one-third of the world's population) chose to secede from the capitalist market economic system to launch a new experiment. It started in the former Russian Empire and Mongolia and spread after World War II to Central and Eastern Europe and the Baltic states before reaching China, the Democratic People's Republic of Korea, Vietnam, and many other countries. It led to the centralization and control of production and the allocation of resources through a system of state planning. And it yielded some remarkable achievements: higher output; industrialization; the provision of basic education, health care, housing, and jobs to entire populations; relative equality in income distribution; and a seeming imperviousness to the Great Depression of the 1930s.[10]

As smart individuals, Yeltsin and Deng would probably acknowledge an indisputable fact: because of CAD-style distortions, the intrinsic inefficiency of their planning system was far less stable than it seemed. Without a well-functioning price system, planners could not get relevant information on production and distribution. The many distortions embedded in the CAD strategy quickly led to the deprivation of firms' autonomy and the suppression of individual incentives.

In my 2007 Marshall Lectures I explained the negative dynamics:

> In order to implement a CAD strategy a developing country government has to protect numerous nonviable enterprises; because these governments usually have limited tax collection capacities, however, such large-scale protection and subsidies cannot be sustained with their limited fiscal resources. The government has to resort to administrative measures—granting the nonviable enterprises in prioritized industries a market monopoly, suppressing interest rates, overvaluing domestic currency, and controlling prices for raw materials—to reduce the investment and operation costs of the nonviable enterprises. Such intervention will cause widespread shortages in funds, foreign exchange, and raw materials. The government, therefore, needs to allocate these resources directly to these enterprises through administrative channels, including national planning in socialist countries.[11]

The overall results of their strategy were disappointing. After recording high annual growth rates in the 1950s—averaging 10 percent according to official estimates, which Yeltsin would agree may have been overestimated—the Soviet economy decelerated: growth averaged 7 percent in the 1960s, 5 percent in the 1970s, and barely 2 percent in the 1980s, and in the 1990s it contracted.[12] This was all the more surprising given that investment rates were quite high. But in contrast to what was happening in industrial economies in the Western world, the return on capital investment was declining steadily—a trend also observed for important social indicators such as life expectancy after the mid-1960s.[13]

Deng would also concede that China's living standards under central planning were suboptimal, to say the least. Despite the government's high rates of investment in heavy industries, the country's total factor productivity declined from 1955 to 1978 under Mao Zedong. The years of the Great Leap Forward in 1959–61 concluded with terrible famines that cost more than 30 million lives. And during the Cultural Revolution in 1966–76, more than 16 million educated urban youth were sent to work in the poor countryside and remote mountain areas due to the lack of jobs in cities. By the 1970s it was clear that socialism had not yielded its promises and that some fundamental changes in the planning economies were needed across Asia and Eastern Europe. Both Yeltsin and Deng took it upon themselves to lead their countries onto the path of fundamental economic reforms.

It could not have been easy. They embarked on that new, difficult endeavor in the midst of sweeping social and political change and thus had to deal with the politics of economic reforms. Harvard University political scientist Samuel Huntington identified a global "third wave" of democratization, which he suggested began in Portugal in 1974 and shook political regimes across the world.[14] While rejecting Huntington's definition of democracy and his temporal division of human history into discrete periods, Yeltsin and Deng would probably agree that the most distinguishing feature of the transition from the socialist planning economy to a market-based economy was its dual nature—difficult economic reforms and challenging political changes had to be implemented simultaneously.

Communist governments in Eastern Europe and Asia were advised by renowned economists to pursue orthodox reforms that involved instituting liberalization, reducing the role of the state in the economy, and expanding the role of the market. No formal regime of private property rights existed in these countries, nor was there any institutional basis for a market economy. Reform pressures mounted to adopt the far-reaching prescriptions of a liberal agenda to transform socialism to capitalism: central planning had to be abandoned, and radically new systems of taxation and social insurance had to be created, prices freed, subsidies and trade restrictions removed, and state enterprises privatized and restructured.

The agenda was daunting, and the stakes were high: dismantling a system that had delivered employment and some sense of social welfare to the national population and political stability to the government. Powerful constituencies had built up behind large consumer subsidies and the large consortium of state corporations and regulations. Economic agents had lived for decades with trade barriers and overvalued exchange rates. The capacity of new leaders in China, Russia, and elsewhere to fundamentally transform the economic structure and accomplish sweeping liberalization in these countries was uncertain. Not surprisingly, some regimes collapsed in the late 1980s and early 1990s.

Yeltsin and Deng faced such challenges and had to address several strategic questions in their countries. First, should political and economic transitions be implemented simultaneously? Second, what was the proper sequencing and policy mix for the economic transition? The answers were hotly debated in academic and policy circles in China and Russia and around the world.

One view was skeptical of the capacity of the new political regimes—especially those striving to replicate the Western democratic model, as was Russia's—to achieve economic stabilization and liberalization in the context of contested multiparty politics. The archetypal experience of General Augusto Pinochet's Chile was given as an example of success in economic reforms under authoritarian regimes. It was therefore argued that economic reforms had to be put ahead of political reforms.

Other political arguments offered by analysts to make the case for "economic reforms first" were built on the examples of Taiwan, China, and the Republic of Korea, where democratization was preceded by two decades of high growth generated by policy and institutional reforms, which a class of technocrats insulated from political pressure and interest groups had engineered. This led some researchers to theorize that democratic environments are less tolerant of the economic sacrifices that stabilization, privatization, and restructuring always entail. As Deepak Lal observed, it was assumed that new opposition parties and freer trade unions would necessarily oppose the end of the socialist welfare state and the move toward a market economy. Therefore, "a courageous, ruthless, and perhaps undemocratic government is required to ride roughshod over these newly created special interest groups" to guarantee the success of transitions.[15]

Looking back, Yeltsin would probably confide that he did not initially take that advice. He thought that political liberalization and economic transition should be simultaneous. His first post-Soviet Russian government, led by Yegor Gaidar, tried to speed change, but the economy began to crumble. The new policies were frequently challenged, ending in a major showdown with the Russian parliament in December 1992. Yeltsin dissolved parliament in September 1993. In early October of that year, a confrontation resulted in hundreds of deaths and injuries, as well as considerable damage to the country's political and economic stability. Just like his predecessor Mikhail Gorbachev, who was more successful with political liberalization (*glasnost*) than with economic restructuring (*perestroika*), Yeltsin could not, by his own admission, successfully implement both processes simultaneously.[16] Undeterred, he once said: "There were no strategic mistakes that could affect Russia's history and its further development. No, there were no such mistakes. Tactical errors were made in some less significant options, problems, and so on. But, on the whole, Russia embarked on a correct path and it changed."

Deng would certainly smile at Russia's rush to solve decades-long problems in a matter of days or weeks. Some of his famous quotes express his pragmatic views on the need for a gradual, yet directed, transition: "Poverty is not socialism. To be rich is glorious. . . . Let some people get rich first . . . free oneself from dogmatisms. . . . Seek truth from facts. . . . No matter whether it is a white cat or a black cat, as long as it can catch mice, it is a good cat. The way to transit from a traditional planned economy to a market economy is just like crossing a river by groping for the stones beneath the surface."

He would then remind his interlocutor that, given China's remarkable progress in recent decades, it is easy to forget the extraordinary dual challenge that China faced in the late 1970s, when the nation started on its journey of economic reform. China was indeed a very poor country in 1979, with a GDP per capita of $182, lower than one-third of Sub-Saharan Africa's average and only one-eighth that of the former Soviet Union. Today China is an upper-middle-income country, the second-largest economy in the world, and on its way to becoming number one within less than a generation.

Deng would probably also be sympathetic to the new conventional wisdom about the relationship between economic reform and democracy. He suggested that "democracy is, at a minimum, potentially compatible with economic stabilization and structural adjustment, and that the success of economic reform is determined by a host of other political, historical, institutional, and international factors that are more or less independent of the gross distinction between democratic and authoritarian regimes."[17]

But Deng would reject the optimistic, and perhaps naïve, argument put forward by some scholars that democracies (defined in the Western liberal sense) are *more* likely to undertake economic reforms because they have a greater legitimacy and greater capacity to place in power new political coalitions ready to impose costs on vested interests.[18] Showing yet again his skepticism toward a uniquely Western way of organizing the polity, he would repeat what he had once said, "The United States brags about its political system, but the president says one thing during the election, something else when he takes office, something else at midterm, and something else when he leaves."[19]

Recognizing the challenges of a dual transition, however, the former Chinese leader would lay out the four main strategic options available to communist countries that attempted to overcome the tensions between political liberalization and economic reforms: they could (1) break abruptly with the past by creating new political institutions ex nihilo if necessary and adopting difficult reforms quickly to take society and vested interests by surprise through political and economic "shock therapy"; (2) pursue the two goals of political and economic reforms not simultaneously but in sequence; (3) await an economic, social, or political crisis so severe as to force social consensus on the need for reform; or (4) choose a pragmatic approach that involves a variety of technocratic and political fixes implemented gradually to achieve the goal of fundamental change without creating unnecessary sociopolitical and economic dislocations. Deng, who rarely quoted Western political leaders, might for once agree with Winston Churchill: "However beautiful the strategy, you should occasionally look at the results." As a pragmatic man, Deng chose the fourth approach.

As the guiding force behind China's early reforms, Deng focused his agenda on economic modernization, which replaced "class struggle" as the national goal.[20] Economic growth became the paramount indicator of success. I was studying Marxist economics at Peking University in the late 1970s and early 1980s when the reform process began. One of the first steps of the transition was the introduction of a new land tenure system in rural areas: the household responsibility system (HRS). The HRS contracted the land to farmers for a fixed period, initially for 1 year and then extended to 3 years, later 15 years, and now 30 years. It allowed them to keep the benefits of their own production after they fulfilled an obligation to sell certain predetermined quotas of agricultural produce to the state at a fixed price and remitted a certain predetermined portion to the production team as collective accumulation. This was not a "Big Bang" privatization of property rights, but it was (and is) an intermediate system to provide enough stable control over land so that farmers would be motivated to produce for their own private benefit while ensuring that the state could distribute enough agricultural products to the urban sectors at low fixed prices.

The HRS was established over 1978–83. It was accompanied by other rural reforms for grain procurement and for pricing and opening access to inputs like fertilizer. In all, the reforms more than doubled agricultural growth rates. At the time, more than 80 percent of the Chinese people lived in rural areas and worked in agriculture, so this transformation dramatically improved their livelihoods. Deng promoted the HRS as a national policy after seeing the results of pilot programs in Anhui and Sichuan Provinces—an experimental approach to reform that would later be used successfully in other areas. He was also a proponent of opening the economy to new ideas and foreign technology as long as they were adapted and tailored to the local reality. His personal management style involved delegating responsibility with clear accountability to trusted colleagues. This approach would also characterize gradual reforms of state-owned enterprises in the transition process.

My research as a graduate student at the University of Chicago focused on that early period of China's rural reform, specifically the HRS. I published results showing that about half the increase in agricultural output was due to the HRS reform.[21] One might refer to this reform as "gradualist," but its impact on productivity was nothing short of revolutionary![22]

Later stages in China's rapid economic transformation involved other complex institutional transitions as the reforms were extended to urban industrial sectors. Throughout the process, however, the transition was managed with care, and the ongoing success of the process can serve as an example for both low-income and middle-income countries confronting the transition from economies with pervasive distortions and strong government interventions to market economies.

China's successful economic transition—as well as those in Mauritius in the 1970s; in Cambodia, the Lao People's Democratic Republic (PDR), and Vietnam in the 1980s; and in Belarus, Slovenia, and Uzbekistan in the 1990s—suggests that gradualism (rather than a Big Bang) may be the better approach. Unfortunately, standard policy prescriptions offered to transition economies in the 1980s and the 1990s under the brand of the Washington Consensus aimed at instantaneously wiping out all distortions with a Big Bang. The main assumption underlying the Washington Consensus was that market resource allocation could be immediately established to replace the old system.

That approach proved to be a failure. It ignored, at a heavy cost, the multiple distortions that were designed to provide necessary subsidies and protections to a large number of nonviable firms in the old economic structure. Without addressing their viability first, the attempt to eliminate those distortions caused an immediate economic collapse and huge unemployment, as well as social and political instability. For fear of prolonging that dreadful result, the government in transition reintroduced various other disguised protections and subsidies, often at costs even higher than those produced by the previous distortions.[23]

Back to Earth: The Economics of Multiple Distortions

One could take a cursory look at the trajectories and achievements of Yeltsin, Deng, and other former socialist leaders and conclude that, beyond politics, philosophy, and personal managerial styles, there were really no major differences among them. Or that the diverging outcomes of Russia and China were mainly due to their different political structures and administrative capacities—or to the fact that the former simply failed to build viable market institutions, whereas the latter succeeded in doing so. Proponents of the Washington Consensus often fell into that trap as they struggled to explain why their policy prescriptions did not deliver results in formerly socialist countries.[24] Such analyses fail to account for the differentiated strategies these two countries adopted to face the realities of multiple distortions. To understand the choices of these two leaders, one must analyze the economic history of socialism in their countries, the context of reforms, and the way Yeltsin and Deng made their strategic choices during the transition.

There is indeed something intrinsic and unique about transition economies. They emerged from an economic structure dominated by state ownership of the means of production. For several decades, they attempted large-scale industrialization administered through large investments in capital-intensive state-owned enterprises. That development strategy had a key similarity to the old structuralism of many developing countries: it led to CAD industrial structures.

Government resources were primarily devoted to capital-intensive heavy industries with three characteristics: their projects required long gestation; most equipment for a project, at least in the initial stage, needed to be imported from more industrialized economies; and each project required a large lump-sum investment.[25] A low-income agrarian economy also had three characteristics: the available capital was limited, so the market interest rate was high; foreign exchange was scarce and expensive because exportable goods were limited and consisted primarily of low-priced agricultural products; and the economic surplus was small and scattered due to the nature of a poor agrarian economy.[26] Because these characteristics of the low-income economy were mismatched with the three characteristics of heavy-industry projects, the spontaneous development of a capital-intensive industry in the economy was impossible.[27]

A set of distorted macro policies was therefore required for the development of a heavy industry–oriented development strategy. To pursue that strategy the Chinese government, for instance, instituted a policy of low interest rates and overvalued exchange rates to reduce the costs both of interest payments and of importing equipment for the priority projects.[28] Meanwhile, to secure enough funds for industrial expansion, a policy of low input prices—which included nominal wage rates for workers and prices for raw materials, energy, and transportation—had to be implemented simultaneously.[29] It was assumed that low prices would enable firms to generate profits large enough to repay the loans or accumulate enough funds for reinvestment.

If firms were privately owned, the state could not be sure that the private entrepreneurs would reinvest the policy-created profits in the intended projects.[30] Eventually private enterprises were nationalized to secure the state's control over profits for reinvestments in heavy-industry projects.[31]

Meanwhile, to maintain the low nominal wage policy, the government had to provide urban residents with inexpensive food and other necessities, including housing, clothing, and medical care.

The low interest rates, overvalued exchange rates, low nominal wage rates, and low prices for raw materials and living necessities constituted the basic macro policy environment in which to pursue a heavy industry–oriented development strategy.[32]

These macro policies led to serious imbalances, however, in the supply and demand for credit, foreign exchange, raw materials, and other living necessities. Because nonpriority sectors were competing with priority sectors for the low-priced resources, a rigid planning system and administrative controls replaced markets as the mechanisms for allocating scarce credit, foreign reserves, raw materials, and living necessities; the government's objective was to ensure that limited resources would be used for the targeted projects. Moreover, the state monopolized banks, foreign trade, and the material distribution systems.[33]

Under that economic model, competition was suppressed and profits ceased to be the measure of an enterprise's efficiency. A Chinese firm that produced inputs for other sectors, such as energy or transportation, would inevitably incur losses because the prices of its outputs were suppressed. By contrast, a heavy machine–building firm was bound to make profit because it could enjoy low input prices and high output prices at the same time.

Central governments controlled all of the activities of state-owned enterprises (SOEs), which implied that these enterprises had a complete lack of decisionmaking autonomy. Government planners decided and then provided all the inputs needed for the SOEs' production. These were laid out in central plans, and a centrally planned budget ensured that all costs were covered. In return, the SOEs were obliged to deliver all outputs and revenues to the government. The state also set the wage rates of SOE workers and managers. Effectively all SOE activities required the state's approval. This degree of central control seems irrational; however, the command structure was in effect a response to the "agency" problems in prioritizing capital-intensive industries in a capital-scarce economy.[34] Any attempt to decentralize decisionmaking would in effect increase the costs of implementing the strategy. For example, the decentralization of wage-setting power to the SOE managers during Gorbachev's years resulted in wage inflation and declining budget revenues. The central government had to rely on administrative control and allocation so that inputs, budgets, and outcomes would fit the central plan.

In that kind of macro policy environment, the challenge at the micro level was to solve the "agency" problem of motivating or "incentivizing" the good performance of SOEs. Because there was no real market test, one could not gather much evidence on the relative performance of SOEs or on their managers' performance. One could examine final sales and inputs and calculate the profitability of each SOE. But there was a serious attribution problem. Because prices were administratively set and internal SOE management decisions were largely controlled by the central government, managers' decisions were of little relevance to firms' eventual profit rates. As a result, one could not reward or discipline managers on that basis.

Another approach might have been to set physical production targets and to benchmark performance against historical levels. Yet again, an attribution problem would have appeared: because the government often failed to meet its own commitments for delivering inputs, it would have been difficult to hold managers accountable even for the physical production outcomes.

Finally, one might have considered an elaborate system for monitoring managerial behavior. But for an economy dominated by SOEs, it would have been prohibitively costly to establish and maintain such a monitoring system. The result was an equilibrium in which "it was imperative for the state to deprive managers of their autonomy and to make the SOEs like puppets in the economic system."[35] SOE reforms aimed at providing more autonomy to SOE managers often failed and reverted back to centralized control by the government.

Rather than learn from their mistakes, policymakers in socialist countries kept launching heavy industries in which their firms could not compete in the global market and devoted large sums of public resources to them. Despite some initial successes, their economies were left with myriad distortions, dominated by large numbers of nonviable firms in the uncompetitive "advanced" sector. In the Cold War atmosphere that dominated most of the second half of the twentieth century, their adversaries in the Western world seemed to follow the recommendation of French general and emperor Napoleon Bonaparte, who once said, "Never stop your enemy when he is making a mistake." It has been argued that former U.S. president Ronald Reagan's 1983 Space Defense Initiative, a defense system in outer space that would protect the country against any incoming nuclear missiles, may have been partly motivated by the desire to encourage the former Soviet Union to continue its CAD strategy of developing advanced heavy industries.[36] After decades of implementing strategies inconsistent with their comparative advantage, Eastern European and many Asian socialist economies were not only in second-best situations but indeed in third-, fourth-, and nth-best situations, and they suffered from the inefficiency caused by the complex effects of multiple distortions.

One peculiarity of socialist or quasi-socialist systems has thus been the additional complications and costs associated with the structural transformation that accompanied their transition from central planning. How could they do that in a way that was politically realistic and economically least disruptive? That is the question that Deng, Yeltsin, and ultimately all leaders of developing countries in Africa, Latin America, and Asia who wrongly pursued CAD, capital-intensive, industry-oriented strategies had to wrestle with when they realized that the transition from a centrally planned system to a market system was almost unavoidable.

Options for Economic Reform: Big Bang or Gradualism?

The crucial issue of economic transition has been to have a strategy of sequencing reforms that removes various distortions to improve incentives and efficiency. Two broad strategic options—each with some nuances—have been implemented by Eastern European and Asian countries in the move from plan to market: the Big Bang, or shock therapy, and the gradualist approach.

Proponents of the Big Bang wanted to eliminate government distortions and interventions in socialist and developing countries and set up well-functioning market systems there as soon as possible. They expected that the installation of market competition and the immediate and quick privatization of SOEs would improve incentives and efficiency. Consequently, the economy would be competitive and prosper.

Postcommunist leaders in Poland were among the most vocal proponents of that approach. When Jeffrey Sachs was invited to advise the reformist movement Solidarity in 1989, he was told by its leaders: "Give us the outline that you see fit. But make it a program of rapid and comprehensive change. And please, start the outline with the words: 'With this program, Poland will jump to the market economy.' We want to move quickly; that is the only way that this will make sense in our society, that it will make sense politically, and—as we understand from experts—the only way it will make sense economically as well."[37]

Perhaps because former Polish trade union leader Lech Walesa was an electrician before he entered politics, he had a lightning approach to policies that seems to have served him rather well. Only four years after creating

Solidarity (the Soviet Bloc's first independent trade union) in the suburbs of Gdansk in 1979, he challenged the military regime of General Wojciech Jaruzelski and was awarded the Nobel Peace Prize (1983). His charisma and strong support from the Western world helped him topple the Polish government, and he became president in 1990. He brought with him a team of radical reformists, such as the brilliant economist Leszek Balcerowicz, who served as deputy premier and minister of finance in the first Solidarity-led government after the fall of communism.

Following the wisdom of seventeenth-century Japanese martial arts master Miyamoto Musashi, who said, "You win battles by knowing the enemy's timing and using a timing which the enemy does not expect," Balcerowicz argued persuasively that the short period of euphoria and "extraordinary politics" after the demise of communist regimes presented a unique opportunity in which reformers had to move rapidly to put in place new democratic and market-oriented institutions and dismantle the massive structural distortions and disincentives of the socialist economy.[38] He therefore made a strong case for the Big Bang or the Washington Consensus on both political and economic grounds. Politically, he asserted that economic reforms were easier to adopt and implement through a comprehensive program than through a lengthy process of piecemeal and often painful measures, which would leave more time for old-liners and conservative forces with the opportunity to oppose it. Economically, Balcerowicz said, radical reform was more likely to control inflation, signal a new era, build confidence, and generate new structures from which there could be no turning back. "Delay will only worsen the macroeconomic situation," he said, while "a gradual or mild stabilization program will most likely fail to overcome inflationary inertia and expectations."[39]

That same Big Bang thesis was advanced by Harvard economist Jeffrey Sachs and many others, including Swedish economist Anders Aslund, who differentiated between "the developed socialist countries of Eastern Europe and the former Soviet Union" and "developing socialist countries like China and Vietnam."[40] Aslund first observed that Western-style democratization appeared to have been a precondition for a successful transition to a market economy. He then went on to suggest, "There are compelling reasons not only for the rapid destruction of the old order, but also for the speedy construction of a new democratic state."[41] The slower the destruction of the old system, he argued, the more trouble and pain the transition would bring: "Given time, communist-holdover officials will find ways to transform their remaining power into property (whether by outright thievery or more subtle methods), thus exacerbating inequalities, undermining public confidence in the state, and preparing the ground for potentially undemocratic populism."[42]

Such a prescription did not take into account the underlying viability problem in the economic system. Decades of central planning and forced industrialization created a massive structure of nonviable firms in the prioritized heavy industries. For the rapid transition to work, the economy would need to effortlessly reallocate resources from those industries to a market-oriented structure. However, equipment and workers in the prioritized heavy-industry sector could not be relocated immediately or at all to light industries and the service sector. The result would have been a collapse of the priority sectors, mass unemployment, and social and political instability.

A more nuanced approach to reform, quite different in practice from the typical Washington Consensus prescription but inspired by it, was advocated by a group of leading macroeconomists who argued that the economic transition from communism should proceed in sequence: stabilization, price liberalization, and privatization had to be implemented rapidly, whereas restructuring should take time (a decade or more).[43] Almost all Eastern European countries entered the postcommunist era with substantial fiscal deficits and excessive money creation. Drawing heavily on the Latin American experience with stabilization programs, the macroeconomists suggested that budget deficits and money creation had to be brought under control at the outset of transition and that prices had to be liberalized, because price control would only perpetuate the shortages recorded under socialism. They also suggested that inflationary shocks be contained, where necessary, by monetary reform involving partial confiscation of nominal assets.

Unfortunately, neither the Big Bang nor the more nuanced version of the Washington Consensus worked smoothly for postcommunist countries. The prevailing wisdom embodied in their prescriptions often failed, and some countries could not come up with viable strategies for managing their structural transformation and guiding their industrial and technological upgrading. In Russia, for instance, most prices were liberalized in January 1992, but macroeconomic stabilization was not implemented because there was not enough political support among key policymakers for the unemployment that would have resulted. In April 1992, the People's Congress instructed the Russian government that the country's priority was to "stabilize production," meaning propping up employment in state firms through credit and thus money creation. As a result, inflation never fell below 9 percent a month in 1992.

But in June the Supreme Soviet approved a plan for fast privatization. State capital was quickly sold at bargain prices to a small group of people, subsequently known as oligarchs, who had financial assets or political connections and could reap extraordinary gains. That, in turn, created new political-economy problems, which Russia is still struggling to address nearly two decades later.[44] Olivier Blanchard and his coauthors, who had recommended the nuanced version of the Big Bang, acknowledged that

> ambitious and clever plans have been disfigured by political compromises, bogged down in political fights, tied down by bureaucratic bottlenecks and foot dragging, sabotaged by those who would lose most from their implementation. . . . The basic lesson is clear: privatization is not about the distribution of assets belonging to "the state," which can dispose of them as it wishes, but about the distribution of assets with many de facto claimants: workers, managers, local authorities, central ministries, and so on. Unless these claimants are appeased, bribed, or disenfranchised, privatization cannot proceed. The main challenge of privatization is thus how to deal with and reconcile those claims.[45]

The new structural economics that I offer in this book provides an alternative explanation for the failure of the Big Bang and its nuanced version.

Socialist economies that had adopted strategies inconsistent with their comparative advantage had a large number of nonviable enterprises in the government's priority sector. Without government protection and subsidies, most of these enterprises were unable to survive in an open and competitive market. In some small postcommunist countries such as Estonia, Latvia, and Lithuania, which had only a limited number of such nonviable enterprises, the output value and employment of those enterprises were limited, and Big Bang reforms could eliminate all government interventions at once. With the abolition of government protection and subsidies, these nonviable enterprises became bankrupt, but given their small relative contribution to the economy, the "transition costs" were small. The originally suppressed labor-intensive sector thrived, especially with inflows of FDI, and newly created employment opportunities in these industries could absorb labor and compensate for the losses from the bankruptcy of nonviable firms. As a result, the economy could grow soon after implementing the shock therapy, with a smaller initial loss of output and employment.

In larger countries, where the number of nonviable firms was large, forceful application of the shock therapy resulted in large-scale bankruptcies and mass unemployment. To avoid such dire consequences and sustain the nonviable enterprises in the advanced industries for political or military purposes, the governments had no choice but to attempt the nuanced approach offered by the leading macroeconomists: immediate stabilization, price liberalization, and privatization, but postponing the restructuring.[46]

But this approach was logically inconsistent and self-defeating. Stabilization could not be achieved if prices were liberalized and nonviable enterprises were privatized while the restructuring was postponed. First, most enterprises in the government's priority sector had certain monopoly powers and would have inflated their prices once controls were lifted. Second, the private entrepreneurs had higher incentives than the SOE managers to use the viability issue as an excuse to lobby for more subsidies from the government because they could directly benefit from such rent seeking.[47] However, government revenues declined in the aftermath of the transition.

Rather than the stabilization its proponents intended, this approach would lead to hyperinflation in the transition. Indeed, that was exactly what happened in many Eastern European and former Soviet Union countries after their transition.[48] The result was "shock without therapy."[49] Easterly has also documented the failure in Eastern European transition economies and provided evidence that it was part of a broader stagnation of developing countries that adhered to the Washington Consensus.[50]

A different and much more effective strategy for economic transition recommended by the new structural economics is a gradual, pragmatic, and dual-track approach that recognizes the endogeneity of the distortions and the viability issue of enterprises in the priority sectors. It recommends that the government provide some transitory protections to nonviable firms in the priority sector to maintain their stability in the transition but liberalize private firms and FDI and facilitate their entrance into sectors in which the country has comparative advantages so as to improve resource allocation, tap the advantage of backwardness, and achieve dynamic growth. The capital accumulation resulting from rapid growth in the new sectors will make many firms in the old prioritized industries viable. Dynamic growth will also create the necessary conditions, including financial resources and job opportunities, for removing the distortions in a manner reminiscent of Kaldor's characteristics of twentieth-century growth, which implies that the policy change will increase the total social welfare and that the losers will be compensated for their losses so no one in the economy loses from the policy change.[51] In this way the policy resistance to the reform can be minimized.

The process is one of opening markets while also providing government support to facilitate the growth of new industries. The latter can be achieved using the six-step operationalization strategy described in Chapter 7. For example, special economic zones are fully compatible with this gradualist approach: reforms and supportive infrastructure are established initially in limited geographic areas and support specific sectors during the economic transition. Elements of this approach have been implemented successfully in transition economies around the world.

Thriving Transitions:
Lessons from China, Slovenia, and a Few Other Countries

American writer Richard Wright suggested that one should not "leave inferences to be drawn when evidence can be presented." So I will follow his advice and provide some evidence to support the thesis that a gradual dual-track approach has a much better chance of success in a transition economy than the Big Bang. China, Vietnam, Slovenia, and Mauritius are good examples. They adopted a pragmatic approach to reforms and development—providing transitory protection or subsidies to nonviable firms in the government's old priority sectors and supporting the sectors consistent with the country's comparative advantages—to achieve dynamic growth.

It is useful to reiterate that when China began its transition from a planned to a market-oriented economy in 1978, it was a poor, inward-looking country with a per capita income of $182 and a trade–GDP ratio of only 9.5 percent. The outcomes over the last 32 years speak for themselves: China's annual GDP growth has averaged 9.9 percent, and its growth in international trade has averaged 16.3 percent.

China's leaders may not have followed a blueprint when they started the reform process, as Dwight Perkins noted.[52] Still, the country's transition followed a rigorous logic. The prior system was based on three integrated components: "(1) a distorted macropolicy environment that featured artificially low interest rates, overvalued exchange rates, low nominal wage rates, and low prices for living necessities and raw materials; (2) a planned allocation mechanism for credit, foreign exchange, and other materials; and (3) a traditional autonomy-deprived micromanagement institution of state enterprises and collective agriculture."[53]

The apparent problem with the economic system was low economic efficiency due to structural imbalances and incentive problems. Therefore, the goals of the reforms in 1978 were to rectify the structural imbalance and improve incentives, but what set the reforms apart from previous attempts were the micromanagement system reforms that made peasants in collective farms and managers and workers in state enterprises partial stakeholders:

"That small crack in the trinity of the traditional economic system was eventually pried open, leading to the gradual dismantlement of the traditional system."[54]

In practice, this translated as continuing government support to nonviable firms in priority sectors. At the same time, however, the government also liberalized and facilitated the entry of private enterprises, joint ventures, and FDI into labor-intensive sectors in which China had a comparative advantage. These sectors had been repressed under the prereform economic strategy. At the start of the reform, the rural sector was critical, given that most of China's population lived in rural areas. The gradual implementation of the HRS, mentioned earlier, allowed farmers to keep a substantial and growing share of their output, thus providing an incentive for their improved agricultural productivity. A new form of collective property— the town and village enterprises—was developed with decentralized control at the local level. That hybrid institutional arrangement evolved over time, but a key feature was that it gave rural farmers and nonfarm workers improved incentives and allowed them to have a say in resource allocation and investment and benefit from the increase in productivity and efficiency.

SOEs were reformed, but only gradually, so that they could adapt to change. Control and decisionmaking autonomy were delegated gradually during the first decade of reforms. The gradual approach was not, by any means, the result of complacency. Deng noted in a 1980 speech:

> Bureaucracy remains a major and widespread problem in the political life of our Party and state. Its harmful manifestations include the following: standing high above the masses; abusing power; divorcing oneself from reality and the masses; spending a lot of time and effort to put up an impressive front; indulging in empty talk; sticking to a rigid way of thinking; being hidebound by convention; overstaffing administrative organs; being dilatory, inefficient, and irresponsible; failing to keep one's word; circulating documents endlessly without solving problems; shifting responsibilities to others; and even assuming the airs of a mandarin, reprimanding other people at every turn,

vindictively attacking others, suppressing democracy, deceiving superiors and subordinates, being arbitrary and despotic, practicing favoritism, offering bribes, participating in corrupt practices in violation of the law, and so on. Such things have reached intolerable dimensions both in our domestic affairs and in our contacts with other countries.[55]

The reform eventually led to largely market-based prices and resource allocation. By 1996 some 93 percent of all retail goods, 79 percent of all agricultural products, and 81 percent of the total sales volume of production factors were priced solely by the market.[56] The realistic transition strategy allowed China both to maintain social stability and to create economic dynamism. Social stability was achieved by avoiding the collapse of the old priority industries, dynamic growth by simultaneously pursuing the country's comparative advantage and tapping its advantage of backwardness in industrial upgrading and diversification. In addition, the dynamic growth in the newly liberalized sectors created the conditions for reforming the old priority sectors. Some SOEs became viable in open, competitive markets because of the rapid accumulation of capital. Others were allowed to go bankrupt because the dynamic growth helped generate job opportunities to employ their workers. In sum, China achieved "reform without losers" and moved gradually but steadily to a well-functioning market economy.[57]

Vietnam followed similar dual-track reforms to dismantle its previous centralized economic system. For example, policymakers began to allow SOE managers to keep revenues from excess earnings when sales exceeded those laid out in the central plan.[58] The Vietnamese government also granted collective farms some autonomy and created a closer link between personal rewards and agricultural production. The Lao PDR, too, followed a reform sequence and phasing very similar to China's.

Many Eastern European and former Soviet Bloc countries chose to follow the Big Bang to reforms, but there were a few exceptions. Slovenia pursued a step-by-step economic reform following the downfall of the Soviet Union and the splitting up of the former Socialist Federal Republic of Yugoslavia.

Slovenia faced a "threefold transition" at the start of the 1990s: the transition from a socialist to a market economy, the transition from a regional to a national economy, and its gradual integration into the EU.[59] Part of the gradualism dates back to before the birth of the nation: a number of reforms to the government-owned sector implied that a quasi-market system was in place. Managers had much more autonomy in running their enterprises than those in some of the former Soviet republics.

Slovenia has recorded balanced growth since the collapse of its output due to the dissolution of the former Socialist Federal Republic of Yugoslavia. But the road to economic transition has been rocky. For a long time its gradual transition maintained parts of its economy sheltered from competition. More than a decade after Slovenia started its economic reforms, state involvement was still significant in many sectors. Regulation kept the pace of restructuring slow. Banking was still dominated by two state-owned banks, and enterprises of public or mixed ownership still produced about half of the total value added and were present in various sectors, from steel to insurance. Capital-account liberalization—a key condition for the country's joining the EU (Slovenia became a member in 2004)—took time. Because it would expose the country's financial system to greater competition, the government also took the time to strengthen the efficiency of the system. The International Monetary Fund expressed concern about the activities of the Slovene Development Corporation, which provided subsidized loans to enterprises. In the face of high structural unemployment in the 1990s, Slovenia also developed an extensive menu of active labor market policies—including job subsidies, public works (for those with a low probability of job reentry), and on- and off-the-job training and retraining programs.

The substantial budgetary resources devoted to such programs raised the eyebrows of experts who advocated radical Washington Consensus prescriptions. But they helped mitigate the social cost of the transition, maintained stability, and allowed the government to achieve its goal of creating "an innovative, entrepreneurial economy" that enjoys "competitiveness, sustainable growth, and social peace."[60] This was an important goal given the region's history and the country's location at the crossroads of the Balkans and Western Europe. Slovenia is now the richest Slavic state. Its GDP per capita increased by three-fourths between 1992 and 2010 and reached 85 percent of the EU27 average, measured in purchasing power parity.

Similarly, Belarus and Uzbekistan, which did not immediately privatize their large state-owned enterprises and adopted a gradual approach to reform, also performed better than other former Soviet Union countries, which followed shock therapy. In spite of its initial attempt to jump to a market economy, Poland also did not privatize its large state-owned enterprises until recently and was a star performer among the Eastern European countries.[61]

Another even more interesting example of the successful implementation of a gradual, dual-track approach to reforms is Mauritius. Fifty years ago, Nobel laureate James Meade famously predicted that Mauritius was an economic and social time bomb: a combination of population growth, single-crop commodity dependence, a small domestic market, distance from major global markets, and socioethnic tensions would inevitably result in economic and social despair.

Fortunately, these predictions did not materialize. To the contrary, Mauritius's economic performance has far surpassed the averages for Sub-Saharan Africa. Its citizens enjoy the highest living standards in the region, with income per capita of nearly $13,000 (in purchasing power parity), an 88 percent literacy rate, and a life expectancy of 73 years.[62]

How did Mauritius achieve this superior performance? Did it simply have better initial starting conditions than were found in other African countries? No; only its life expectancy was higher. On many other variables, Mauritius had no advantage. And although Mauritius avoided the pitfalls of many of its landlocked neighbors, it faced the barrier of sheer distance, located in the southern part of the Indian Ocean, thousands of kilometers from the major market centers of Asia, Europe, and North America.

Mauritius began its independence in 1968 with a largely single-crop (sugar) economy, combined with a dominant state apparatus. While maintaining the policy distortions in its domestic economy as a legacy of its old import substitution strategy, it created an export-processing zone in the 1970s and actively attracted textile and garment enterprises from Hong

Kong SAR, China, motivating them to relocate their production to Mauritius. In the zone, in addition to having good infrastructure and efficient administration, labor and other regulations were liberalized. Many observers attributed Mauritius's success to favorable external factors: preferred import status for textiles entering the United States as well as favorable treatment for sugar imports into the EU because of its low-income status. Although these favorable conditions definitely helped Mauritius achieve success, I would highlight that those favorable conditions existed in other low-income countries, and, compared to them, Mauritius had many unfavorable conditions, as just noted.

But Mauritius was one of the most successful countries in exploiting those favorable conditions. I submit that its successes are due, first, to its dual-track approach to transition (on one track maintaining economic and social stability by retaining transitory protections to old sectors and, on the other, allowing the economy to tap its comparative advantages as an engine of growth in the new sectors) and, second, to the government's correct identification of industries with latent comparative advantages and its effective facilitation of those industries' growth. In the 1970s, Hong Kong SAR, China, was the world's major exporter of labor-intensive garments and textiles. With its dynamic growth, wages were increasing and the enterprises in those sectors were looking for opportunities to relocate their operations. Mauritius's per capita income in 1970 (in purchasing power parity and 2000 international dollars) was $2,945, about 50 percent that of Hong Kong SAR, China, in the same year ($5,695).[63]

Because the garment and textile industry was in line with Mauritius's latent comparative advantage, once the enterprises from Hong Kong SAR, China, brought in their production, management, and marketing know-how, many local entrepreneurs also entered the sector. Today about 70 percent of the textile and garment enterprises in Mauritius are owned by Mauritians.[64]

While the dual-track approach allows a transition economy to maintain stability and achieve dynamic growth, it also entails social and economic costs. The transition to a well-functioning market economy will not be complete until the remaining distortions in the first track are eliminated. China's transition is a good example. It achieved enviable stability and growth in the past three decades but was troubled by structural problems: most notably, disparities in income distribution and an imbalance between consumption and savings and the external account. When the transition started, China was a relatively egalitarian society, but with rapid growth its income distribution became more unequal.[65]

During the transition the Chinese government retained some market distortions to provide continuing support to nonviable firms in the priority industries. Major remaining distortions include the concentration of financial services in four large state-owned banks and the equity market; the almost zero royalty on natural resources; and the monopolies in major service industries, including power, banking, and telecommunications. These distortions facilitated stability and dynamic growth during China's transition.

Most firms in the old priority sectors have become viable because of the rapid accumulation of capital and other reforms. But they continue to receive subsidies through the remaining distortions, contributing to the rising income disparity and economic imbalances. Only large companies and the wealthy have access to capital in the equity market and the credit provided by the large banks. Capital costs and interest rates are artificially repressed. As a result, large companies and wealthy individuals are receiving subsidies from small equity investors and bank depositors who have no access to the capital markets or to banks' credit services. The concentration of profits and wealth in large companies and the widening of income disparities are unavoidable. The low royalty levies on natural resources and the monopolies in the service sector have similar effects. Because rich individuals and large corporations have a high saving propensity, their high profits and access to bank credit and equity market capital allow them to make large investments, expanding China's production capacity rapidly. However, China's domestic absorption capacity was repressed as the income share of the relatively poor, who have a higher consumption propensity than the rich and large corporations, dwindled. The consequence of these two trends has been a widening of China's trade surplus.

For China to address the structural imbalances and complete its transition to a well-functioning market economy, it will have to remove the remaining distortions in the financial, natural resource, and service sectors more generally. I suggest that it adopt the following key reforms: remove financial repression and allow small and local financing institutions, including local banks, to fully develop; levy an appropriate royalty on natural resources; and encourage entry into and competition in the power, finance, and telecommunications sectors.[66]

The exact prescriptions for further reforms in countries that adopted a dual-track approach will need to be tailored to their specific economic, social, and political environments (especially in the case of those that achieved stability and dynamic growth over their dual-track transition). But all will need to remove remaining distortions in the first track if they want to have a well-functioning market economy. Governments in those countries will need to facilitate their structural transformation to avoid the middle-income trap and to continue to grow dynamically when they reach high-income economy status, the topic of the next chapter.

Fostering Structural Change
at Higher Levels of Development

I T IS DIFFICULT FOR ANYONE TO VISIT VIETNAM EVEN TODAY without having to fight back some elusive memories and thoughts of the 21-year-long war that tragically put the country on the international agenda in the 1960s and 1970s. The war took place while I was still a young student in Taiwan, China. Like anyone else, I grew up seeing television images and newspaper pictures of the brutality, destruction, and horror, which seem to always reemerge subconsciously whenever I am back in Hanoi. When the plane prepares for landing at Noi Bai airport, flying over the plains of North Vietnam, where many rivers flow eastward to the sea in scenery so similar to that of my own hometown, Yilan, in the northeast corner of Taiwan, China, I often find myself looking through the windows as if semiconscious, in search of the ghosts of the soldiers, peasants, and ordinary men and women who perished for their nations in one of the worst conflicts of the twentieth century. Some 58,000 American soldiers were killed in action, while an estimated 1.1 million Vietnamese soldiers and an additional 4 million civilians (totaling nearly 13 percent of the country's population, according to the Vietnamese authorities) died during the more than two decades of the war.[1]

Things have changed dramatically, and each time I visit the country—most recently in the summer of 2010, the year of the city's 1,000th birthday—I can see economic progress under way, often amid the difficulties of the vibrant new urban life there. The 28-mile trip from the airport to downtown Hanoi is always fascinating. The narrow road is congested and polluted due to the constant flow of vehicles into and out of town. Reports by the city's Traffic Safety Board note that people living nearby suffer daily from exhaust fumes and dust—and that severe traffic jams, some lasting for hours, are common. A large number of vehicles get stuck at intersections, with thousands of cyclists and motorists crisscrossing the commercial and administrative parts of Hanoi.

The congestion and difficulties of urban life also reflect the dynamism of a country whose long history has been characterized by resilience. Hollywood blockbuster movies such as *Platoon, Apocalypse Now,* and *Full Metal Jacket* recount how bombs and guns killed millions of people and destroyed what little infrastructure the country had in the 1960s and 1970s. But the destruction could not overcome the indomitable spirit and ingenuity of a people who have a long experience of battling adversity. Few analysts could have predicted the economic progress made only a generation after the Vietnam War had claimed so many lives. The country still defines itself as a socialist republic, but reforms in the late 1980s and early 1990s, particularly those returning responsibility for agricultural production to individual farmers and permitting household enterprises, led to dramatic increases in agricultural production. These reforms turned Vietnam into a dynamic middle-income country with a GDP per capita in 2010 of nearly $3,000 (in purchasing power parity).

Vietnam has embarked on preparing its new 10-year National Socioeconomic Development Strategy, the guiding framework for two consecutive five-year plans. On my last trip to Hanoi I attended a high-level workshop titled "Vietnam: Looking towards the New Decade and Beyond," chaired by Prime Minister Nguyen Tan Dung and organized to gather comments from a wide range of experts on the government's draft strategy document, brainstorm about industrial policy in developing countries, and draw lessons from the many failures of the past. At the workshop I outlined how one might apply the GIF framework to a country like Vietnam. My main point was that a developing country that follows its comparative advantage has the best chance to be competitive globally; successfully upgrade its endowment structure (which can evolve), tapping into the potential of late-comer advantages; sustain industrial upgrading; raise its national income; and reduce poverty. The preconditions for such a successful strategy are a well-functioning, competitive market system and a facilitating state.

I was impressed by the quality of the debate and the very open tone of the discussions among academics, policymakers, political leaders, and development partners. When I met privately with Prime Minster Nguyen Tan Dung and other senior government officials, I realized that they were happy with the country's development performance so far but mostly preoccupied with difficult strategic issues ahead—and rightly so. Although the current development model—which Vietnam has relied on for more than two decades since *Doi Moi*—has led to rapid economic growth in the past two decades (with per capita income growing almost 10-fold), the continuation of dynamic growth cannot be taken for granted.[2] Vietnam is still a globally competitive low-wage manufacturer and commodity producer. But new governance, poverty, and inequality challenges are emerging, and joining the World Trade Organization is bringing both rewards and risks.

Who could blame Vietnamese policymakers for worrying about the long-term sustainability of their country's excellent economic performance? After all, many other countries have performed quite well for a period before stalling inexplicably in their development. The Russian Federation, for instance, has been trapped as a middle-income country for nearly 200 years despite trying very hard to join the select club of high-income countries. Some high-income countries have even slipped to become middle-income countries. As a recent World Bank report pointed out, in 1900 Argentina was the sixth-largest economy and had one of the highest incomes in the world. In 1950 República Bolivariana de Venezuela was ranked highest in per capita GDP in Latin America, with the same income as Australia and Canada. Yet today the per capita incomes of Argentina and Venezuela are below that of middle-income Malaysia.[3]

Many people in Vietnam are closely watching China, my own country, which faces the same challenges despite its remarkable economic achievements in the past three decades. The 2008 Olympics there were a tremendous success. The government managed well the complexities of hosting an event of such magnitude and global renown. The theme for the event was "One World, One Dream." In many ways, to host the games was a landmark in China's progress, both in its economic development and its international role. The Olympics indeed provided an opportunity to showcase China's growing capacity on many fronts: the coordination of the activities for the event itself, the high quality of the public infrastructure, the creativity and innovation in the design of the "Bird's Nest" stadium, and the mix of high-tech production with traditional music and dance at the opening and closing ceremonies. These achievements were on television for the world to see as they followed the athletes' achievements on the ground.

But just like the Argentines, Venezuelans, or Vietnamese, the Chinese have good reasons to be modest in their triumph: 40 years earlier, Mexico hosted the summer Olympics. Despite some concerns over the high altitude and urban air pollution, the event was well attended and generally viewed as an extremely well-organized international event. It also represented a landmark in Mexico's economic development and world role. At that time, Mexico's economy had already put it in the middle class of nations. Its GDP per capita was $3,461 (in 2000 U.S. dollars). Since then, there have been dramatic improvements in many social indicators in the country, including access to basic services and educational attainment, and in 2008 (before the global financial crisis) its GDP per capita had nearly doubled, to $6,592 (in 2000 U.S. dollars). There has also been growth in new industries and a strong opening of the economy to international trade. Yet, on the global scale of things, Mexico's economy still belongs essentially to the middle class rather than the upper class of nations—despite its membership in the OECD. Its GDP per capita has remained about 19 percent that of the United States.

Too many economies, even after emerging from a low-income trap, have not been able to continue closing their gap with the highest-income countries. The question, then, is how can they avoid relative stagnation and continue to close their gap with the highest-income country in the world? What could have helped Mexico come substantially closer to the living standards of the United States or Europe over the past four decades? China has grown from a low-income country to an upper-middle-income country and is now the world's second-largest economy and a global leader in manufacturing. How can China continue to grow rapidly and reach advanced-economy status? What steps can ensure that the next generation of citizens in Vietnam, Russia, Argentina, and other middle-income countries will enjoy the privileges and opportunities of living in a truly advanced economy?

Policymakers in various parts of the world face those questions. Even in richer Western European countries such as Greece, Italy, and Spain, the anxiety of getting stuck at an income far below that of the United States is haunting, a reflection of the financial and economic crises of recent years. Many middle-income countries seem to have fallen into a trap of painfully slow growth over the past half century: they simply are not "catching up." And there are examples of highly advanced economies that have entered prolonged periods of nearly zero economic growth—Japan over the past two decades is a prime example. In a globalized world, economic competition is, as the Chinese proverb says, "like rowing upstream; not to advance is to drop back." And policymakers need all the wisdom they can draw upon to continue to promote prosperity. The new structural economics and its GIF framework can provide answers and outline the path toward the big dreams of reaching high-income status that all middle-income countries are entitled to.

A key theme of this book is that an economic structure should evolve over time at different levels of development no matter whether a country is low, middle, or high income. Both its observed and its latent comparative advantage will change throughout that process, and in a market economy the government should play a facilitating role to address the coordination and externality issues that will inevitably arise in the dynamic process. As Chapter 7 showed, the GIF framework proposes an approach for a country to use to develop according to the changes in its comparative advantages and tap the potential advantage of backwardness in its industrial upgrading. The key challenge is to determine the sectors at a higher level of development and policies to encourage or support their development.

This chapter deals with that challenge for middle- and high-income countries. I start by describing the main long-term challenges that policymakers in successful developing countries must keep in mind—most notably the "middle-income trap." Then I discuss how some countries are dealing with this challenge through policy decisions consistent with the new structural economics and the GIF framework, which are applicable to virtually all economies. For policymakers in middle-income countries, the dream of reaching high-income status should not be an end in itself because, even at that level, continuing technological and industrial upgrading and structural transformation will remain the most important driving forces for improvements in welfare, job creation, and social stability. I conclude by highlighting examples of government facilitation to sustain structural transformation in high-income countries and showing how these policies are consistent with the principles in my analytical framework.

Fighting Off the Middle-Income Curse

Let us start with a clarification: what exactly are the concerns of policymakers in China, in Vietnam, and certainly in other developing countries that are still trying to catch up with more advanced economies? What is a middle-income country, and what is the middle-income trap? Broadly speaking, the characteristics that we want to capture when describing a country as "middle income" are those of an intermediate state of development. It seems, then, that if we want to classify countries as middle income, it would be better to use some absolute threshold of income per capita. One could then adjust those thresholds over time to take into consideration the impact of inflation. It turns out that for years the World Bank has been doing just that. The World Bank classifies a country as middle income if its income per capita (gross national income, in accounting terms) is greater than $1,006 and less than $12,275. Within that group, countries in the range of $1,006–$3,975 are considered lower middle income, and those in the range of $3,976–$12,275 upper middle income.[4]

A middle-income country may still suffer from some of the symptoms of "backwardness"—lower human and physical capital than the richest countries on earth and less technological and institutional sophistication. For a typical middle-income country, the adult literacy rate is about 80–90 percent, infant mortality is 20–40 per 1,000 live births, and life expectancy is around 70 years. In addition, the typical middle-income country possesses sectors or industries that may be highly developed—and even at the global technological frontier. For example, a middle-income country might have producers of some household appliances, such as microwaves, DVD players, air conditioners, and washing machines, as in China, or have a middle-range regional aircraft manufacturer, such as Embraer in Brazil, that have reached the global technological frontier in those categories of products. But the technologies in most other sectors still trail those in the high-income countries, and some high-value-added sectors in high-income countries are missing from the country's industrial structure.

Structural change and economic development represent a continuing struggle across the levels of development. Descriptions of everyday life in *Oliver Twist,* Charles Dickens's well-known novel, remind us that Britain was still quite poor in the early nineteenth century even though it was the most developed country in the world at that time. And, by today's standard, all countries had poor agrarian economies before the eighteenth century. Successful countries today have kept the growth process going—not only from low income to middle income but also from middle income to high income—and have maintained dynamic growth throughout their high-income stage.

Unfortunately, some countries that moved beyond low-income status by virtue of their industrialization efforts or their windfall of natural resources in earlier periods find themselves in a precarious situation of further narrowing their gap with advanced countries. Many of them have not engineered the structural evolution for advancing most of their industries to the global technological frontier and competing head to head with other developed countries, except in a few sectors. In concrete economic terms, the middle-income trap is a slowing of growth and structural change as economies are caught between low-wage manufacturers and high-wage innovators.

We can thus define such a trap, in structural terms, as a country's inability to continue on the path of industrial upgrading—resulting in stagnation of its income per capita relative to global leaders. On average, Latin America as a whole is stuck at a fixed ratio of income per capita relative to the United States (Figure 9.1). And this phenomenon has persisted for much of the last century. Clearly, that is a problem to be resolved.

Even in countries that can be seen as success stories, some particular anomalies raise concerns. The following economies have moved from middle income to high income, according to World Bank definitions, since 1987 (each economy with an asterisk next to its name was actually high income at one point, fell back to middle income, and later returned to high income): Antigua and Barbuda, Aruba*, Bahrain, Barbados*, Croatia, Cyprus, the Czech Republic, Equatorial Guinea, Estonia, Greece, Guam, Hungary, the Isle of Man*, the Republic of Korea, Latvia, Malta*, the Netherlands Antilles, New Caledonia, the Northern Mariana Islands*, Oman, Poland, Portugal, Puerto Rico, Saudi Arabia*, the Slovak Republic, Slovenia, and Trinidad and Tobago.

Note that many of these economies are European countries whose per capita incomes were also very close to those of high-income countries before they joined the EU, and they enjoyed substantial assistance in the process. There are also several small island economies—some still territories rather than sovereign countries. And there are the special cases of resource-rich countries (for example, Equatorial Guinea, Oman, Saudi Arabia, and Trinidad and Tobago).

How fast did middle-income countries become high income? Taking a longer time frame and using data from Angus Maddison, one can extract some clues about the uncertainty and flexibility of the process from the following factoids:

- Taiwan, China; Japan; and the Republic of Korea all took about 35 years to go from an income of $1,500 to $15,000 (measured in 1990 "Geary–Khamis" [GK] dollars).

- Israel took 46 years to go from $2,800 to $15,000 (1990 GK dollars).

- Spain took 50 years to go from $2,000 to $15,000 (1990 GK dollars).

- Mauritius took 58 years to go from $2,500 to $14,500 (1990 GK dollars) (with a "take-off" in 1985).

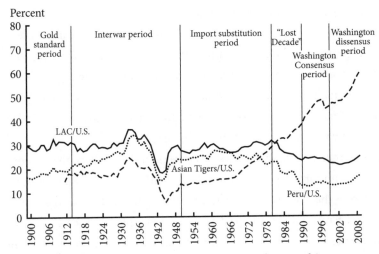

Figure 9.1 GDP per capita of selected regions relative to the United States, 1900–2008
Source: Maddison (n.d.).
Note: LAC: Latin American countries. Asian Tigers: an average of Hong Kong SAR, China; Taiwan, China; the Republic of Korea; Singapore; and South Korea.

Some high-income countries have also found themselves in stagnant income traps, with their economic transformations seemingly coming to a halt as they struggle to find industries in which their firms can make productivity gains and pursue the dynamics of industrial and technological upgrading. This has been the case throughout modern times. The United Kingdom became the global leader during the Industrial Revolution and set the standard for economic development. It was the leader in creating the new technologies for manufacturing. The United States, by accelerating its technological invention and diffusion and strategically upgrading its infrastructure, eventually surpassed the United Kingdom, its "colonial master," in the twentieth century. It went from being a colonial supplier of raw materials to a global leader in advanced technology over about 150 years.

Even more puzzling is the situation of countries that reached high income but were not able to raise their living standards and converge with the richest countries in their group. For example, Ireland was already high income in the 1950s by a purely quantitative standard. But its per capita income remained about 40 percent that of the United States up to the 1980s.

What happened, and how did so many countries fall into the low-growth trap even after achieving some success? English poet William Blake once observed, "The fox condemns the trap, not himself." Stagnating income traps are not self-perpetuating failures or insurmountable impasses, as the cases of Finland and Ireland demonstrate (Figure 9.2): their policymakers eventually managed to restore sustained growth and transform their economies into two of the wealthiest in the OECD.

In the 1980s Finland embarked on economic reforms that eventually spurred an important degree of "catch-up" with the United States—despite a recession in the early 1990s (due in part to the dismantling of the neighboring Soviet Union). Over the past 25 years, a key new sector was developed: IT industries, including the transformation of the Nokia business conglomerate into a global household name specializing in electronics, particularly cellular phones. Few people remember that Nokia started as a pulp mill and rubber shoe maker at the end of the nineteenth century. It diversified its activities into a wide variety of sectors: from natural resources like forestry and rubber to consumer electronics like television.[5] IT industries increased their share of the total value added in Finland from 4.2 percent in 1980 to 15.3 percent in 2001.[6] About two-thirds of this rise was due to telecom equipment—heavily influenced by Nokia's rise as a global leader in cell phones, which were responsible for about 20 percent of its total factor productivity growth in the late 1990s.[7]

The ICT sector is organized around high-technology clusters. The Finnish National Technology Agency, Tekes, supports both public and private R&D activities. Total R&D expenditures have reached nearly 4 percent of GDP, with about three quarters of that R&D done by the private sector.[8] Empirical studies have found that Tekes subsidies increase their productivity growth in small and medium enterprises and in firms close to the technological frontier.[9]

Ireland's relative stagnation before the 1980s had led to a massive exodus of its people to Great Britain and the United States for a couple of centuries. Its progress began in the late 1970s but really accelerated in the 1990s. One element of its starting condition was that a disproportionate share of its pop-

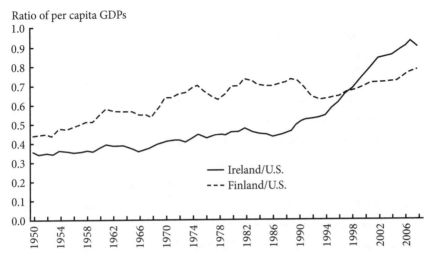

Figure 9.2   Irish and Finnish "catch-up" performances relative to the United States, 1950–2008

Source: Data from Maddison (n.d.).

ulation was still employed in agriculture—nearly a quarter of workers as late as 1973.[10] Although its output per worker outside agriculture was similar to Britain's, the agricultural output per worker was only 60 percent of Britain's at that time. Clearly a more accelerated rural–urban transition was part of a potential that could be exploited to secure some of the productivity gains required for catch-up.

Improving education produced more qualified labor by the 1980s, and the English language was another advantage in attracting investment from multinational companies. Ireland's low tax rate combined with declining international costs for trade also played a role in the Irish success story.[11] Improved infrastructure was another factor, and the generous contributions of the EU helped finance particularly rapid improvements.[12]

But those favorable conditions were in place long before the economic take-off in the late 1980s. As discussed in Chapter 7, a major reason for Ireland's success was that it went from using general incentives in support of any export-oriented investment to targeting selected industries and proactively attracting multinationals in industries in countries with per capita incomes about 100 percent higher. The government identified potential winners and targeted both soft and hard infrastructure interventions through special processing zones to foster the emergence of competitive clusters. Here again we see the combined power of following a country's comparative advantage—playing to its strengths—while also using the helpful hand of government to provide the enabling environment for the creation of new capacities for production and growth.[13]

These successes confirm the predictions of the new structural economics. Income stagnation in low- and middle-income countries reflects a failure to design and implement strategies for dynamic structural transformation. Some middle-income countries may be trapped because of the old structuralist policies (heavy industrialization and broad-based protectionism) that allowed them to build a substantial industrial base, but at the cost of serious distortions and inefficiencies. This has been the case in many transitional and Latin American economies. They pursued CAD development strategies, establishing a predictably distorted and ultimately unsustainable economic structure. Although they enjoyed some initial success, the distortions led to frequent crises and ultimate stagnation.

Governance problems—outright corruption or political capture—made the system self-perpetuating. The governance regime was itself a legacy of the CAD strategy: a last-ditch effort to protect some "modern" industries established during the import substitution era that had once been on the global frontier but had become technologically antiquated. The rationale for keeping them alive was the need to protect some jobs and to satisfy some political (often urban) elites. Such situations were particularly pervasive in middle-income countries where the initial ability to finance the investment and to sell to growing and protected domestic markets allowed some of these industries to reach substantial sizes—implying higher financial and political costs either to continue with the subsidies or to dismantle the unsustainable ventures. The debt crisis of the 1980s opened a new phase in their history: several Latin American countries became serial debt defaulters and suffered from frequent, periodic, and deep recessions. It was time for decisions.

In the previous chapter I suggested a dual-track approach to maintain stability in the reform process. But the question of how middle-income countries can facilitate the growth of new dynamic sectors remains to be answered. Even some middle-income countries that may have avoided the pitfalls of the old structuralist policies and followed their comparative advantages and export-oriented growth found themselves in a competitiveness trap. They must now compete with dynamic low-income countries "taking advantage of backwardness." But they cannot compete against more advanced economies that use their greater capital stocks, superior infrastructure, and knowledge base to upgrade and diversify into producing more sophisticated goods. The question is now what should they do next?

The common mistake is to follow the misguided strategy that Ireland tried before the 1980s: to avoid engaging growth identification and facilitation policies that are required to overcome the inherent coordination and externality issues in the process of industrial upgrading and diversification of the economy. The challenge for countries facing stagnation is for their governments to design and implement positive interventions that can unleash the power of industrial upgrading and diversification and open the way for dynamic growth toward high-income status and beyond. The new structural economics and GIF framework offer a methodology of finding the narrow path past these competitive pressures. There are some subtle differences in how the methodology should be applied in middle-income countries, which is the topic that I will now explore.

Keeping Pace with the Times

An important question is how would the policy implications of the new structural economics and the GIF framework differ in middle- and high-income environments? "Keeping pace with the times," Chinese political wisdom, advises the government to adjust policies in accord with changing opportunities and challenges. A well-known African proverb stating that dancers change their choreography when the music changes provides governments with similar advice. How would things have to be done differently in countries with intermediate or more advanced economic structures?

As a general rule and stylized fact of economic development, middle-income countries—even those lagging Latin American countries highlighted in Figure 9.1—are likely to have some industries on the global technological frontier. High-income countries must give up some mature industries in which they are no longer competitive—because of the increase in their capital endowments (human and physical) and wage rates—and shift resources to newer, higher-value-added industries. Otherwise they will not be able to generate new sources of productivity gains and continuing income growth. That sequential pattern of development has been likened to that of "flying geese." The Japanese economist Kaname Akamatsu coined that phrase in a seminal paper analyzing empirical patterns of development in Asia.[14]

That same pattern describes different dynamics: how an individual industry upgrades its processes as it goes through a cycle of importing, then producing, and finally exporting; how a variety of industries diversify and upgrade from simple to more sophisticated technologies; and how a latecomer in the development process can benefit from the graduation of industries in a more advanced, dynamically growing economy with similar features.

The third interpretation of the flying geese metaphor outlines an international division of labor based on comparative advantage. In that case, it postulates that low- and middle-income countries will catch up with high-income countries as part of a general hierarchy in which the production of commoditized goods and services continually moves from the more advanced countries to the less advanced. The less-developed economies could be considered to be "aligned successively behind the advanced industrial nations in the order of their different stages of growth in a wild-geese-flying pattern."[15]

We see these patterns recurring over time. For example, the textile industry was the most advanced capital-intensive industry in the eighteenth and early nineteenth centuries, but now it is one of the most labor-intensive industries. Similarly, the electronics industries—such as those making radios, televisions, washing machines, refrigerators, and microwaves—were among the most advanced industries in the early twentieth century, but today they are mature, lower-value-added industries in comparison with many of today's high-tech industries.

Other examples include the industries for the design of computer chips, the manufacture of equipment (production lines) for their fabrication, their fabrication itself, and their assembly into final ICT products. The United States was the dominant country before the 1970s in all these processes. The fabrication and assembly of chips migrated to Taiwan, China, in the 1980s. Taiwan, China, remains the most advanced economy in chip fabrication, but the assembly has migrated to the mainland. The United States retains its lead, however, in the design of chips and innovation of the production line from 4 inches of waffle to 6 inches, 8 inches, and 12 inches.

For policymakers in middle-income countries who are confronted with the challenge of continuous industrial and technological upgrading and economic diversification, a fair question is whether the new structural economics approach and the GIF framework proposed in this book would be reliable tools for designing and implementing policies. Skeptical readers of theories of economic development may wonder whether these analytical tools may be appropriate only for low-income countries.

The answer is that these tools can still be used advantageously in higher-income countries. Although a few adjustments would actually be necessary to the basic framework presented in previous chapters to work well in middle- and high-income countries, much of the difference in application is one of emphasis rather than substance. The GIF framework provides a step-by-step approach to identifying industries that are part of a country's latent comparative advantage and, with the right support, could be the new growth sector. For middle-income countries, a key element and starting question is which high-value-added industries that exist in advanced countries are missing from their industrial structures and among their existing industries that are still within the global technological frontier (even if more advanced than rudimentary sectors in low-income countries), and which are already on the global technological frontier? Most middle-income countries have economic structures that include all three types of industries. Even high-income countries possess those three types of industries, but often most of their existing industries are already at the global technological frontier. A preliminary step should be to separate existing domestic industries into categories and adjust the sequential GIF steps accordingly. The main rules of thumb will remain: to follow a country's comparative advantage or play to its strengths (as a recent World Bank study put it) and to create capacity and opportunities through government facilitation.[16]

For industries that are missing or still within the global technology frontier, middle-income countries should continue to apply the GIF framework to tap the potential of latecomer advantages and support industrial upgrading and diversification. But they must also acknowledge that some of their industries are on or close to the global technology frontier—especially upper-middle-income countries. To assist further technological innovation and upgrading in these types of industries, middle-income countries should do what high-income countries do: they should have a national innovation system that brings together education for skill development, an incentive framework for private-sector R&D, public finance for basic scientific research, and collaboration between the public and private sectors. A successful example of that strategy is seen in Finland, which moved from natural resource–based industries to more high-tech sectors using an effective national innovation system.

GIF Principles and Continued Structural Transformation

"Facts are stubborn things; and whatever may be our wishes, our inclinations, or the dictates of our passions, they cannot alter the state of facts and evidence," American president John Adams observed. Those comments are consistent with wisdom from Chinese culture—*shishiqiushi* (finding truth from the facts), *jiefangsixiang* (freeing one's mind from dogmatism), and *yushijujin* (keeping pace with the times)—and could guide any government engaged in the quest for prosperity anywhere in the world. So I will focus here on examining facts.

Examples abound of middle-income countries whose successful industrial and technological upgrading strategies can be explained by the GIF framework. India is well known for the recent rapid growth of its ICT industries, and it is one of the most successful middle-income countries in this sector. Public-sector support was critical to this success. Information service outsourcing firms require computer hardware for their call centers, programming, and so on. They need the latest cutting-edge technology to be productive in providing those services. During the early years of this sector's development in India, the government provided support through special privileges to import hardware.[17] Naturally, earlier public investment in tertiary education and the timely development of land-based telecommunications to replace high-cost satellite communication were also important.

India's economic history also provides examples of government facilitation in more traditional agricultural sectors compatible with the country's comparative advantage in labor-intensive activities. These industries are typically within the global technological frontier. With government support, farmers engaged in technological upgrading and thus improved productivity. For grape production, government action was consistent with the GIF framework: small growers were conducting successful experiments to increase production, and this caught the government's attention. Policymakers then initiated public–private partnerships to support technological upgrading and market development that promoted grape exports.[18]

Sometimes supporting technological upgrading requires various sectoral reforms. India's successful maize production also illustrates the effectiveness of that strategy. First, the government decided to liberalize the sector, lifting a ban on imported maize seed technology. This created healthy competition between domestic and foreign laboratories (including government research centers) to adapt imported technology to local conditions. Second, it was deemed necessary for the state to play a direct role in unleashing the potential of the sector; there was strong public investment in maize research, and producers were given public access to breeding materials the government developed. Without this government support, domestic companies probably would not have entered the seed sector and competed with multinationals.[19]

Brazil also offers examples of effective growth identification and facilitation both in its traditional agricultural sectors and in newer, higher-technology ones. It has been an important producer of agricultural commodities since colonial times. For example, coffee was the traditional export crop that was the basis of the wealth of landowning elites in the state of São Paulo in the nineteenth century. More recently, Brazil has become an innovative global force in agriculture as the world's largest exporter of many products, including beef. And controversial, long-standing government support for biofuels production has put Brazil at the global technological frontier in that "new age" product. Consistent with the new structural economics and GIF principles, the government identified key constraints to private initiatives and provided key public goods in the form of basic research for use by private firms.

An important government organization behind Brazil's success is EMBRAPA, the national agricultural research and extension agency. R&D allowed the country to improve its productivity in both traditional and new crops and to transform previously underused areas, such as its savannahs. Econometric studies show that R&D and infrastructure improvements were essential to increasing agriculture's productivity.[20]

Note that industrial upgrading and technological innovation are typically associated with large externalities and coordination issues. For a country to upgrade or diversify to new industries that are within the global technological frontier, the six steps in the GIF framework are useful to address the issues. In the case of industries that have already been on the global technological frontier, if the country intends to stay in those industries, firms in the industries need to continuously create new processes, new products, and new technologies—thus advancing the frontier. The government's policy should be to support a national innovation system. A good innovation system spans a wide variety of activities. It starts with a high-quality education system that generates the human capital capable of working at the technological frontier. It also includes government budget support and a tax system amenable to R&D by firms, as well as direct government spending on basic research (justified by the fact that fundamental scientific advances often develop knowledge that is a pure public good, or very close to being a pure public good: it is a "nonrival" good because several individuals can consume the same good without diminishing its value, and "nonexcludable" because an individual cannot be prevented from consuming the good).

The process does not stop there. Firms need the legal basis and enforcement of a patent system to capture rents for a reasonable period for the exclusive innovative products or processes that they create. Otherwise, pioneer firms would have no incentive to invest in their own proprietary R&D. A government can also use its procurement policy to support new products and allow production to quickly reach an economic scale.

The Republic of Korea provides a good illustration. As a low-income country in the early 1960s it launched an industrial-upgrading program focused on exports and moved quickly from low-income to middle-income and now to high-income status. As chronicled by Wonhyuk Lim, "After exploiting its comparative advantage to develop labor-intensive downstream industries, Korea sought to indigenize intermediate inputs imported from foreign upstream industries through technology acquisition, human resource development, and construction of optimal-scale plants aimed for the global market. For instance, in the chemical-textile value chain, Korea systematically built the links backward from export of textiles to production of synthetic fibers, to development of basic petrochemicals."[21]

The rural sector was also included in the process. The central government provided funding for local communities to develop their own infrastructure, and innovations in local management were used for peer learning across local governments. Government support also helped introduce improved crop varieties and greenhouse infrastructure, reducing the rural–urban income gaps.[22]

As part of the upgrading, the Korean government recognized that skills development had to be a key component. In 1973 a National Technical Certification Law was passed, and technical high schools were established to meet the projected future demand for technical skills. The government also initially led the way in R&D activities in the 1960s and 1970s, paving the way for rapid growth in private-sector R&D given the skills base and institutional basis for patents. Total R&D spending increased from under 0.5 percent of GDP in the 1970s to about 3 percent of GDP in the mid-2000s as the private share rose from 20 to 75 percent.[23]

Although the Korean government did protect certain sectors with high trade barriers and in some cases took an aggressive approach to industrial upgrading by moving into capital-intensive industries, the results have been remarkable. Over the past 40 years the country has achieved remarkable GDP growth rates and performed impressively in upgrading into such industries as automobiles and semiconductors. Yet it did not push ahead of its comparative advantage. In the case of automotives, early in the growth period, Korean manufacturers concentrated mostly on assembling imported parts—which was labor-intensive and in line with their comparative advantage at the time. In electronics the focus was initially on household appliances, such as TVs, washing machines, and refrigerators, and then on memory chips, the least technologically complex segment of the chip industry.

Korea's technological ascent has been rapid, but so has its accumulation of physical and human capital due to the conformity of Korea's main industrial sectors to its comparative advantage, and thus the changes in its underlying comparative advantage. Equally important, Korea's government has a record of managing protected sectors in ways that subject them to market discipline, making large deviations from the economy's comparative advantage impossible. Industries benefiting from protection and subsidies were required to prove on export markets that their competitiveness was increasing over time. In addition, the government worked hard to make sure that Korean manufacturers could acquire intermediate inputs at world prices—for example, through duty drawbacks and exemptions and through export processing zones. It clearly recognized that comparative advantage mattered and that successful technological upgrading depended on firms' being influenced by world prices for both inputs and outputs. In sum, Korea's government served as a facilitating state to lift its economy from low to middle to high income.

Understanding the Economics of Wealth and Greatness

Countries much richer than Brazil and Korea also facilitate growth to keep their structural transformations going. Germany has long been known for its high-tech manufactures, with success so great that "German engineering" has become a sort of brand name. Neither an accident nor a spontaneous result of market forces, this success came from a partnership between the government and the private sector to develop industrial clusters and ensure the development of the skill base necessary to support private industry. Still, Germany is not exempt from competitive pressures in the globalized economy, and its government has pursued a well-developed industrial policy to ensure Germany's continuing leadership in advanced manufacturing. In particular, the government has identified several challenges that need to be overcome to maintain the country's competitiveness: high wage and nonwage labor costs, high electricity and energy costs, a shortage of engineers (an emerging issue), and stagnation in patent applications (unlike in China and the United States).[24]

Consistent with the new structural economics principles, the German government is responding. The Kompetenznetze Deutschland works with businesses to bring together the top-performing innovation clusters. The Wissenschaftsfreiheitsinitiative promotes market relevance. And the Central Innovation Program for SMEs is supporting 10,000 small-business innovation projects. The government is also working with the subnational Länder and with municipalities to improve educational quality by investing more funds in and improving the adaptability of vocational training programs. On the energy front, the government promotes alternative energy technologies and works with European neighbors to improve cross-border energy markets. These are just a few examples of the government's partnership with industry to promote innovation at the technological frontier.

Other rich-country governments have relied on different policies to support continuing structural transformation. Take the United States, the most technologically advanced economy, which still ensures that government resources are available to support innovation. During the late nineteenth and early twentieth centuries, as the United States closed its gap with Great Britain in economic development, much U.S. technological innovation was accomplished by individuals rather than firms.[25] As R&D evolved and became more capital intensive, firms began to take the lead in patenting new technologies. And government financing of basic research grew through U.S. federal agencies and programs, including science and engineering research for defense.

In 1950 the National Science Foundation (NSF) was established to "promote the progress of science; to advance the national health, prosperity, and welfare; to secure the national defense."[26] On its 60th anniversary the NSF had an annual budget of about $6.9 billion—roughly equal to the GDP of Chad or Nicaragua.[27] It uses these funds to finance research, identify research needs, and collect data on research activities in universities and research centers across the country. In allocating research funds it has to pick projects that are likely to remove the current technological bottlenecks and expand the technology frontier.

Political leaders in the United States and the United Kingdom, which one would not think of as industrial policy advocates, have therefore engaged in activist government policies fully consistent with the new structural economics. In December 2010, U.S. President Barack Obama signed a two-year retroactive extension of the R&D tax credit through 2011, providing incentives for companies to invest in America's future. John Holdren, his science and technology advisor and director of the White House Office of Science and Technology Policy, explained:

> The bipartisan passage of the America Competes Act represents a major milestone on this Nation's path to building an innovation economy for the twenty-first century—an economy that harnesses the scientific and technological ingenuity that has long been at the core of America's prosperity and applies that creative force to some of the biggest challenges we face today. Whether it's developing new products that will be manufactured in America, or getting and using energy more sustainably, or improving health care with better therapies and better

use of information technology, or providing better protection for our troops abroad and our citizens at home, innovation will be key to our success. And that is exactly what the Competes Act is all about.[28]

The Act authorizes the continuing growth of the budgets of several government agencies that "are incubating and generating the breakthroughs of tomorrow."[29] It also bolsters the U.S. administration's activities to enhance education—"to raise American students from the middle to the top of the pack and to make sure we are training the next generation of innovative thinkers and doers."[30] It authorizes ongoing support for Arpa-E, the novel energy research program that promises to give rise to "leapfrog" technologies that will reduce America's dependence on foreign energy sources and stimulate a green economy while producing steady, high-quality jobs for the future.

Giving a great boost to the cause of generating novel solutions to tough national problems, which need to be identified and picked, the America Competes Act gives every department and agency the authority to conduct prize competitions: "Prizes and challenges have an excellent track record of accelerating problem-solving by tapping America's top talent and best expertise wherever it may lie. The [U.S.] Administration has supported this approach as part of its all-hands-on-deck approach to stimulating innovation, and under Competes we can expect a further blossoming of new ideas from citizen solvers across the land."[31] President Obama, in his 2011 State of the Union address, referred to a new "Sputnik moment" as part of a rallying cry to accelerate technological innovation.

Similar forms of industrial policy, all consistent with the new structural economics, are also being adopted by conservative U.K. prime minister David Cameron, who has launched the upgrading of his country's soft and hard infrastructure. In a speech he said:

This is where so much of the promise of new jobs and opportunities lie [sic] and that's why, as part of our strategy for growth, we've made a really important decision. We're not just going to back the big businesses of today, we're going to back the big businesses of tomorrow. We are firmly on the side of the high-growth, highly innovative companies of the future. Don't doubt our ambition. Right now, Silicon Valley is the leading place in the world for high-tech growth and innovation. But there's no reason why it has to be so predominant. Question is: where will its challengers be? Bangalore? Hefei? Moscow? My argument today is that if we have the confidence to really go for it and the understanding of what it takes, London could be one of them. All the elements are here. And our ambition is to bring together the creativity and energy of Shoreditch and the incredible possibilities of the Olympic Park to help make East London one of the world's great technology centers.[32]

Suggesting that outmoded U.K. copyright laws have chilled innovation on the Internet, where a bottom-up, no-permission-needed approach has often proved most successful, Cameron indicated that his goal is to change U.K. law and change the United Kingdom's approach to industrial policy. His strategy also includes helping to create the right framework so that it will be easier for new companies to start up, for venture capital firms to invest, for innovations to flourish, and for businesses to grow, providing equity finance for businesses with high growth potential. He hopes to significantly boost U.K. Trade & Investment's help to technology companies that are either starting up in the United Kingdom or trying to expand into new markets. Cameron's strategy also will open government procurement budgets to small and medium firms. And it will build facilities and transportation infrastructure to foster industries consistent with the country's latent comparative advantage.[33]

One can simply imagine what the political leaders of developing economies —say, Korea's Park Chung Hee; Taiwan, China's, Chiang Ching Kuo; or Singapore's Lee Kuan Yew, all of whom had to fight mainstream development thinking to (successfully) pursue similar policies—would think when listening to such a prescription. Perhaps they would feel vindicated. Or they might just think about what Nelson Mandela once said about the challenges of leadership: "It always seems impossible until it is done."

To sum up: economic development is not a zero-sum game in which countries compete against each other and one's loss becomes the other's gain. It is a continuing process of discovery in which industrial and technological upgrading is the main driver, constrained only by human imagination and creativity. So there is reason to hope for continuing improvements in living standards for all human beings.

Middle-income countries stuck at certain incomes and incapable of catching up with countries at the highest levels of development are generally those where policymakers have failed to understand their countries' evolving factor endowments or identify their latent comparative advantages. All have sectors within or at the technological frontier. The former should just follow the principles of the GIF framework and foster their structural transformation, as Ireland did after the 1980s. Their governments need to work closely with the private sector to understand the coordination and externality issues that must be overcome for competitive firms to enter industries with potential for productivity gains. The latter need government support to encourage R&D, just as in high-income countries—that is what Korea and Finland have done. A key to avoiding middle-income traps or high-income stagnation is thus to maintain the focus on exploiting countries' current and latent comparative advantages.

Unfortunately, policymakers in countries that successfully embark on the path of economic development run the risk of falling into the trap of complacency. Seventeenth-century French writer François de la Rochefoucauld rightly warned, "Self-love is the greatest of all flatterers." But some self-esteem and—more important—knowledge and appreciation of one's factor endowments is essential to take full advantage of the opportunities out there. The same is true for economic development: understanding a country's endowment structure and its dynamics over time and facilitating the growth of new industries consistent with the latent comparative advantage determined by dynamic change in the country's endowment structure are the secrets of prosperity.

TEN

A Recipe for Economic Prosperity

THE FIELD OF ECONOMICS, AS DEFINED BY THE TITLE of Adam Smith's seminal book, is for inquiring into the nature and causes of the wealth of nations. Yet ironically, in spite of all the time economists spend on their work, economics is still often referred to as "the dismal science."[1] The recent global crisis, with its heavy financial, economic, and human costs, has not helped the discipline's cause. The sociopolitical instability across the world is also raising questions about the usefulness of economic knowledge accumulated at least since Adam Smith. Regardless of whether these crises are due to cyclical factors, such as the bursting of financial bubbles, or fueled by structural factors such as low growth, low productivity, youth unemployment, or poverty, they are often the consequences of inappropriate economic strategies and misguided policies.

Educated in Confucian tradition, I have always wanted to find a way of contributing to the prosperity of my country so that our people would be free from the fear of poverty and hunger, of which I hold vivid childhood memories. Economics is a perfect subject for such a purpose. However, I would not have become an economist without an unexpected encounter. To understand the logic of China's socialist system, I went to study Marxism at Peking University in 1979. Professor Theodore W. Schultz, the 1979 Nobel laureate, accompanied by Professor D. Gale Johnson, chairman of the Economics Department at the University of Chicago and Schultz's former student at Iowa State University in the 1940s, was invited to visit Fudan University in Shanghai for a month in the fall of 1980. They made a stop in Beijing on their way back to Chicago, and each gave a lecture at Peking University. I was assigned to be Professor Schultz's interpreter for his lecture.

After he and Johnson returned to Chicago, I unexpectedly received a letter from him, thanking me for my help and offering me a scholarship. I had never had any plan to study abroad. But who could resist such an invitation? I very much enjoyed the rigorous training, scholarly debates, and research on real-world development issues and their solutions I experienced in Chicago, which I consider the principal sources and purposes of my knowledge. I hoped that through the study of modern economic development theories, I could help my country's government do the right things and avoid the wrong decisions. During my student years at the University of Chicago and in the course of professional interactions later on, I found that many fellow economists from developing countries share the same pursuit—helping their nations. The position of chief economist of the World Bank Group has given me the platform to interact and explore with them closely and to reflect with them on the best ways to promote prosperity in developing countries.

As the chief economist of the World Bank Group, the head of its research department, an economic advisor to the Bank's president, and a member of the senior management team, I have no direct lending responsibility in any particular country. But my team of experts must conceptualize the world we live in, outline broad strategic directions for development thinking, and constantly come up with new ideas that may be of use to others. I have been delighted to take up the challenge. As soon as I joined the World Bank in June 2008, the world was immediately hit by the most serious financial crisis since the Great Depression. My immediate mission was obviously to try to understand the nature of the crisis and its likely impacts on the developing countries and to recommend policy responses for the Bank and its client countries. I will soon publish a separate book discussing my views of the causes of and ways out of the crisis as well as the evolution of a multipolar-growth world in the coming decades. However, I have tried not to forget that economic development will forever be a challenge to the Bank and the world's economists. I wrote this book with the hope of making a contribution in this context.

I have great admiration for Abraham Lincoln and Winston Churchill, whom I have quoted several times in this work. But despite their glorious minds and impressive political skills, they were wrong to downplay the importance of policies. Lincoln once said, "I never had a policy; I have just tried to do my very best each and every day." Churchill made a similar point, more cynically and humorously: "I always avoid prophesying beforehand, because it is a much better policy to prophesy after the event has already taken place."

I disagree. Beyond politics, which by definition is their main activity, almost all political leaders everywhere in the world are motivated by two basic impulses: trying to stay in power as long as they can, and having a good name in history when their staying in power is not threatened. Contributing to his or her nation's prosperity is the best way for a political leader to stay in power and to have a good name in history. In my reading of history and my personal encounters with political leaders around the world as the World Bank's chief economist, I have not found political leaders whose initial motivations for engaging in politics were to harm their people and ruin their nations. If presented with policies that they think will bring prosperity to their nations and enhancing the possibility of their staying in power, they will most likely embrace and implement them.

However, as I reviewed in Chapter 2, existing economic theories, as I learned through my student and professional years, have failed to provide such policy recommendations to developing countries, despite more than two centuries of research by the many brilliant economists who took up the challenge after the publication of Adam Smith's *An Inquiry into the Nature and Causes of the Wealth of Nations*. As a result, a political leader in today's world is likely to make mistakes by adopting policies that cause unintended damage to the welfare of people and the prosperity of his or her nation. To stay in power, a leader may adopt self-serving and self-protecting policies that inflict further costs and harm on his or her people and nation.

I conclude this book with a few thoughts on the sacred importance of policies aiming at long-term development, especially in the aftermath of the recent global crisis. I summarize the new structural economics and anticipate some of the skepticism of those who oppose any suggestion of any type of proactive state role in facilitating industrial development.

Understanding the True Nature and Causes of Economic Development

Edgar Allan Poe, one of the great nineteenth-century American writers, offered an interesting spiritual allegory about self-discovery, uncertainty, and fear in his story *The Narrative of Arthur Gordon Pym of Nantucket*. Toward the end of its action-packed plot, he briefly tells the story of a "savage" man from an indigenous tribe on a mysterious island in the Antarctic who looks in a mirror for the first time in his life and falls down, horrified by what he sees. After the 2008–09 Great Recession, some economists seem to have been through a somewhat similar and traumatic experience. They have been surprised and even frightened not only by the sudden eruption and intensity of the crisis but also by the finding that some of their most sacred theoretical frameworks had become brutally ineffective in explaining the world we live in. Like Edgar Allan Poe's character, these economists saw unknown if not strange images of themselves in the mirror of a new reality. As a result, some have suffered self-doubt to the point of questioning the very essence of their discipline.

Who could blame them? For several decades, notably from the mid-1980s to the late 2000s, an intriguing feature of the economic landscape was the substantial decline in the macroeconomic volatility of both output and inflation—the Great Moderation.[2] Markets improved around the world, making economic planning easier and reducing the resources devoted to hedging inflation risks. The Great Moderation was characterized by more stable employment and less economic uncertainty confronting households and firms. And it validated the new consensus on macroeconomic theory.

Moreover, recessions became less frequent and less severe, and economic growth lifted hundreds of millions of people out of poverty.

The crisis came as a great surprise to most. Many developing countries had shown remarkable foresight leading up to the crisis, putting their fiscal and financial affairs in order. Their economies proved to be quite resilient as they faced the shock waves from a disaster that—this time—emanated from the high-income countries. The impressive coordinated policy response of the G-20 nations also helped avoid an even worse outcome.

The economic recovery is fragile, because most of the large high-income countries still suffer from high unemployment and low capacity utilization. These economies still constitute about 70 percent of global GDP, so their lackluster growth continues to be a drag on global economic growth. The magnitude of the shocks has forced economists to confront their own theories, analytical tools, and basic assumptions.

Indeed, the crisis provides a good opportunity for rethinking economic development. Despite a robust global recovery, developing countries still face daunting challenges in maintaining dynamic growth to close their gap with the developed countries. Some 1.4 billion people still go to bed hungry every night, and more than a sixth of humanity (the "bottom billion," as Paul Collier put it) remains trapped in poverty.[3] But rapid population growth and the gloomy predictions of Malthusian economics have not materialized, and the world is not facing starvation and death. Sustained economic growth, the foundation for reducing poverty and converging to high income, is now understood to be the result of incessant structural change through continuing technological innovation and industrial upgrading and diversification— a process that can be bounded only by human creativity. The main question on the global intellectual agenda should therefore be how can we rethink long-term strategies for growth and renew the catch-up policies that can allow developing countries to close the gap with the most advanced ones?

The most enduring foundations for sustained global growth must be envisaged at the national level, where economic policies are designed and implemented. How to promote economic growth has been a main topic of economic discourse and research since the publication of Adam Smith's *An*

Inquiry into the Nature and Causes of the Wealth of Nations in 1776. Development economics has provided us with some broad remarkable theoretical insights. But as a subdiscipline of economics, it has so far been unable to offer a convincing policy agenda for generating and distributing wealth in poor countries. The recent global crisis offers an opportunity to identify new areas of research not only on how to help the developed and developing countries cope with the challenges of the crisis and prevent similar crises in the future but also on how to achieve sustainable inclusive growth in developing countries.

Theories and empirical evidence show that market mechanisms are essential for valuing the basic ingredients for production (factor endowments) and providing the right price signals and appropriate incentive systems for the efficient allocation of resources. However, modern economic growth—a fairly recent phenomenon in human history, as Simon Kuznets pointed out— is a process of continuing technological innovation, industrial upgrading, and diversifying and improving the infrastructure and institutional arrangements that constitute the context for business development and wealth creation.[4] Market mechanisms may not be sufficient, and governments can help firms overcome the various problems of information, coordination, and externality inherent in modern economic growth.

This book has focused on the long-term development challenges and the fundamental elements of successful growth-increasing strategies. It has discussed the evolution of development thinking since its inception and suggested a framework to enable developing countries to achieve sustained dynamic growth, eliminate poverty, and narrow their income gap with the developed countries. Drawing lessons from experience and from economic analysis, the book has presented the key principles of a new structural economics, a neoclassical approach to structures and their dynamics in the process of economic development. The proposed approach suits countries at all incomes—low, middle, and high.

The book suggests that the starting point for an analysis of the ways an economy can achieve sustained economic development should be the economy's endowments, that is, what the economy has. Endowments are given in an economy at any specific time and are changeable over time. Following the tradition of classical economics, economists tend to think of a country's endowments as consisting only of its land (or natural resources), labor, and capital (both physical and human). These are, in fact, factor endowments, the total budgets in an economy that firms can use in production. Conceptually, it is useful to add infrastructure as one more component of an economy's endowments. Infrastructure includes hard (or tangible) infrastructure and soft (or intangible) infrastructure. Examples of hard infrastructure are highways, port facilities, airports, telecommunications systems, electricity grids, and other public utilities. Soft infrastructure consists of institutions, regulations, social capital, value systems, and other social and economic arrangements. Infrastructure affects an individual firm's transaction costs and the marginal rate of return on investment.

The new structural economics highlights the importance of endowments and differences in industrial structures at various levels of development. It analyzes the implications of distortions stemming from past misguided interventions by policymakers whose belief in the old structural economics led them to pursue plans for industrial development inconsistent with the comparative advantages determined by their endowment structures. That fundamental mistake caused firms in priority sectors to be nonviable. It inevitably led to subsidies or protection, through various distortions, for firms' initial investments and continuing operations. The new structural economics also points out that policies advocated under the Washington Consensus often failed to take into consideration the structural differences between developed and developing countries and ignored the sources of various types of distortions in developing countries.

In the past decade the World Bank has initiated research projects to draw lessons from the experience of successful economies. These projects, reported in *The East Asian Miracle* (1993), *Economic Growth in the 1990s* (2005), and *The Growth Report* (2008), have produced many useful stylized facts for determining the success or failure of economic development.[5] The new approach proposed in this book continues that effort. It is not an attempt to substitute another ideologically based policy framework for those that have dominated development thinking in past decades while largely ignoring the empirical realities of individual countries. Instead it brings attention to the endowment structure and level of development of each country, suggesting a path toward country-based research that is rigorous, innovative, and relevant to development policy. This framework stresses the need to better understand the implications of structural differences at various stages of a country's development—especially the appropriate institutions and policies and the constraints to and incentives for the private sector in the process of structural change.

Economic development is a process of continual industrial upgrading and diversification, with corresponding improvements and adaptations in infrastructure—a process with intrinsic coordination and externality issues. All countries that have transformed from agrarian economies to modern advanced economies—including those old industrial powers in Western Europe and North America as well as the newly industrialized economies in East Asia—had governments that helped individual firms overcome coordination and externality problems in their structural transformation. Indeed, the governments of high-income countries today continue to play that role.

The sad fact is that almost every government in the developing world has also attempted, at some point in its development process, to play that facilitating role, but most have failed. In this book I have argued that these pervasive failures in developing countries are mostly due to the inability of governments to come up with good criteria for identifying industries that are appropriate for a given country's endowment structure and level of development. The propensity of governments to target industries that are too ambitious and not aligned with their countries' comparative advantages largely explains why their attempts to pick winners resulted in their picking losers. To protect jobs, the governments in both developed and developing countries may have also supported old declining industries in which their countries had already lost comparative advantages. Such policies have been costly as well.

By contrast, the governments in successful developing countries have, spontaneously or intentionally, targeted mature industries in dynamically growing countries with endowment structures similar to theirs and with levels of development not much more advanced than theirs. The main lesson from development history and economic analysis is straightforward: the government's policy to facilitate industrial upgrading and diversification must be anchored in industries with a latent comparative advantage so that, once the coordination and externality issues are overcome and new industries are established, they can quickly become competitive domestically and internationally.

The secret recipe to economic success is thus the one that helps policymakers in developing countries identify the industries in which their economies may have latent comparative advantages (that is, what they can do well) based on their endowment structures (that is, what they have) and remove binding constraints to facilitate private firms' entry into and operation in those industries. This is not necessarily an easy task, I admit, given the poor track records of so many countries that have embarked on that uncertain path. But it certainly is not an impossible one, given that Brazil, China, Finland, Indonesia, Ireland, Japan, the Republic of Korea, Malaysia, Mauritius, Singapore, and Vietnam recorded rapid growth in the second half of the twentieth century. Policymakers there designed and successfully implemented an industrialization process that has quickly transformed their subsistence agrarian economies and lifted several hundred million people out of poverty in the space of one generation.

Industrial Policy in Action

Active economic policies developed by developing countries' governments to promote growth and industrialization have generally been viewed with suspicion by economists, and for good reasons. Experiences show that such policies have too often failed to achieve their stated objectives. Yet every country in the world, intentionally or not, pursues an industrial policy. Even if one does not like the idea of industrial policy, countries are using it.

There are two main reasons for the controversy and confusion about industrial policy in developing countries. First, economists who have studied the matter have tended to focus their attention on the failed policies implemented by developing countries, not on the objectives and the broader strategic choices of the successful cases. Second, very different types of government interventions are too often lumped together in regression analyses, with little consideration as to which ones may have attempted to facilitate the emergence of industries that were consistent with their countries' latent comparative advantages, and which ones promoted new industries far beyond their levels of development or protected sunset industries in which the countries had lost comparative advantages.

This book has introduced an important distinction between two types of government interventions. First are policies that facilitate structural change by overcoming information, coordination, and externality issues that are intrinsic to industrial upgrading, diversification, and structural change. Such interventions aim to provide information, compensate for externalities, coordinate entry into an industry, and improve both the hard and soft infrastructure so that the private sector can grow in sync with the dynamic change in an economy's comparative advantage. Second are policies aimed at protecting some selected firms and industries that defy the comparative advantage (determined by the existing endowment structure) either in new sectors that are too advanced or in old sectors that have lost comparative advantage.

That analysis opens up a dilemma for economists. First, they can adopt a hardline position against active government intervention and stay on the sidelines to issue general technical pronouncements that aim to criticize it or explain why it should not be attempted. Second, they can step in with advice on how it should be done with a maximum likelihood of success. Besides, lessons from history and from economic analysis show clearly that the state has always facilitated structural change and helped the private sector sustain it across time in all successful economies. In all countries that have transformed from agrarian to modern, advanced economies—including the old industrial powers in Western Europe and North America as well as the newly industrialized economies in East Asia—governments helped overcome the challenges of coordinating various investments by private firms that launched new industries, provided incentives to pioneer firms to compensate for the risks they assumed as first movers, and supplied useful technology and industrial information to firms in the economy.

Even before the recent global crisis, governments around the world often provided financial support to the private sector through direct subsidies, tax credits, or loans from development banks.[6] The recession has justified a more active role for governments in economic policy. Recent policy discussions at many high-level economic summits of major nations have aimed at stepping up other less controversial features of industrial policy. These include the public provision or financing of hard infrastructure and the constant upgrading of soft infrastructure. In the wake of the Great Recession, industrial policy has arguably become more expansive: it should facilitate the design of government-sponsored economic programs in which the public and private sectors coordinate their efforts to develop new infrastructure, technologies, and industries.

As an economist concerned with practical policy issues and results on the ground, I have chosen the second option, that of stepping in with advice. That is the justification for the new structural economics proposed in this book. I am an admirer of Wang Yangming, who taught, "Knowing is the beginning of action; action is the completion of knowing." And I fully agree with the great German playwright Johann Wolfgang von Goethe's observation: "Knowing is not enough; we must apply. Willing is not enough; we must do." I recognize that policymakers around the world—notably in developing countries—may find the theoretical framework of the new structural economics a useful guide for strategic thinking but may still face a few major questions: How can this framework be applied concretely to specific conditions and issues in their countries? How can industries that may hold latent comparative advantage be identified? How can binding constraints be removed and private firms' entry into those industries be facilitated?

The GIF framework is the implementation tool for the new structural economics. It suggests a way of designing and implementing industrial policies with maximum chances of success, thereby ensuring that economic growth remains a process of continual industrial and technological upgrading. Its key features apply to both high-income and developing economies. In advanced countries most industries tend to be on the global frontier, which means upgrading requires an original innovation. In addition to ex post measures such as giving a patent for a successful innovation or supporting a new product through procurement, a government may also use ex ante measures such as supporting basic research or imposing a mandate for use of a new product, such as ethanol.

For upgrading and diversifying to new industries in developing countries, governments may tap into the advantage of backwardness by following the following six simple steps:

- *Step 1:* Policymakers should select dynamic growing countries with similar endowment structures and with about 100 percent higher per capita incomes. They must then identify tradable industries that have grown well in those countries for the past 20 years.

- *Step 2:* If some private domestic firms are already present in those industries, they should identify constraints to technological upgrading or further firm entry and take action to remove those constraints.

- *Step 3:* In the cases of industries in which no domestic firms are present, policymakers may try to attract FDI from the countries listed in Step 1 or organize new firm incubation programs.

- *Step 4:* In addition to the industries identified in Step 1, the government should also pay attention to spontaneous self-discovery by private enterprises and support the scaling up of successful private innovations in new industries.

- *Step 5:* In countries with poor infrastructure and bad business environments, special economic zones or industrial parks may be used to overcome barriers to firm entry and FDI and encourage the formation of industrial clusters.

- *Step 6:* The government should be willing to compensate pioneer firms in the industries identified earlier with tax incentives for a limited period, cofinancing for investments, or access to foreign exchange.

These six steps provide an actionable framework for policymakers to use first to identify sectors likely to be consistent with a country's latent comparative advantage and then to facilitate the entry and operation of private firms into those sectors by removing binding constraints and providing incentives to the first movers.

Being Too Cautious: The Greatest Risk of All

The Greek philosopher Aristotle observed, "Criticism is something we can avoid easily by saying nothing, doing nothing, and being nothing." Having discussed these ideas in academic and policy circles in recent years, I am aware of some of the questions they may raise.[7]

Responding to the new structural economics and the GIF framework, some of my fellow economists argue that targeting industries in richer comparable countries and then following comparative advantage accordingly may be problematic. Their skepticism is based on two ideas: first, the economic structure of the richer country could be the result of distorting policies, and second, a formidable set of policies is required to go beyond the mere identification of potential products.

That is a valid warning. Even in successful cases, carrying out industrial policy is never smooth. It always involves trial and error from governments that put in place good mechanisms and channels to learn from mistakes, adjust economic strategies, and minimize the potential costs of bad decisions. However, the GIF framework recommends choosing the target countries not only because they are richer but also because they have recorded dynamic growth for a long period. If they have grown dynamically for several decades, it is unlikely that they have followed strategies that defy their comparative advantages. It is also unlikely that any government could have afforded to subsidize a dynamically growing tradable industry for several decades if it were inconsistent with comparative advantage. The rising wages in target countries due to their dynamic growth will cause them to lose comparative advantages in industries that used to be in line with their comparative advantages. The GIF framework recommends that latecomers be realistic (and even modest) in their choice of reference countries and targeted industries.

Other skeptics observe that world trade has undergone remarkably rapid changes in style and that there are fewer stable products and industries to be targeted today than several decades ago. The truth is that despite changes in style and product customization, the division of labor among countries at different levels of development is still the same. For example, television has evolved from black-and-white to color and then to flat panel today. The main producing countries have changed from the United States before the 1950s to Japan in the 1960s–80s, Korea in the 1980s–2000s, and China today. A latecomer entering the market today could go into labor-intensive assembly of flat-panel TVs first, just as forerunners did a few decades ago when they decided to compete in the black-and-white and color TV markets.

Globalization provides huge potential for industrialization through specialization. Several decades ago, many low-income countries faced the constraints of their limited market sizes, high transport costs, and trade barriers—and so could not take advantage of the opportunities offered by large-scale manufacturing. With globalization, almost any country can identify production activities in which it has overt or latent comparative advantage, scale them up, and create its own niche in the world market. Precisely because of globalization, the economic development strategy in each country should follow comparative advantage closely.

Multinational firms are more likely to exploit any small difference in production costs in determining their production or procurement locations. Globalization also makes the government's role in facilitation even more important, because only with good hard and soft infrastructure, which reduces transaction costs, can the production cost advantage based on endowment structure and specialization be realized.

Questions are also often raised about the supposedly impressive amount of knowledge about targeted industries that government officials would need to have to design a successful industrial policy and the capacities of governments in developing countries to meet those requirements.[8] First, all low-income countries tend not to have high capacity by definition. Ha-Joon Chang reminds us that, not so long ago, it was not unusual to refer to "lazy Japanese and thieving Germans."[9] With economic development, capacity will be enhanced in any society. More important, some of the requirements are likely to be relevant only to more advanced industries in high-income countries. For industries with low technical content, the list should be streamlined considerably. Moreover, rather than analyzing the technical nature of various industries to find out the knowledge underpinning them, private-sector and government officials can rely on the advantage of backwardness and observe what the dynamically growing countries with similar endowment structures are already doing. These successful countries must have already overcome those knowledge challenges either by trial and error or by analysis.

Finally, some economists make persuasive arguments about the political-economy difficulties of implementing any type of public policy, some of which are well known. The body politic may be tempted to ignore economic rationality and pursue more sophisticated sectors in their zeal to emulate advanced countries. And the possibility of extending even successful policies well beyond their effective time span may create opportunities for rent seeking. These general governance issues are well studied in the economic and political science literature.[10]

The various concerns are legitimate, but only for the traditional industrial policy that encourages firms to enter CAD industries. Firms in those industries are not viable in an open, competitive market. Their entry and continuing operation depend on large subsidies and protection, which create opportunities for rent seeking and corruption and make it difficult for the government to give up the interventions and to exit from the distortions.[11] The new structural economics and its GIF framework promote something quite different: the development of industries consistent with an economy's latent comparative advantage. Firms are viable once the constraints to their entry and operation are removed. The incentives the government provides to the first movers, such as tax holidays for a few years, are to be temporary and small, only to compensate for their information externality. In that context, pervasive rent seeking and the persistence of government interventions beyond their initial timetable can be mitigated. Is the approach proposed in this book risky? It probably is, to a certain extent. But I would submit that it is the least risky development strategy among those available today. Jawaharlal Nehru spoke well when he said: "The policy of being too cautious is the greatest risk of all."

"No country can depend on development aid forever," Rwandan president Paul Kagame recently said in an interview. "Such dependency dehumanizes us and robs us of our dignity."[12] The fundamental issue at the heart of development could not be expressed more elegantly. Beyond the usual rationale for growth and poverty reduction (higher incomes, employment opportunities, improved human welfare, and a more stable world), the real justification for sustained growth is to allow each human being to fulfill the most intimate and most precious goal of life: improving his or her self-esteem as a member of a well-functioning society. So development thinking is really about the economics of dignity.

Before my appointment to the World Bank and throughout my tenure, I have met heads of state, prime ministers, central bank governors, government officials at all levels of authority, leaders of nongovernmental organizations, researchers, academics, entrepreneurs, and ordinary citizens who all struggle every day to reach that goal. In the past development economists focused on what developing countries did not have and could not do well, using what advanced countries had and could do relatively well as references. They advised the developing countries to correct their shortcomings, for example, through the development of advanced heavy industries in the import substitution strategy advocated by structuralism and the privatization, marketization, and liberalization advocated by the neoliberal Washington Consensus. The results of various efforts based on that thinking by the developing countries and by international development communities were disappointing.

In this book I propose a change in the development mindset. Economists and the international development community should work with governments in developing countries to pragmatically identify and scale up what they can do well (that is, their comparative advantages) based on what they have now (that is, their endowments). Success will breed success.

Modern economic growth is by nature a process of continual structural change in technologies, industries, infrastructure, and socioeconomic institutions. I believe that all developing countries, including those in Sub-Saharan Africa, can grow at 8 percent or more for several decades, significantly reduce poverty, and become middle-income or even high-income countries in the span of one or two generations. But they can do this only if their governments have the right policy frameworks to tap into their latecomer advantages and facilitate the private sector's development along the lines of their comparative advantages.

Political leaders' goals are to stay in power and to have good names in history if their staying in power is not under threat. As Keynes wrote in the last sentence of his great book *The General Theory of Employment, Interest, and Money*, "But, soon or late, it is ideas, not vested interests, which are dangerous for good or evil." Vested-interest groups exist in any country at any time. Political leaders always have some discretionary powers and are not necessarily hostages of vested interests. With the right ideas, political leaders will have the incentives and capability to change the fates of their nations. I hope this book, which challenges accepted wisdom while drawing from economic history and analysis, contributes to every developing country's realization of its potential for growth and its quest for prosperity.

GLOSSARY

advantage of backwardness   Any country can learn from those that are more advanced, a practice that reduces the cost and risk of innovation. Modern economic growth is in essence a process of continuous structural change in technology, industry, and socioeconomic and political institutions. The advantage of backwardness in industrial upgrading and technological innovation provides developing countries the potential to grow several times faster than advanced countries.

comparative advantage   A situation in which a country can produce a good at a lower opportunity cost than a competitor. This idea was originally put forth by British economist David Ricardo, who made the strong theoretical case that each country should specialize in those activities in which it has lower opportunity cost. Its main implication is that trade between two countries will lead to an increase in the real incomes of both. Swedish economists Eli Heckscher and Bertil Ohlin extended Ricardo's concept to include countries with different factor endowments. It prescribes that countries produce goods and services requiring their relatively abundant factors as inputs, thus incurring lower costs compared with other countries producing the same goods. Take the case of a developing country that is endowed with relatively abundant labor or natural resources but has relatively scarce capital.

As a result, the price of labor or natural resources there should be relatively low and the price of capital relatively high in the absence of distortive policies. Under those circumstances, a developing country will have comparative advantage in labor-intensive industries and a comparative disadvantage in heavy industry, which requires large capital inputs and small labor inputs, in open, competitive markets.

comparative advantage–defying (CAD) strategy   A situation in which a government's economic development strategy does not follow the comparative advantage determined by the country's endowment structure. For example, in many developing countries projects selected to reach development goals were too capital intensive for an economy characterized by relatively scarce capital. Because developing countries are relatively rich in labor and natural resources but not in capital, advanced capital-intensive industries were not adapted to their endowment structures—or aligned with their comparative advantage. As a result, firms were not viable in an open, competitive market. Advised by the dominant development thinking after World War II, in the 1950s and 1960s governments in many developing countries adopted a CAD strategy, attempting to build up capital-intensive industries despite having scarce capital and abundant unskilled labor. Firms in these industries required the government's subsidies and protection for their investment and continuous operation. After an initial period of investment-led growth, the strategy resulted in repeated crises and stagnation in many developing countries.

comparative advantage–following (CAF) strategy   A set of policies that a developing country implements to foster the development of competitive industries that are consistent with its comparative advantage as determined by its factor endowments. Modern economic growth is essentially a process of continuous industrial and technological upgrading. Developing countries that choose to start that process by developing industries and adopting technology according to their comparative advantage will be most competitive in domestic and international markets, have the greatest economic surplus and return on investment, and accumulate capital the fastest. With capital accumulation, the country's endowment structure will upgrade to having a higher relative abundance of capital than it used to and its comparative advantage will change, requiring industries to upgrade accordingly. The CAF strategy is the fastest way for a country to develop its economy. For firms to follow an economy's comparative advantage to choose technologies and industries, the relative factor prices should reflect their relative abundances in the factor endowments of the economy. Only in a well-functioning market can relative factor prices have such a property. The CAF strategy thus requires the government both to maintain the competiveness of markets and also to overcome the coordination and externality issues inherent in the process of industrial upgrading.

Dutch disease   Generally, the deindustrialization of certain economies, which occurs when the discovery of a natural resource (typically oil) increases the value of the domestic currency. The currency appreciation makes the country's other products less price competitive on the export market. It also leads to higher levels of cheap imports. The end result is much less competitive manufactured goods (in comparison with other countries), decreased exports, and increased imports. The term originated in Holland after the discovery of North Sea gas and the economic crisis of the 1960s. It has been extended in the economic literature to refer to the negative impact on an economy of anything that gives rise to a sharp inflow of foreign currency, including large amounts of foreign aid.

growth identification and facilitation (GIF) framework   The implementation tool for the new structural economics. It suggests a way of designing and implementing industrial policies with maximum chances of supporting industrial upgrading and diversification according to the country's comparative advantages, thereby ensuring the economy's dynamic and sustained growth. Its key features apply to both high-income and developing economies. For upgrading and diversifying to new industries in developing countries, governments may follow six simple steps that provide an actionable framework for policymakers to use to identify sectors likely to be the country's latent comparative advantage, then facilitate the entry and operation of private firms into those sectors by removing binding constraints and providing incentives to the first movers. This framework suggests that policymakers identify tradable industries that have performed well in fast-growing countries with similar endowments and with per capita incomes about double their own. If domestic private firms in these sectors are already present, policymakers should identify and remove constraints to those firms' technological upgrading or to entry by other firms. In industries in which no domestic firms are present, policymakers should aim to attract foreign direct investment from the countries being emulated or organize programs for incubating new firms. The government should also pay attention to the development of new and competitive products discovered by domestic private enterprises and support the scaling up of successful private-sector innovations in new industries. In countries with a poor business environment, special economic zones or industrial parks can facilitate firm entry, foreign direct investment, and the formation of industrial clusters. Finally, the government might help pioneering firms in the new industries by offering tax incentives for a limited period, cofinancing investments, or providing access to land or foreign exchange.

latent comparative advantage   A situation in which a country's factor costs of production in an industry are competitive globally, that is, have comparative advantage in that industry based on its factor endowment structure. However, due to high transaction costs related to logistics, transportation, access to power, red tape, and other factors, the industry has not yet been competitive in domestic and international markets. For example, low-income countries should have comparative advantages in labor-intensive industries, such as garments, footwear, and toys, for which labor is the most important cost component. However, few of them are competitive globally in those industries due to high transaction costs. The growth identification and facilitation framework provides a practical approach for the government to use to coordinate necessary efforts to reduce transaction costs and assist the private firms to develop those latent comparative advantage industries competitively.

middle-income trap   A situation in which a country fails to rise above middle-income status over a long period. The World Bank currently classifies a country as middle income if its income per capita (gross national income, in accounting terms) is greater than $1,006 and less than $12,275. Between 1950 and 2008 only 28 economies in the world were able to reduce their per capita income gap with the United States by 10 percentage points or more. Among them only 12 were non-Western economies or were not oil- or diamond-producing countries. In other words, more than 150 countries in the world have remained trapped in middle- and low-income status. Most countries that have moved beyond low-income status by means of their industrialization efforts or windfalls of natural resources in earlier periods still find themselves in a precarious situation in terms of further narrowing their gap with advanced countries.

new structural economics   A modern application of a neoclassical approach to the study of the determinants of economic structure and the causes of dynamic changes in the economic structure of a country over time. Following the convention of neoclassical economics, this field should be named "structural economics." However, there already was a structuralist school in development economics in the past, and in order to distinguish it from the past, this new approach is named the "new structural economics." This new structural economics postulates that the industrial structure of an economy is endogenous to its factor endowments, which are given at any specific time and changeable over time. The factor endowments determine the total budgets of the economy, and the relative abundance of factors in the endowments determines the relative factor prices in the economy at any specific time. The basic message of the new structural economics is that a developing country that follows its comparative advantage has the best chance to be competitive globally, successfully upgrade its endowment structure, tap into the potential of latecomer advantages, sustain industrial upgrading, increase its national income, create jobs, and reduce poverty. It recommends that, to maintain stability in economic transition, developing countries' governments that deal with distorted economic environments should provide some transitory protections to nonviable firms in the priority sector set up previously by misguided development policy. At the same time, the government should liberalize and facilitate the entry of private firms and foreign direct investment into sectors in which the country has comparative advantage so as to improve resource allocation and achieve dynamic growth. The dynamic growth will also create the necessary conditions for removing the remaining distortions, which will increase the total social welfare. The process is one of opening markets while also providing government support to facilitate the growth of new industries. The latter can be achieved using the six-step operationalization strategy of the growth identification and facilitation framework.

structuralist economics   An early wave of development economics developed mostly by economists in Latin America after World War II. Those economists emphasized the importance of structural change, attributed the lack thereof to market failures, and proposed government interventions to correct them, most notably via import substitution strategies. Many of those attempts in developing countries failed because their targeted industries went against the countries' comparative advantages; the firms in the priority industries were nonviable in open, competitive markets; and their investment and continuous operations relied on their governments' protection and subsidies through various distortions.

Washington Consensus   The name given to the neoliberal policies that dominated development thinking in the 1980s and 1990s and the subsequent structural adjustment package of policy reforms from Bretton Woods institutions, which encouraged developing countries' governments to remove market distortions, radically reform social programs, and stay away from industrial policy. Standard Washington Consensus policy prescriptions aimed at instantaneously wiping out all distortions in a "Big Bang" approach—replacing the old system with market resource allocation. Wide-ranging reforms were meant to ensure fiscal discipline, "competitive" exchange rates, trade and financial liberalization, privatization, and deregulation—that is, to ensure minimal state involvement in economic development. Although the Washington Consensus embodied the broad neoclassical principles of macroeconomic stabilization, it ignored the key policy issues facing developing countries: how to ensure the survival of a large number of nonviable firms in former priority sectors that were a legacy of the development strategy previously adopted by the government for jobs and stability and how to promote entry into industries with an actual or latent comparative advantage so that poor countries could embark on the process of industrial and technological upgrading and structural transformation. The prescriptions of the Washington Consensus did not always yield the intended or satisfactory results.

NOTES

Prologue

1. Lin 2009b.
2. Pinkovsiy and Sala-i-Martin 2009; Young 2010; Leke et al. 2010.
3. Radelet 2010.
4. The number of state-based armed conflicts in Sub-Saharan Africa fell from a peak of 16 in 1999 to 5 in 2005 and 7 in 2006 but went back up to 11 in 2008 and 2009. As a result, the number of battle-related deaths shrank from about 64,000 in 1999 to 1,400 in 2005, the lowest figure in decades, but it increased to 6,000 in 2008 (World Bank 2011).
5. World Bank 2009a, p. i.
6. Zoellick 2010.

Chapter One:
New Challenges and New Solutions

1. Angola's GDP declined more than 20 percent in 2008–09.
2. Ghana and Kenya, two of the most important economies of the region, had to postpone sovereign bond offerings worth more than $800 million, delaying major infrastructure projects.
3. The Gleneagles Summit official communiqué (G-8 2005, p. 25) noted that "a substantial increase in official development assistance, in addition to other resources, is required in order to achieve the internationally agreed development goals and objectives, including those contained in the Millennium Declaration (the Millennium Goals) by 2015, as we agreed in Monterrey in 2002. Fulfilling this commitment is needed in order to consolidate and build on recent progress in Africa, to stimulate the growth that will increase other resources and to enable African and other poor countries over time to reduce their aid dependency. . . . The commitment of the G-8 and other donors will lead to an increase in official development assistance to Africa of $25 billion a year by 2010, more than doubling aid to Africa compared to 2004." Such bold commitments did not materialize.

4. A key response occurred when the International Monetary Fund contended that all countries with low debt and a track record of disciplined policies could be prudently encouraged to undertake a fiscal boost equivalent to about 2 percent of GDP. That recommendation was based on the assumption of a multiplier of one—a conservative assumption if indeed the fiscal stimulus is well targeted—and therefore envisioned a 2 percent increase in global growth. As of January 2009, the fiscal stimulus packages announced by G-20 countries amounted to 2.7 percent of total GDP, with tax cuts and infrastructure each representing 0.8 percent and other expenditures 1.2 percent (Freeman et al. 2009).

5. In the United States, there were 140 bank failures in 2009—the largest number on record since the Great Depression.

6. An article based on this speech was published with the title "Beyond Keynesianism: The Necessity of a Globally Coordinated Solution" (Lin 2009a).

7. Oliver Blanchard rightly points out that interest rates are a poor tool to use to deal with excess leverage, excessive risk taking, or apparent deviations of asset prices from fundamentals. He also notes that "the crisis has shown that interest rates can actually hit the zero level, and when this happens it is a severe constraint on monetary policy that ties your hands during times of trouble" (Blanchard, quoted in Clift 2010)." Elsewhere he notes: "To the extent that monetary policy, including credit and quantitative easing, had largely reached its limits, policymakers had little choice but to rely on fiscal policy" (Blanchard, Dell'Ariccia, and Mauro 2010, p. 9).

8. Care certainly needs to be exercised to ensure that "temporary" fiscal stimulus packages in many countries do not become a means of avoiding some of the difficult adjustments that will be needed eventually in the most advanced economies (rethinking budget priorities and allocations, enforcing public expenditure controls, undertaking entitlement reform, and implementing new strategies for revenue generation).

9. See Lin and Doemeland 2012 for a discussion of issues of Ricardian equivalence and the need to move beyond Keynesianism.

10. Blanchard, Dell'Ariccia, and Mauro 2010, p. 3.

11. Ibid.

12. The report was released in 2008 and titled *The Growth Report: Strategies for Sustained Growth and Inclusive Development* (Commission on Growth and Development 2008). The Commission comprised 20 experienced policymakers and two Nobel prize–winning economists, Michael Spence and Robert Solow. Its work has been supported by the governments of Australia, the Netherlands, Sweden, and the United Kingdom; the William and Flora Hewlett Foundation; and the World Bank Group.

13. Comparative advantage is typically defined as a situation in which a country, individual, company, or region can produce a good at a lower opportunity cost than a competitor. It differs from absolute advantage, where the good can be produced at a lower cost per unit than the cost at which any other entity produces that good. It was first discussed by eighteenth-century British economist David Ricardo in *On The Principles of Political Economy and Taxation* (1817).

Chapter Two:
A Battle of Narratives and Changing Paradigms

1. Sage 1992, p. 149.
2. Maddison 2001.
3. Cameron 1993.

4. Barro and Sala-i-Martin 1995, p. 6.

5. Kuznets 1971.

6. Schultz 1964.

7. A few technological innovations before modern times, such as the introduction from America to the rest of the world of corn and sweet potatoes, which were byproducts of the discovery of the new continent, can be analyzed as exogenous technological shocks. Most other technological innovations before modern times were byproducts of daily practices of craftsmen or farmers.

8. Kuznets 1966; Perkins 1969; Clark 2007.

9. Bairoch 1993; Maddison 2006.

10. Smith 1776; Cipolla 1980; Pomeranz 2000.

11. Shiue and Keller 2007.

12. Lin 1995; Landes 1969, 1998.

13. Mokyr 1990.

14. Romer 1986; Lucas 1988.

15. Braudel 1984; Baumol 1994.

16. Pritchett 1997.

17. DeLong 1997, p. 44.

18. See, for example, the 13 economies studied in Commission on Growth and Development 2008.

19. Collier 2007.

20. Barro 1997, back cover.

21. Conditional convergence is a key property in Solow–Swan models. It is conditional because in these models, the steady-state levels of capital and output per worker depend on characteristics that vary across economies: the saving rate, the population growth rate, and the position of the production function. Many recent empirical studies have suggested that many other sources of cross-country variations, such as government policies or the initial stock of human capital, should be included in the analysis.

22. The Cass (1965) and Koopmans (1965) versions of the neoclassical model, which built on Ramsey's analysis of consumer optimization, attempted to provide an endogenous determination of saving rates. Although this extension helped preserve conditional convergence, it did not solve the problem of long-run growth's being determined by exogenous technological progress.

23. See Robinson 1933, 1956; Solow 1998.

24. Maddison n.d.; see also *The World Economy: Historical Statistics,* available at www .ggdc.net/maddison/.

25. Commission on Growth and Development 2008.

26. Romer 1986.

27. See Romer 1987, 1990; Lucas 1988; Aghion and Howitt 1992 .

28. In economics, a good is considered "rival" when its consumption by one consumer prevents simultaneous consumption by others. Most private goods (food, clothing) meet that definition. By contrast, a "nonrival" good can be used simultaneously by many others. Typical examples include intangible goods such as clean air and most intellectual property. A good is considered "excludable" when it is possible to prevent consumers who have not paid for it from having access to it and "nonexcludable" when it is not possible to do so. Goods that are both "nonrival" (several individuals can consume the same good without diminishing its value) and "nonexcludable" (an individual cannot be prevented from consuming the good) are called public goods.

29. Jones 1998.

30. Acemoglu and Robinson 2001; Glaeser and Shleifer 2002.

31. For surveys, see Jones 1998; Barro and Sala-i-Martin 2003; Helpman 2004.

32. Lucas 2002, p. 2.

33. Lucas 1988, p. 5.

34. Lucas 2002, p. 16.

35. Ibid.

36. Robert Lucas made a similar point in his 1997 Kuznets lectures at Yale University, where he considered the interaction of human capital growth and the demographic transition in the early stages of industrialization. He also used a diffusion model to illustrate the possibility that the vast intersociety income inequality created in the course of the Industrial Revolution may have already reached its peak and that income differences would decline during the twentieth century.

37. Lucas 2002, p. 18.

38. See Landes 1969; Lin 1995.

39. A good illustration of this peculiar dynamic is observable in the financial sector: in developed countries, where large capital-intensive firms and high-tech firms prevail in the economy, the financial system is dominated by equity markets, venture capital, and big banks, which are more efficient in mobilizing or allocating financial resources, spreading or sharing risks, and promoting economic growth. By contrast, small and less risky labor-intensive firms are the main engine for economic growth in developing countries, where appropriate financial structures are characterized by the dominance of banks, especially small local banks.

40. See, in particular, Schultz 1962; Becker 1992; Lucas 2002; Hickman 2006.

41. See Mankiw 1995.

42. Deaton 2009, p. 45.

43. From 1870 to 1990, the ratio of per capita incomes between the richest and the poorest countries increased by roughly a factor of five. See Pritchett 1997.

44. Maddison 2006.

45. That is the view expressed by Baumol (1986) and Barro and Sala-i-Martin (1992). Prescott (1999) is even more optimistic, expressing the view that continued divergence is not an option and that the world distribution of income will eventually converge.

46. Rosenstein-Rodan 1943.

47. Dutt and Ros 2003.

48. The new field of development economics was regarded as covering underdevelopment because "conventional economics" did not apply (Hirschman 1982). Early trade and development theories and policy prescriptions were based on some widely accepted stylized facts and premises about developing countries (Krueger 1997). These included the ideas that developing economies' production structures were oriented heavily toward primary commodity production; that if developing countries adopted policies of free trade, their comparative advantage would forever lie in primary commodity production; that the global income elasticity and the price elasticity of demand for primary commodities were low; and that capital accumulation was crucial for growth and, in the early stage of development, it could occur only with the importation of capital goods. Based on these stylized facts and premises, it was a logical next step to believe that the process of development was industrialization and that industrialization consisted primarily of the substitution of domestic production of manufactured goods for imports (Chenery 1958).

49. Rosenstein-Rodan 1943; Nurkse 1953.

50. Lewis 1954.

51. Backward linkages refer to the various channels through goods, services, and money flow between a firm and its suppliers and create a network of economic interdependence. They exist when the growth of an industry leads to the growth of the industries that supply it. The typical example is the growth of the textile industry, which may encourage the growth of the cotton industry, lead to higher incomes for cotton farmers, and create a greater demand for goods and services in rural areas. Forward linkages generally refer to the distribution chain connecting a producer or supplier with the customers. They exist when the development of an industry leads to the growth of other industries that use its output as input or when the output of an industry fosters another industry. For example, it has been observed in many countries that the development of agriculture or manufacturing has helped create services in the transportation sectors.

52. Taylor 1983, 1991.

53. The Washington Consensus involved 10 reforms: fiscal discipline; reordering public expenditure priorities, most notably by switching expenditure from things like indiscriminate subsidies to basic health and education; constructing a tax system that would combine a broad tax base with moderate marginal tax rates; liberalizing interest rates; adopting a competitive exchange rate; liberalizing trade; liberalizing inward foreign direct investment; privatization; deregulation; and ensuring property rights (Williamson 2002).

54. See Easterly 2001.

55. For a good summary of the critique, see Naím 2000 and Birdsall and de la Torre 2001.

56. Stiglitz 2003, p. 35.

57. Rodrik 2006, p. 974.

58. I discuss these issues further in the next chapters of this book.

59. See Coase 1937, 1960; North 1981, 1990, 1994.

60. See Williamson 2000, p. 599.

61. As Zagha, Nankani, and Gill (2006, p.9) note, "Whereas reforms can help achieve efficiency gains, they will not put the economy on a sustained growth path unless they also strengthen production incentives and address market or government failures that undercut efforts to accumulate capital and boost productivity." Pritchett (2006) suggests that economists abandon the quest for a single growth theory and focus instead on developing a collection of growth and transition theories tailored to countries' particular circumstances.

62. World Bank 2005, p. xiii.

63. Hausmann, Rodrik, and Velasco 2006, p. 12.

64. Ibid.

65. The methodology proposed for the identification of the binding constraints to growth relies on shadow prices. Even in countries where data on shadow prices are widely available, it is not clear that these data would accurately identify areas in which progress is most needed in each country. For example, one could imagine a simple model of growth for a low-income country where technology and human capital were complementary. In such a country, the returns to both education and technology adoption would be low due to low levels of human capital and technology. An exclusive focus on shadow prices and an ignorance of cross-country comparison of levels would then suggest no need to improve education levels and encourage technology adoption.

66. Ravallion 2009, p. 2.

67. See the discussions about the need to be cautious about applying past experiences and existing theories to solve the current issues in my book *Benti and Changwu: Dialogues on Methodology in Economics* (Lin 2012).

Chapter Three:
Economic Development

1. Biney 2008, p. 129.
2. Nkrumah 1957.
3. Cooper 2002, p. 161.
4. Nkrumah 1960.
5. Convention People's Party 1962, pp. 393–394.
6. Ibid.
7. A variant of old structuralist policies, the "big push" theory aimed at achieving the industrialization of developing countries. Its proponents viewed the small size of domestic markets as the main constraint and advocated strong government intervention to accelerate the process. They recommended coordinated and simultaneous public investments in a particular sector as a way of generating demand and enlarging the size of markets in other sectors (Rosenstein-Rodan 1943).
8. Nkrumah himself acknowledged this idea. In introducing the Plan to Parliament on March 4, 1959, he commented: "It is, however, apparent that our ability to execute this great plan of development will largely be influenced by what we can do to obtain capital from overseas" (Government of Ghana 1959, p. 2). The steady deterioration of the terms of trade made matters worse: in 1957, when Ghana attained independence, a ton of cocoa beans could be used to purchase about 110 barrels of crude oil. By 1966 cocoa prices had plummeted, and the same ton was worth only 40 barrels of crude oil (Yeboah 1999).
9. Aryeetey and Fosu 2008.
10. Maddison n.d.
11. Lal 1983; Krueger 1992; Lin 2009b.
12. See, for instance, Grossman and Helpman 1994; Sokoloff and Engerman 2000; Acemoglu 2007.
13. These explanations are presented, respectively, by North 1981; Alesina and Rodrik 1994 and Persson and Tabellini 1994; Besley and Coate 1998 and Acemoglu and Robinson 2002.
14. White elephants are defined in the economic literature as investment projects with negative social effects.
15. Socially efficient projects do not have this feature because all politicians can commit to build them, and they thus have a symmetric effect on political outcomes. So white elephants may be preferred to socially efficient projects if the political benefits are greater than the surplus generated by efficient projects.
16. See, for instance, Gordon and Li 2005.
17. These authors advocated the need to change the international division of labor and, particularly, the need for developing countries to become producers and exporters of manufactures, but some of their views on inward-looking policies evolved over time. Prebisch, for example, became an early critic of the excesses of import substitution–industrialization in

the late 1950s and argued for a mix of import substitution–industrial strategies with export promotion (diversification) and regional integration. He rejected the "unequal world order" and was a believer in the existence of asymmetries in the international economic system, including in trade and finance. But that view was hardly unique to Prebisch or "old structuralists"; it was shared by international organizations, including the World Bank, which was created in part to help redress those inequalities.

18. Gerschenkron 1962.

19. The idea of comparative advantage was initially proposed by David Ricardo in 1819 (see Ricardo 1921). I will discuss it in more depth later in this chapter and also in Chapter 6.

20. Arndt 1985.

21. Lin 2009b.

22. The success of the Stalinist model of modernization that inspired many developing countries' leaders was misleading: the Soviet Union was able to achieve apparent success in the first 40 years and sustain its system for 60 years, until the late 1980s, because it had the world's richest per capita natural resource endowment and a large population of 290 million in the early twentieth century. So it was possible for the state to mobilize enough resources and subsidize a large number of nonviable firms for a long period. Many developing countries following a similar strategy failed quickly because they were not equally endowed and their populations were typically much smaller (Lin 2009b).

23. Even Cambodia's Saloth Sar, the man who became Pol Pot, is described by some of his biographers as having been preoccupied with having a good reputation. In his account of the tragedies of the Khmer Rouge, Philip Short (2004) suggests that some of their egregious acts were the results of slovenly incompetence. In his political biography of Stalin, Robert Service (2005) notes that the former Soviet leader too was obsessed with his grandiose legacy. The book explains Stalin's long-lasting appeal by describing him not just as a dictator but also as a man fascinated by ideas and an avid reader of Marxist doctrine and Russian and Georgian literature, as well as an internationalist committed to ensuring that Russia assumed a powerful role on the world stage.

24. I will discuss the secrets of successful countries in Chapter 4.

25. Monga 2006, p. 243.

26. During the years 1960–94, Africa invested 9.6 percent of GDP (measured at international prices), whereas the rate for other developing countries was 15.6 percent (Hoeffler 1999). Africa's investment rate was therefore thought to be lower than the 11 percent believed to be required for a country to start the take-off stage of its modern economic growth (Rostow 1960). But any statement about whether African investment was the source of poor performance would have to take into consideration the composition of that investment—and whether more public investment, an instrument under government control, would have benefited the continent. Devarajan, Easterly, and Pack (2002) have analyzed the productivity of economywide investment across countries and tried to obtain some insight into the underlying process generating the aggregate results through a case study of the evolution of the manufacturing sector in Tanzania. They found that low investment has not been the major constraint on development in Africa. Recognizing that private investment is endogenous, they used the method of instrumental variables (with the level of private investment at the beginning of the period as the instrument). Their basic finding was that public investment has not been correlated with growth in Africa. Private investment was also not correlated with growth unless Botswana was included in the sample. The reason is that Botswana

is the only country in Africa to have experienced high rates of private investment and growth.

27. Lin 1990.

28. Balakrishnan 2007.

29. "As more or less an accounting scheme the Mahalanobis model was exclusively a supply-side model. There was no recognition of a possible demand constraint to capital accumulation and little scope for slackening demand growth to subvert the growth process. A model based on the purely physical relationship between inputs and outputs made sense in the Soviet Union, the classical 'command economy' where investment can be decreed by planners and enforced by commissars. Not so in India, with a ubiquitous private sector that invests only in response to growing profits or its anticipation" (Balakrishnan 2007, p. 13).

30. Glassburner (2007) estimates that Indonesia's real per capita income in 1966 was 3.6 percent below the 1958 level.

31. Mabro 1974; Mabro and Radwan 1976.

32. For a theoretical discussion, see Lin and Tan 1999; Lin and Li 2008.

33. According to Maddison (2006), Egypt's per capita GDP increased from $905 in 1956 to $1,254 in 1970 (1990 international Geary–Khamis dollars).

34. Abu-Bader and Abu-Qarn 2005.

35. Rocheteau 1982, p. 240.

36. Rocheteau 1982.

37. Chang 2002.

38. Chang 2007, 2008c.

39. The strategy of giving priority to the capital goods industry was supported by respectable theories, such as the economic development model created by a famous Indian statistician, P. C. Mahalanobis, in 1953, which became the foundation for India's second five-year plan (Bhagwati and Chakravarty 1969); those discussed in Amartya Sen's dissertation at Cambridge University, later published as a book (1960); and those proposed recently by Murphy, Shleifer, and Vishny (1989).

40. Lin 2009b.

41. Lin and Li 2009.

42. Selim 2006.

43. See Lin 2009b; Lin and Li 2009. There are alternative hypotheses about the government interventions and distortions in developing countries, especially in Latin American countries. In the models of Olson (1982), Grossman and Helpman (1996 and 2001), Engerman and Sokoloff (1997), and Acemoglu, Johnson, and Robinson (2001, 2002, 2005), government intervention and institutional distortions arise from the capture of government by powerful vested-interest elites. Logically, their models can explain some observed interventions and distortions, such as import quotas, tax subsidies, entry regulations, and so on. Their theories cannot, however, explain other important interventions and distortions—for example, they cannot explain why publicly owned enterprises are pervasive in developing countries even though this is against the interests of the powerful elites or why most distortions to protect the industrial sectors were introduced in the 1940s and 1950s, when most power elites were of the landed class. Nevertheless, once the government introduces a distortion, a group of vested interests will be created even if the distortion is created for noble purposes. The vested-interest argument could be appropriate to explain the difficulty of removing distortions.

44. See Lin and Tan 1999; Lin 2009b.
45. Krueger 1974; see Krugman 1993 for a general exposition of these issues.
46. World Bank 1995.
47. Hausmann and Klinger 2008, p. 2.
48. Demery 1994.
49. Leechor 1994, p. 153.
50. Maddison 2006.
51. World Bank 2002.
52. Blanchard et al. 1993.
53. World Bank 2002.
54. Stiglitz 1998, 2002.
55. Schopenhauer 1890, p. 80.

Chapter Four:
Lessons from Successful Catch-Up Countries

1. Commission on Growth and Development 2008, p. 33.
2. Spence 2011, p. 72.
3. Bold 1982.
4. Kaldor 1961.
5. Solow 1969, p. 2.
6. Jones and Romer 2009.
7. These previous studies include, among others, *The East Asian Miracle: Economic Growth and Policy* (World Bank 1993), *Economic Growth in the 1990s: Learning from a Decade of Reform* (World Bank 2005), and *World Development Report 2008: Agriculture for Development* (World Bank 2007).
8. Commission on Growth and Development n.d.
9. Commission on Growth and Development 2008, p. x. The way the Commission organized its work was also quite unusual. First it defined themes and issues deemed important for growth and development. Then it invited world-renowned academics, practitioners, and experts to write papers exploring the state of knowledge on these themes and issues; the papers were reviewed and discussed at workshops. A working group, which interacted with academics and commissioners, reviewed and commented on the papers throughout the process. The working group also supported the chairman in drafting the final report by reviewing interim drafts and providing comments.
10. Commission on Growth and Development 2008, p. 2.
11. The list of economies includes Botswana; Brazil; China; Hong Kong SAR, China; Indonesia; Japan; the Republic of Korea; Malaysia; Malta; Oman; Singapore; Taiwan, China; and Thailand.
12. Because growth rates of this magnitude for such long periods were unheard of before the latter part of the twentieth century, the authors acknowledge that their work could have been called a report on "economic miracles" if they didn't believe the term to be a misnomer; unlike miracles, sustained high growth can be explained and repeated.
13. Rilke 1984, p. 90.

14. Commission on Growth and Development 2008, p. 22.

15. For Weber's position, see Weber 1958.

16. Myrdal 1968; Chang 2008b.

17. The ant is said to have worked all summer long, built a house, and saved food in preparation for the winter. Meanwhile the grasshopper had a good time and thought it was not smart to work so hard. Then the winter came, and it was time for reckoning. The grasshopper had no food or shelter and could not cope with changing weather conditions.

18. Kroeber and Kluckhohn 1952.

19. Jamieson 1980.

20. Montiel and Servén 2008.

21. For Schumpeter's position, see Schumpeter 1942, p. 82.

22. Mkapa 2008, p. 5.

23. Commission on Growth and Development 2008, p. 68.

24. Zellner 1979.

25. Brady and Spence 2010, pp. 35–36; see also Brady and Spence 2009.

26. Ibid.

27. WTO n.d.

28. Ibid.

29. Smith 1776, IV.2.12.

30. See Torrens 1815; Irwin 1996. Comparative advantage became an important idea in economics upon the 1848 publication of *Principles of Political Economy* by John Stuart Mill (Mill 1848).

31. Krugman suggests that comparative advantage is hard to understand because it relies on three assumptions that economists use implicitly. First, the basic Ricardian model envisages a single factor (labor) that can move freely between industries in which the economy has a comparative advantage; as a result, wages are determined in a national labor market. Second, the standard textbook version of the model assumes full employment in both countries (not only because international trade is a long-run issue and, in the long run, the economy has a natural self-correcting tendency to return to full employment, but also because, in today's world, central banks actively work to stabilize employment around the nonaccelerating inflation rate of unemployment). Third, the standard textbook presentation of the Ricardian model is usually a one-period model in which trade must be balanced (Krugman 1996).

32. At any given moment, a country's total endowment determines its economy's total budget at that time. Likewise, its endowment structure, together with households' preferences and the technologies available to firms, determine the relative factor and product prices in the economy. Total budgets and relative prices are two of the most fundamental parameters in economic analysis. However, the endowments and their structure, which are given at any specific time, are also changeable over time. These properties make factor endowments and the endowment structure the best starting points for analyzing economic development. However, in Heckscher-Ohlin trade theory, the economic profession has not given enough attention to the implications of factor endowments and endowment structures, which I discuss more in Chapter 5.

33. A high-income country will accept migrant workers to complement its labor force but not to the extent of lowering its capital–labor ratio to the level of a developing country; the high-income country's capital will also flow to developing countries but not to the extent

of making capital–labor ratios there as high as in rich countries. If either scenario happened, the incomes in both countries would be equalized.

34. Porter 1990.

35. Lin and Ren 2007.

36. Commission on Growth and Development 2008, pp. 21–22.

37. Lin and Chang 2009.

38. Harrison and Rodríguez-Clare 2010.

39. Today industries in advanced developed countries are typically located on the global frontier and face uncertainty as to what the next frontier industries will be. This explains why government policy measures to support pioneer firms in such countries are usually in the form of general support to research in universities, which has externality to private firms' R&D, patents, preferential taxes for capital investments, mandates, defense contracts, and government procurement. Support in the form of preferential taxes, defense contracts, and government procurement is industry or product specific. Support for basic research also needs to be prioritized for certain types of potential industries or products because of budget constraints. Except for the case of patents, which are ex post rewards, the government is required to pick winners. But the government's attempt to pick winners in developing countries, especially low-income countries, has often failed. One of the most important reasons for such failures is the attempt by governments in low-income countries to support firms in industries that are inconsistent with their economies' comparative advantages, as discussed in Chapter 3.

40. An industry is consistent with a country's latent comparative advantage if, based on the country's endowment structure, it has comparative advantage in this industry but, due to the inadequate infrastructure and clustering, firms' transaction costs in this industry are too high and the industry is not competitive in domestic and international markets.

41. I define the development strategy here in the same way as Rodrik (2005), as referring to the policies and institutional arrangements adopted by the government in a developing country to achieve economic convergence with the living standards prevailing in advanced countries.

42. Botswana is the exception on the list. The country relies on diamonds and has good governance indicators. But the government did not play an active role in facilitating structural transformation. As a result, the manufacturing sector contributes only 4.2 percent to its GDP, unemployment is extremely high, and social indicators are poor. Compared with the other 12 successful economies on the list, Brazil has been more aggressive in its industrial development. It can do so because it is very rich in natural resources and has a large population (194 million). It can afford to provide large subsidies and protection to selected advanced industries. The question often posed is why Russia, a country with a similar resource endowment and population size, has not performed equally well. The answer is that Brazil's industrial development is not as ambitious as Russia's and thus is not too far away from its comparative advantages. For example, Brazil's aerospace industry features middle-range airplanes, whereas Russia competes directly with the United States in the space industry.

43. Countries at similar stages of development may specialize in different industries. But the capital intensity in their industries will be similar. For example, in recent years China achieved dynamic growth by specializing in labor-intensive manufacturing industries such as electronics, toys, and textiles, whereas India's growth relied on specializing in call centers,

programming, and business process services, which are labor-intensive parts of the information industry.

44. Akamatsu 1962; Ito 1980; Kim 1988. In a similar spirit, Hausmann and Klinger (2006) recently investigated the evolution of a country's sophistication in exports and found that this process was easier when the move was to "nearby" products in the product space. This is because every industry requires highly specific inputs such as knowledge, physical assets, intermediate inputs, labor skills, infrastructure, property rights, regulatory requirements, and other public goods. Established industries have somehow sorted out the many potential failures in managing all these inputs. The barriers preventing the emergence of new industries are less binding to nearby industries, which require only slight adaptations of existing inputs.

45. For a discussion of the conformity of Korea's industrial upgrading to its evolving comparative advantage, see Lin and Chang 2009.

46. Noland and Pack 2003.

47. See the discussion of specific-country cases in Chapter 3 of this book.

48. Recent work by Acemoglu and Robinson (2005) suggests that democracy is more a consequence than a cause of economic growth.

49. Brady and Spence 2010, pp. 38–39. Empirical analysis also shows that, as a general rule, the effects of leaders on economic growth are far stronger (in both positive and negative directions) in more autocratic settings than in more democratic ones. See Jones and Olken 2005.

50. List's book covers the rise of economic powerhouses in a variety of contexts, from Italian cities such as Venice to Hanseatic cities such as Hamburg and Lübek, as well as countries such as France, Germany, the Netherlands, Portugal, Spain, the United Kingdom, and the United States.

51. Chang 2002.

52. Trebilcock 1981.

53. I will elaborate the latter point in Chapter 7.

54. The European Coal and Steel Community was created in 1951, the European Atomic Energy Community in 1957.

55. European Commission 1994.

56. In October 2005 the European Commission announced seven new horizontal initiatives to (1) consolidate the EU's legal framework in the area of intellectual property, (2) take into account the links between the issues of competitiveness and environmental protection, (3) adapt the trade policy with a view to developing the competitiveness of European industry, (4) simplify the law governing certain industrial sectors (construction, the food industry), (5) remedy the shortage of skilled labor in certain sectors (new technologies, textiles), (6) anticipate and support the structural changes in industry by taking this objective into consideration in other EU policies (structural funds, in particular), and (7) adopt an integrated European approach to industrial research and innovation (Commission of the European Communities 2005).

57. Several proposals are under consideration to stimulate innovation and growth in France. The recently issued Juppé–Rocard report by two former prime ministers (a socialist and a conservative) recommends that France raise 35 billion euros ($52 billion) through public borrowing to be spent on universities and research (providing them with endowments and incentives to merge or become independent and private), the green economy,

and high technology to propel growth (Juppé and Rocard 2009). Among the projects are plans to expand high-speed Internet, develop green cities, and support innovative small businesses and France's cutting-edge aerospace and nuclear industries. Of the 35 billion euros to be raised, 13 billion will come from the reimbursed bailout packages given to French banks, with the remaining 20 billion to be raised on the financial markets.

58. Her Majesty's Government 2009.

59. Jäntti and Vartiainen 2009.

60. Kosonen 1992.

61. Romer 1993, p. 66.

62. Ibid.

Chapter Five:
A Framework for Rethinking Development

1. Helpman 2004.

2. Skidelsky 2003.

3. A convention in neoclassical economics: when the subject of research is agriculture, the field is typically called agricultural economics, and when it is finance, the field is referred to as financial economics. Following that convention, my proposed field is named structural economics. However, there were early contributions by structuralist economists such as Prebisch (1950) and Furtado (1964, 1970) and recent contributions by structuralist economists such as Taylor (1983, 1991, 2004) and Justman and Gurion (1991). They studied the same subject but applied an approach that is sensibly different from mine. I refer to their work as old structural economics and call my research new structural economics. That is also a convention in neoclassical economics. When Coase, North, Williamson, and other economists applied a neoclassical approach to a study of institutions in the 1960s, they named their field new institutional economics to distinguish their research from that of the institutional school, which applied a Marxian approach and existed in the United States in the late nineteenth and early twentieth centuries.

4. GNI per capita is given here in terms of purchasing power parity (World Bank 2010b).

5. CIA n.d.; World Bank 2010a.

6. Leibenstein 1957.

7. The factor-price equalization theorem in international trade will not hold in reality due to transportation costs, specialization, differences in technology across countries, and so on. The mobility of capital will not be able to equalize the capital–labor ratio across countries, either. Therefore, in a closed economy as well as in an open economy, the relative factor prices are determined largely by the structures of factor endowments.

8. Lin 2003, 2009b.

9. Heckscher and Ohlin 1991; Lin 2003.

10. Schumpeter 1975; Aghion and Howitt 1992.

11. Harrison and Rodríguez-Clare 2010; Jones and Romer 2009.

12. Incidentally, Adam Smith discussed both factor endowments and infrastructure endowments (public works and institutions) in Book V of *The Wealth of Nations* (Smith

1776). But the role of infrastructure was often neglected by later economists. For example, there is no discussion of infrastructure in Alfred Marshall's *Principles of Economics* (Marshall 1890).

13. The continual introduction of new and better technology in an existing industry is an important aspect of modern economic growth. Most people in low-income countries depend on agriculture for their livelihood. Improvements in agricultural technology are key to increasing farmers' income and reducing poverty. But without diversifying and upgrading from existing industries to new, more capital-intensive industries, the scope for sustained increase in per capita income will be limited. Therefore, the discussion here will focus more on industrial upgrading and diversification than on technological innovation in existing industries, although the basic principles for facilitating industrial upgrading and diversification also apply to the case of technological innovation.

14. Cross-border labor mobility is still very limited. Financial capital is more mobile than labor. But due to the limitation of infrastructure endowment, the returns to large capital inflows to the industrial sectors in developing countries are likely to be low. Such capital inflows are unlikely to be large enough to reduce the capital scarcity in developing countries. So despite the globalization of factor markets, the factor endowment in any developing country can be taken as a given at any specific time.

15. Ju, Lin, and Wang 2009.

16. Dinh et al. 2012.

17. When a country reaches middle-income status, some of its industries locate on the global technological frontier and enter business segments being vacated by high-income countries' firms. With success come new responsibilities: middle-income countries' firms reaching that level have to rely on indigenous innovations for new technology and products in those industries.

18. Technological innovation, product innovation, and managerial capacity all contribute to the overall level of risk associated with firms, but their relative importance varies greatly from one industry to another and from one level of economic development to another. This has implications for the efficiency of alternative financial institutions in reducing information asymmetries and in sharing risk (Lin, Sun, and Jiang 2009).

19. The difference between factors of production and infrastructure is that the supply and demand of the former are determined individually by households and firms, whereas the latter are supplied by the community or governments in a form that cannot be part of the decisions of individual households or firms because they require collective action.

20. This pattern, which was documented in the literature by Chenery (1960) and Akamatsu (1962), is formalized by Ju, Lin, and Wang (2009).

21. Lin, Sun, and Jiang 2009.

22. The proposition that countries need to specialize in industries consistent with their comparative advantage at each level of their development is just like the one that countries need to have free, competitive markets. It provides a theoretical framework for organizing an economy efficiently. In reality, just as no country will have a free, competitive market in the perfect sense in the real world, no country will follow its comparative advantage perfectly, especially given the fact that it changes over time and industrial change is not instantaneous. We do know that deviation too far from the free market is likely to reduce economic efficiency. Likewise, a large deviation from a country's comparative advantage is likely to create distortions, reduce the growth rate, increase macro instability, and worsen income

distribution. For empirical testing on the impact of deviations from comparative advantage, see Lin (2009b).

23. Lin 2009b; Lin and Chang 2009.

24. For a theoretical discussion, see Krugman 1979.

25. Harrison and Rodríguez-Clare 2010.

26. Note that this is different from the coordination role often proposed in the past for developing countries' governments. That "big push" line of argument stressed the idea that if each potential firm's viability depends on inputs from another firm that does not yet exist, none of the potential firms may emerge. In that case, the government can theoretically move the economy to a higher welfare equilibrium with a big push that leads to the concurrent emergence of upstream and downstream firms (Rosenstein-Rodan 1961; Murphy, Shleifer, and Vishny 1989). But changing global conditions have made the traditional big push argument less compelling. The reduction in transport and information costs in recent decades has led to global production networks in which many countries, both developed and developing, produce only certain parts of a final product according to each country's comparative advantage.

27. Lin 1989.

28. In the aftermath of the crisis, the Bush administration created a large emergency fund to buy up the so-called "toxic" mortgage debts that sparked the global financial crisis. Henry Paulson, then U.S. Treasury secretary, indicated that the underlying problem was "illiquid assets" that were "choking off the flow of credit," a vital tool for keeping the country on track. "To restore confidence in our markets and financial institutions so that they can fuel continued growth and prosperity, we must address the underlying problem," he said on September 19, 2008 (Paulson 2008). U.S. President Bush authorized his administration to enact a nearly $1 trillion financial rescue package, backed the purchase of investment bank Bear Stearns and stocks in leading banks, engineered a government takeover of mortgage giants Fannie Mae and Freddie Mac, supported guarantees to money market fund holdings, and funneled billions of dollars to stabilize troubled insurance giant American International Group. He also supported government loans and subsequent takeovers of private automobile companies.

29. Krugman 1991.

30. Matthew 9:17, King James Bible.

31. Such interventions are due to the need to protect nonviable firms in priority industries identified in the government's industrial policy in violation of comparative advantage (Lin and Li 2009).

Chapter Six:
What Would Be Done Differently?

1. Believers in Keynesianism sometimes offer as evidence of success the expansionary policies applied in social democratic Sweden and even Nazi Germany in the early twentieth century. They also cite U.S. President Franklin Delano Roosevelt, who thought that insufficient buying power caused the Great Depression. He implemented various elements

of Keynesian economics, especially after 1937, when the United States suffered a second wave of recession. Even more notable are economic policies he implemented at the onset of World War II, considered by economic historians to have stimulated the world economy.

2. Christina Romer, the former chair of U.S. President Barack Obama's Council of Economic Advisors, estimates the spending multiplier in the United States to be around 1.6 after about a year and a half (Romer 2009).

3. The term *voodoo economics* was first used by George H. W. Bush to mock the economic policies of his future running mate Ronald Reagan, who favored reduced tax rates on income and capital gains to boost economic growth.

4. Barro 2009.

5. O'Rourke 1991, p. xxiv.

6. The basic idea behind the Ricardian equivalence trap (developed by David Ricardo and fleshed out by Robert Barro) is that government attempts to stimulate the economy with public expenditures will always fail. This is because the public will expect taxes to be raised at some point in the future to pay off the debt incurred by the government to finance these expenditures. It will therefore anticipate tax increases by saving its excess money. Those who challenge the Ricardian theory—mainly Keynesians—underline the unrealistic assumptions on which it is based, such as the existence of perfect capital markets, the ability for households and firms to borrow and save whenever they want, and the willingness of private agents to save for a future tax increase even though they may not see it in their lifetimes (see Chapter 1).

7. Francesco and Pagano 1991.

8. Several empirical studies have shown that although fiscal policy is generally either acyclical or countercyclical, in developing countries it is, by and large, procyclical. Gavin and Perotti (1997) first made that observation; despite some challenges, that view has recently been confirmed by Ilzetzki and Vegh (2008).

9. See Lin 2009a.

10. Banco Central de Cuba n.d.a.

11. Banco Central de Cuba n.d.b.

12. In addition to steering interest rates by managing liquidity, the central bank can also signal its monetary policy stance to the money market. This is usually done by changing the conditions under which the central bank is willing to enter transactions with credit institutions. The central bank also aims to ensure proper functioning of the money market and to help credit institutions meet their liquidity needs smoothly. This is achieved by providing regular refinancing to credit institutions and facilities that allow them to deal with end-of-the-day balances and to cushion transitory liquidity fluctuations.

13. There is a wide consensus among neoclassical economists that in the long run—after all adjustments in the economy—a change in the quantity of money in the economy will be reflected in a change in the general level of prices. But it will not induce permanent changes in real variables such as real output or unemployment. This general principle, referred to as "the long-run neutrality of money," underlies all standard macroeconomic thinking. Real income or the level of employment is, in the long term, essentially determined by real factors, such as technology, population growth, or the preferences of economic agents.

14. Bernanke 2004.

15. Ibid.

16. Blanchflower 2009.

17. Mankiw 2006, p. 44.

18. Grauwe 2008.

19. The likely mechanism of a liquidity trap in a developed country confronting excess capacity is as follows: many firms will have poor performance, and some may go bankrupt or reduce employment. This will aggravate the slack in the labor market and reduce wage rates and job security. As long as job security is poor, consumption is likely to remain low, even if interest rates are reduced. In fact, the reduction of interest rates may not stimulate investment because of two factors: the lack of profitable opportunities for investing in the existing industries with excess capacity and the uncertainty of upgrading from the existing global technological frontier to new industries.

20. See Blankenburg, Palma, and Tregenna 2008.

21. Following a dispute over pending payments by the country's state oil company to some private business partners, in 2010 the government announced the nationalization of a large fleet of oil rigs that had been idle for several months. Oil Minister Rafael Ramirez was quoted by Reuters as saying that companies that refused to put their rigs into production were part of a plan to weaken the government and that the rigs were being nationalized to bring them back into production.

22. See Bates 1981.

23. IMF 2001.

24. See Hausmann and Klinger 2006.

25. Collier 2010.

26. That is, 250 percent of cost (UNCTAD n.d.).

27. See Hirschman 1958. Gerschenkron (1962) made a similar point, arguing that the private sector alone cannot effectively address the problems of access to finance in weak institutional environments.

28. See Rocheteau 1982.

29. See McKinnon 1973 and Shaw 1973. For an empirical analysis of the negative impact of financial repression on economic growth, see Roubiniand and Sala-i-Martin 1992.

30. See Monga 1997.

31. See Caprio and Honohan 2001.

32. Equity markets do not offer a suitable financial arrangement for small firms and farms because of the high fixed costs of listing and financial disclosure. Large banks generally discriminate against small firms and farms because of their lack of financial records and the high transaction costs per unit of fund loaned to them. Microfinance is too small to provide funds for business purposes, even for small firms and farms.

33. See Lin, Sun, and Jiang 2009.

34. Eichengreen et al. 1999.

35. See OECD 2002.

36. Aitken, Hanson, and Harrison 1994.

37. Blomström, Lipsey, and Zejan 1994.

38. An IMF report cautions: "Low policy rates, although necessary under current conditions, can carry longer term threats to financial stability. With growth remaining sluggish in the advanced economies, low rates are appropriate as a natural policy response to weak economic activity. Nevertheless, in many advanced economies some sectors are still trapped in the repair-and-recovery phase of the credit cycle because balance sheet repair has been incomplete, while a search for yield is pushing some other segments to become more lever-

aged and hence vulnerable again. Moreover, low rates are diverting credit creation into more opaque channels, such as the shadow banking system. These conditions increase the potential for a sharper and more powerful turn in the credit cycle, risking greater deterioration in asset quality in the event of new shocks" (IMF 2011, pp. ix–x).

39. Lucas 1990.

40. Fischer 2001, p. 2.

41. Fischer 2003, p. 3.

42. Kanbur 2009.

43. Naughton 1995; Lau, Qian, and Roland 2000; Subramanian and Roy 2003; Lin 2009a.

44. Pritchett 2001.

45. Becker 1975; Jones and Romer 2009.

46. Schultz 1961.

47. Lucas 2002.

48. Carneiro and Heckman (2003) have demonstrated the importance of both cognitive and noncognitive skills that are formed early in life in accounting for gaps in schooling among social groups and other dimensions of socioeconomic success. They have provided empirical evidence of a high return to early interventions and a low return to remedial or compensatory interventions later in life.

49. Osman-Gani 2004.

Chapter Seven:
Putting the New Structural Economics into Practice

1. See ILO n.d.

2. The first "modern zone" was established in Ireland in 1959. In recent decades a variety of different zone setups have evolved that are typically grouped under the special economic zone concept. Free trade zones (also known as commercial free zones) are fenced-in, duty-free areas offering warehousing, storage, and distribution facilities for trade, transshipment, and reexport operations. Export processing zones are industrial estates aimed primarily at foreign markets. Hybrid export processing zones (EPZs) are typically subdivided into a general zone open to all industries and a separate EPZ area reserved for export-oriented, EPZ-registered enterprises. Enterprise zones are intended to revitalize distressed urban or rural areas through tax incentives and financial grants. Freeports typically encompass much larger areas and accommodate all types of activities (including tourism and retail sales), permit on-site residence, and provide a broader set of incentives and benefits. Single-factory EPZ schemes, similar to bonded manufacturing warehouse schemes, provide incentives to individual enterprises regardless of location; factories do not have to locate within a designated zone to receive incentives and privileges. And specialized zones include science or technology parks, petrochemical zones, logistics parks, and airport-based zones (FIAS 2008).

3. See the short economic history of modern growth in Chapter 4.

4. Chang 2002, p. 31.

5. The European Coal and Steel Community was created in 1951, the European Atomic Energy Community in 1957.

6. In October 2005 the European Commission announced seven new horizontal initiatives to (1) consolidate the EU's legal framework in the area of intellectual property, (2) take into account the links between the issues of competitiveness and environmental protection, (3) adapt the trade policy with a view to developing the competitiveness of European industry, (4) simplify the law governing certain industrial sectors (construction, the food industry), (5) remedy the shortage of skilled labor in certain sectors (new technologies, textiles), (6) anticipate and support the structural changes in industry by taking this objective into consideration in other EU policies (those for structural funds, in particular), and (7) adopt an integrated European approach to industrial research and innovation (Commission of the European Communities 2005).

7. The GIF framework was presented in Lin and Monga 2011.

8. For the African success stories, see Chuhan-Pole and Angwafo 2011.

9. Porter 1990; Krugman 1991.

10. Menon 2010.

11. Sweeney 1999, p. 127.

12. In 1980 Ireland's per capita income was $8,541—about 46 percent of the U.S. per capita income of $18,577. So the selection of those four industries from Germany, the United Kingdom, and the United States was consistent with the criteria for the GIF framework, elaborated in the next section. The list was subsequently extended in the 1990s to include financial services and teleservices.

13. Two factors were often used to explain Ireland's success: access to the European common market, and the low corporate income tax (Romalis 2007). But these cannot be the main factors. Ireland has been a member of the European Economic Community since 1973, and its corporate income tax increased from zero to 10 percent (replaced by 12.5 percent in 2003) after joining the Community. Ireland's success came only after its industrial policy changed from "hands off" to "picking winners" in the later 1980s (Sweeney 1999). Ireland's troubles after the 2008 global financial crisis were due to the bursting of its housing bubble, financed mainly by foreign banks, and the government's decision to provide blanket guarantees to those foreign banks after the crisis. Ireland's industrial sector remains very competitive.

14. *Tradable goods* refers to manufactured products, agricultural products, and fisheries products as well other natural resource products. Because of the ascendance and dominance of international production networks in manufacturing industries, here *manufactured goods* refers not only to the final products but also to intermediate inputs of final products in manufacturing industries.

15. Katz 2006.

16. Sawers 2005.

17. Japan's per capita income in 1950, 1960, and 1965 was $1,921, $3,986, and $5,934, respectively, while that of the United States was $9,561, $10,961, and $13,419. The ratios were as follows: 20, 36, and 44 percent. The numbers for 1960 and 1965 are consistent with the general principles I suggest. The 1950 figure was lower than the "normal" threshold. This is probably due to the fact that Japan was still recovering from the war, and its human capital and soft and hard infrastructure were greater than those indicated by its per capita income; a strong indication is the fact that Japan's per capita income in the 1930s had already reached about 40 percent of that of the United States (for example, $2,120 versus $5,467 in 1935).

18. Maddison n.d.

19. For a discussion of industrial policies in these countries, see Chang 2002. For the estimations of per capita income for these countries, see Maddison 2006.

20. See Lin and Monga 2011; Chang 2002. For estimations of the per capita income of these countries, see Maddison 2006.

21. Carroll 1865.

22. My definition of government refers to both the central and local entities, and the process I am advocating can also be followed by all development stakeholders (multilateral development agencies and nongovernmental organizations) willing to promote industrial upgrading and diversification.

23. Hausmann and Klinger 2006.

24. Gelb et al. 2007.

25. Hesse (2008) has done some research about the quote and concludes that Lincoln never said it. He liked a similar anecdote about a cow.

26. An example of these micro analyses is a study by Ayyagari, Demirgüç-Kunt, and Maksimovic (2008), which presents the mean reported values for a number of investment climate variables in a sample of more than 6,000 firms in 80 countries. In the overall sample, taxes and regulation, political instability, inflation, and financing are reported as the greatest obstacles to firm growth.

27. François Bourguignon, my predecessor as World Bank chief economist, observes: "'Extracting means' is the way I would characterize the Investment Climate Assessment exercises that the Bank is now carrying out. Like the Doing Business indicators, these are undoubtedly useful. However, what they give us is essentially new and better right hand side variables in cross-country regressions, not necessarily better data for country-specific analysis. The goal should be to use investment climate surveys to measure the sensitivity of firms of different types to investment climate variables, as another way of determining exactly which variable corresponds to a major obstacle to growth" (Bourguignon 2006).

28. Hausmann, Rodrik, and Velasco 2008.

29. The methodology proposed for identifying the binding constraints to growth is not always straightforward. Even if data on shadow prices were widely available, it is not obvious that they would accurately identify areas of progress most needed in each country. For example, one could imagine a simple model of growth for a low-income country where technology and human capital were complementary. In such a country the returns to education and technology adoption would be low due to low levels of both human capital and technology. An exclusive focus on shadow prices and ignorance of cross-country comparisons of levels would then suggest no need to improve education levels and encourage technology adoption.

30. Duflo 2004.

31. Benavente 2006.

32. Naik 2006a.

33. Larraín, López-Calva, and Rodríguez-Clare 1996.

34. Ibid.

35. Du, Harrison, and Jefferson 2011.

36. Rhee 1990; Rhee and Belot 1990; Mottaleb and Sonobe 2011.

37. Menon 2010.

38. Sawers 2005.

39. UNCTAD 2006, p. 1. See also Katz 2006.

40. Maddison n.d.

41. Spar 1998; Dulfano 2003. During the IMF–World Bank spring meetings in Washington in 2010, I had a meeting with a minister from Costa Rica who told me that Costa Rica's president at that time personally led a government team, including several ministers and other officials, that went to Intel's headquarters in Santa Clara, California, to persuade the company to make that investment. He proudly told me that he was a junior member of that team.

42. MIGA 2006.

43. In 2008 India's information technology exports were close to $60 billion (Bhatnagar 2006).

44. Harrison and Rodríguez-Clare 2010.

45. In his Ph.D. dissertation, Zelalem T. Chala (2010) contends that the implemented export promotion policy that encouraged FDI flows in selected agricultural activities could not really transform the livelihoods of many poor people. His results show that investment in flowers, vegetables, and other cash crops could not reallocate many underemployed or unemployed laborers still held in subsistence coffee and food. But he acknowledges that data limitations may have constrained his analysis. Other empirical studies are much more positive in their assessment of Ethiopia's cut-flower industry (see, for instance, Melese 2007).

46. O'Brian and Rodriguez 2004.

47. Djik and Szirmail 2006.

48. *The Economist* 2008.

49. Henckel and McKibbin 2010, p. 2.

50. World Bank 2009b.

51. Calderón, Moral-Benito, and Servén 2009.

52. Mistry and Treebhoohun 2009.

53. Mathews 2006.

54. Aghion 2009; Romer 1993.

55. I owe this idea of ex-post rewards to Professor Shang-Jin Wei.

56. The study shows that foreign firms that were targeted and received tax subsidies were more likely to generate positive externalities through backward linkages (from producers of final goods to domestic suppliers) than were other types of foreign firms. The effect of tax breaks was stronger than that of tariffs (Du, Harrison, and Jefferson 2011).

57. Lin 2009b.

58. See, for example, Di Maio 2008; Agosin, Larraín, and Grau 2009.

Chapter Eight:
Identities and Trajectories of Transition Economies

1. Isaacson 2007.

2. Maddison n.d.

3. Ibid.

4. Yeltsin was elected to the Russian parliament and selected chairman (president) of the Russian Republic in May 1990. Later that year, he formally resigned from the Commu-

nist Party. In the fall of 1991 he and other republic leaders declared the independence of their respective republics, and in December the presidents of Russia, Ukraine, and Belarus (Belorussia) formed the Commonwealth of Independent States (CIS), declaring that they would no longer recognize the Soviet Union as of January 1, 1992. Eight other republics joined the CIS, and four became completely independent. Gorbachev resigned before year's end, and as of January 1, 1992, the Soviet Union no longer existed.

5. Salisbury 1992, p. 328. Also cited in Shambaugh 1993, p. 457.

6. Remarkable identities are mathematical expressions that can be evaluated or expressed in such a way that one can easily understand or solve a problem.

7. See Yeltsin 1990, 1995, 2000.

8. Xiaoping 1984, 1992, 1994.

9. Lin 2011a.

10. See World Bank 1996.

11. Lin 2009b, p. 31. For a formal model of the dynamics, see my paper, coauthored with Feiyue Li, "Development Strategy, Viability, and Economic Distortions in Developing Countries" (Lin and Li 2009).

12. World Bank 1996.

13. See Easterly and Fischer 1995.

14. According to S. P. Huntington, the first two "waves" of global democratization occurred in 1828–1926 and 1943–62 and were each followed by reversals. His Third Wave is based on the analysis of the transition in some 35 countries, mainly in Asia and Latin America, from nondemocratic to democratic political systems during the 1970s and 1980s. Huntington identifies four broad categories of political transitions: "transformations," in which the elites in power took the lead in bringing about democracy (Brazil, Hungary, India, and Spain); "replacements," in which opposition groups took the lead in bringing about democracy (Argentina, East Germany, Portugal, and Romania); "transplacements," in which democratization occurred through joint action by government and opposition groups (Bolivia, Czechoslovakia, Nicaragua, and Poland); and "interventions," in which democratic institutions were imposed by an outside power (Grenada and Panama; Huntington 1992). Many researchers have questioned Huntington's western-centric approach to democracy (see, for instance, Monga 1996).

15. Lal 1983, p. 33.

16. On Gorbachev, see Diamond and Plattner 1995.

17. Diamond and Plattner 1995, p. xi.

18. S. Haggard and R. R. Kaufman, for instance, suggest that "over the long term, the opportunities that democratic institutions provide for debate and peaceful contestation offer the best hope for finding durable compromises for the social conflicts and ongoing policy dilemmas" associated with economic reforms" (Haggard and Kaufman 1995, p. 8).

19. Whitman 2003, p. 72.

20. Shambaugh 1993.

21. Lin 1992.

22. For a detailed discussion of China's economic transition, see Lin 2011a.

23. World Bank 2002.

24. See, for instance, Portes 1993; Aslund 1994.

25. The construction of a light-industry project, such as a small textile factory, takes one or two years. The construction of a large heavy-industry project generally takes much lon-

ger. For example, in China the average construction time for a metallurgy plant is seven years, for a chemical plant five to six years, and for a machine-building plant three to four years (Li and Zheng 1989).

26. A real interest rate of 3 percent per month was a normal rate in the informal financial markets that existed before the adoption of the development strategy in China. It is equivalent to 36 percent per year. This is also the interest rate charged by many microfinance institutions in many low-income countries.

27. Spontaneous development of heavy industry was impossible for several reasons. First, the high interest rates would have made any project that required a long gestation unfeasible. For example, it takes, on average, seven years in China to complete the construction of a metallurgy plant. In the early 1950s the market interest rate in China was about 30 percent per year (2.5 percent per month). Suppose the fund for the project was borrowed at the market rate and repayment was made after the completion of the project. The principal and interest payment, calculated at a compound rate, would be $6.27 for each dollar borrowed in the first year of the project. It is obvious that no project would be profitable enough to compensate for such a high interest burden. Second, because most equipment had to be imported from industrial countries, the limited supply of foreign exchange again made the construction of heavy-industry projects expensive under the market-determined exchange rate. Third, because the agricultural surplus was small and scattered, it was difficult to mobilize enough funds for any lump-sum project.

28. For example, the interest rate on bank loans was officially reduced from 30 percent per year to about 5 percent per year. For a $1 fund borrowed at the beginning of a seven-year project, the principal and interest payment at the time that the project was completed would be reduced from $6.27 to $1.41.

29. Although the real GNP per capita tripled between 1952 and 1978, the nominal wage was kept almost constant, increasing only 10.3 percent during the same period (State Statistical Bureau 1987). For a more detailed discussion of the formation of low nominal wage policy, see Wu 1965; Cheng 1982. It is worth noting, however, that because of in-kind subsidies, the real wages paid to urban workers were not as low as suggested by the evolution of the nominal wages. Urban wage rates might have declined sharply if the restriction on rural–urban migration had been removed (Rawski 1979).

30. Even with all these price distortions facilitating heavy-industry development in China, the period required for a heavy-industry project to earn back the capital investment was, on average, about four to five times longer than the period required for a light-industry project. Therefore, a profit-maximizing private owner would have higher incentives to invest in a light-industry project. See Li (1983).

31. Under the new democracy policy adopted by the Chinese Communist Party in the late 1940s, private enterprises were supposed to coexist with state-owned enterprises for an extended period after the Revolution. The enterprises, however, were nationalized after 1952, when the government adopted a development strategy oriented toward heavy industry. The attempt to secure profits for heavy-industry projects was the motivation for the government's change in position toward private enterprises.

32. The government could use subsidies instead of distorting the price signals as a means of facilitating the development of capital-intensive heavy industry in a capital-scarce economy. It can be shown theoretically that the subsidy policy is more efficient economically than the policy of price distortion. However, with a subsidy policy, heavy

industry would incur a huge explicit loss and the government would have to tax other sectors heavily to subsidize the loss. In such a situation, the government would find it difficult to defend its position of accelerating the development of heavy industry. Moreover, the government in a developing economy may not be able to collect large amounts of taxes. This may explain why governments, not only in socialist economies but also in capitalist economies, use price distortions instead of subsidies to facilitate the development of priority sectors.

33. Many authors who have written about China and other socialist countries presume that the distorted policy environment and the administrative controls were shaped by socialist doctrines. The socialist ideology might have played a role in the formation of these policies, but there was also an economic rationale. These policies facilitated the implementation of a development strategy oriented toward heavy industry in a capital-scarce economy. This explains why nonsocialist developing economies such as India had a similar policy environment and administrative controls when they adopted the same development strategy under similar economic conditions.

34. The "principal–agent" problem arises when one party, the principal (in this case the central government) expects its agent (in this case the SOEs) to perform specific duties that may or may not be in their mutual interest. In such case the nature of the incentives system in place is a determining factor, because the principal faces information and risk asymmetry with regard to whether the agent will effectively perform as expected.

35. Lin, Cai, and Li 1998, p. 424.

36. Broad (1992) argues that the proponents of the project had to work against the constraints of the "Nitze Criterion," a rule of thumb devised by the American arms expert Paul Nitze that held that before the United States invested in a strategic defense system, it had to be sure that the system would be cheaper than the extra weapons it would take for the Soviets to overwhelm it. Broad also comments that the proposed program was "most dangerous" because the Soviets were terrified by it.

37. See Sachs 1993, p. 43.

38. Balcerowicz 1995.

39. Ibid., p. 92.

40. Sachs 1993; Aslund 1995, p. 74.

41. Ibid., pp. 75–76.

42. Ibid., p. 75.

43. See Blanchard et al. 1991.

44. Freeland 2000.

45. Blanchard et al. 1993, p. 5.

46. Blanchard et al. 1991.

47. See Lin and Tan 1999; Lin and Li 2008.

48. World Bank 2002.

49. Galbraith 2002.

50. Easterly 2001.

51. Lin 2009b.

52. Perkins 1988.

53. Lin, Cai, and Li 1996, p. 203.

54. Ibid., pp. 212–213.

55. Xiaoping 1980.

56. Lin, Cai, and Li 2003.

57. See Naughton 1995; Lau, Qian, and Roland 2000; Lin, Cai, and Li 2003.

58. See Lin 1997.

59. See Mrak, Rojec, and Silva-Jáuregui 2004.

60. IMF and Republic of Slovenia 2001, p. 12.

61. World Bank 2002. Admittedly the growth performance of a gradual approach to transition in Slovenia, Poland, Belarus, and Uzbekistan was not as remarkable as in China and Vietnam, partly due to the governments' lack of proactive facilitation of new competitive industries after transitions in those countries.

62. World Bank 2010c.

63. Maddison n.d.

64. Subramanian and Roy 2003.

65. The Gini coefficient, a measure of income inequality, increased from 0.31 in 1981 to 0.49 in 2007 (World Bank 2010c; Li, Luo, and Sicular 2011). Meanwhile, household consumption dropped from about 50 percent of GDP to about 35 percent, while investment in fixed assets increased from around 30 percent of GDP to more than 45 percent. Net exports, which started at roughly zero, rose as high as 8.8 percent of GDP in 2007.

66. For a detailed discussion of China's dual-track approach to transition and the remaining reform issues, see Lin 2011a.

Chapter Nine:
Fostering Structural Change

1. Smith 2010.

2. *Doi Moi* is the Vietnamese Communist Party's term for reform and renovation in the economy. This term was coined in 1986, when Vietnam began transitioning from its centrally planned command economy to a socialist-oriented market economy. *Doi Moi* favors gradualism and political stability over radical change, with economic restructuring introduced before privatization.

3. World Bank 2010c.

4. These numbers are based on "Atlas dollars," where the "Atlas" measurement smoothes out short-term changes in countries' exchange rates. In years when the currency has been fairly stable, the Atlas dollar GNI per capita is very close to a GNI per capita based on market exchange rates. More information is available at http://data.worldbank.org/about/country-classifications.

5. Daveri and Silva 2004.

6. Ibid.

7. Ibid. Jalava and Pohjola (2007) find similar results for a period that extends to the first half of the 2000s. It should be noted that Daveri and Silva find the linkages from Nokia to other parts of the economy to be "thin."

8. Maliranta (2010) finds that much of the acceleration in productivity growth in Finland was due to more churning through the entry and exit of firms. He does not quantify the impact of innovation policy on experimentation by firms.

9. See, for example, Piekkola 2007.

10. Honohan and Walsh 2002.

11. Romalis 2007.

12. Bailey, de Ruyter, and Kavanagh 2007.

13. Although economic activity in Ireland dropped sharply in 2008–10 because of the world financial crisis, the story of Ireland and its strong growth performance, which averaged 6 percent in 1995–2007, deserves serious consideration by policymakers facing income stagnation.

14. Akamatsu 1962.

15. Ozawa 2005, p. 9. See also Kojima 2000.

16. De Ferranti et al. (2002) used the phrase "play to one's strengths" with a particular emphasis on natural resource endowments in their World Bank regional report on Latin America, *From Natural Resources to the Knowledge Economy: Trade and Job Quality*.

17. Bhatnagar 2006.

18. Naik 2006a.

19. Naik 2006b.

20. Mendes, Teixeira, and Salvato 2009; Sá Barreto and Almeida 2009.

21. Lim 2011, p. 199.

22. See Lim 2011 for a more detailed discussion of the Korean experience.

23. Lim 2011.

24. German Federal Ministry of Economics and Technology 2010.

25. Nicholas 2010.

26. NSF n.d.

27. Budget figure ibid.

28. Holdren 2011.

29. Ibid.

30. Ibid.

31. Ibid.

32. Cameron 2010.

33. Such an active industrial policy is not unprecedented for a conservative U.K. leader. David Merlin-Jones notes that "contrary to popular belief [former Prime Minister Margaret] Thatcher and her ministers were not very laissez-faire in their industrial policy." Rather, Mrs. Thatcher's government had used grants, loans, and subsidies to "buy time" so that companies could restructure and become fit enough to face international competition. Mrs. Thatcher recognized that a "pragmatic involvement in industry should outweigh any political obedience to an entirely market driven economy when recession looms and jobs are at risk" (Merlin-Jones 2010, p. 1).

Chapter Ten:
A Recipe for Economic Prosperity

1. The origin of the term *dismal science*, coined by Scottish historian Thomas Carlyle, is itself puzzling. Carlyle criticized the economists' belief in supply and demand, which stood in sharp contrast to his idealized view of slavery, which he considered a model for society. He therefore disliked economics because it provided analytical support for equality and freedom for all people, black emancipation, and the ending of slavery (Carlyle 1849).

2. The most convincing empirical evidence was provided by Blanchard and Simon (2001).

3. Collier 2007.

4. Kuznets 1966.

5. World Bank 1993, 2005, 2007.

6. Rodrik 2009.

7. See Lin 2011a, 2011b; Lin and Monga 2011.

8. See H. Pack's thoughtful comments (2011) at the symposium on the GIF paper in *Development Policy Review.*

9. Chang 2008a.

10. Tollison and Congleton 1995; Robinson and Torvik 2005.

11. Lin 2009b.

12. Chu 2009.

REFERENCES

Abu-Bader, S., and A. Abu-Qarn. 2005. "Financial Development and Economic Growth: Time Series Evidence from Egypt." MPRA Paper 1113. University Library of Munich, Germany.

Acemoglu, D. 2007. "Modeling Inefficient Institutions." In *Advances in Economics and Econometrics, Theory and Applications: Ninth World Congress of the Econometric Society,* ed. R. Blundell, W. K. Newey, and T. Persson. London: Cambridge University Press.

Acemoglu, D., and J. A. Robinson. 2001. "A Theory of Political Transitions." *American Economic Review* 91: 938–963.

———. 2002. "Economic Backwardness in Political Perspective." NBER Working Paper 8831. National Bureau of Economic Research, Cambridge, MA.

———. 2005. *Economic Origins of Dictatorship and Democracy.* New York: Cambridge University Press.

Acemoglu, D., S. Johnson, and J. A. Robinson. 2001. "The Colonial Origins of Comparative Development: An Empirical Investigation." *American Economic Review* 91: 1369–1401.

———. 2002. "Reversal of Fortune: Geography and Institutions in the Making of the Modern World Income Distribution." *Quarterly Journal of Economics* 117: 1231–94.

———. 2005. "Institutions as the Fundamental Cause of Long-Run Growth." In *Handbook of Economic Growth,* Vol. 1, Part A, ed. P. Aghion and S. N. Durlauf, 385–472. Amsterdam: Elsevier Science (North-Holland).

Aghion, P. 2009. "Some Thoughts on Industrial Policy and Growth." Documents de Travail de l'OFCE 2009–09. Observatoire Français des Conjonctures Économiques, Paris.

Aghion, P., and P. Howitt. 1992. "A Model of Growth through Creative Destruction." *Econometrica* 60 (2): 323–351.

Agosin, M., C. Larraín, and N. Grau. 2009. "Industrial Policy in Chile: A Proposal." Working Paper 294. Departamento de Economia, Universidad de Chile, Santiago. http://www.econ.uchile.cl/uploads/publicacion/c00d45b0-c1e0-46af-9c1e-2730e6c54c67.pdf. Accessed February 7, 2012.

Aitken, B., G. Hanson, and A. Harrison. 1994. "Spillovers, Foreign Investment and Export Behavior." NBER Working Paper 4967. National Bureau of Economic Research, Cambridge, MA.

Akamatsu, K. 1962. "A Historical Pattern of Economic Growth in Developing Countries." *Journal of Developing Economies* 1 (1): 3–25.

Akerlof, G. 2009. *Animal Spirits: How Human Psychology Drives the Economy, and Why It Matters for Global Capitalism.* Princeton, NJ: Princeton University Press.

Alesina, A., and D. Rodrik. 1994. "Distributive Politics and Economic Growth." *Quarterly Journal of Economics* 109: 465–490.

Arndt, H. W. 1985. "The Origins of Structuralism." *World Development* 13 (2): 151–159.

Aryeetey, E., and A. K. Fosu. 2008. "Economic Growth in Ghana: 1960–2000." In *The Political Economy of Economic Growth in Africa, 1960–2000: Country Case Studies,* ed. B. Ndulu et al., 289–324. Cambridge, England: Cambridge University Press.

Aslund, A. 1994. "Lessons of the First Four Years of Systemic Change in Eastern Europe." *Journal of Comparative Economics* 19 (1): 22–38.

———. 1995. "The Case for Radical Reform." In *Economic Reform and Democracy,* ed. L. Diamond and M. Plattner, 74–85. Baltimore: Johns Hopkins University Press.

Ayyagari, M., A. Demirgüç-Kunt, and V. Maksimovic. 2008. "How Well Do Institutional Theories Explain Firms' Perceptions of Property Rights?" *Review of Financial Studies* 21 (4): 1833–1871.

Bailey, D., A. de Ruyter, and N. Kavanagh. 2007. "Lisbon, Sapir and Industrial Policy: Evaluating the 'Irish Success Story.'" *International Review of Applied Economics* 21 (3): 453–467.

Bairoch, P. 1993. *Economics and World History: Myths and Paradoxes.* Chicago: University of Chicago Press.

Balakrishnan, P. 2007. "Visible Hand: Public Policy and Economic Growth in the Nehru Era." Centre for Development Studies Working Paper 391. Centre for Development Studies, Trivandrum, Kerala, India.

Balcerowicz, L. 1995. "Understanding Postcommunist Transitions." In *Economic Reform and Democracy,* ed. L. Diamond and M. Plattner, 86–100. Baltimore: Johns Hopkins University Press.

Banco Central de Cuba. n.d.a. "Home." www.bc.gov.cu/English/home.asp. Accessed February 6, 2012.

———. n.d.b. "Monetary Policy." www.bc.gov.cu/English/home.asp. Accessed February 6, 2012.

Barro, R. J. 1997. *Determinants of Economic Growth: A Cross-Country Empirical Study* (*Lionel Robbins Lectures*). Cambridge, MA: MIT Press.

———. 2009. "Government Spending Is No Free Lunch." *Wall Street Journal,* January 22.

Barro, R. J., and X. Sala-i-Martin. 1992. "Convergence." *Journal of Political Economy* 100 (2): 223–251.

———. 1995. *Economic Growth.* Cambridge, MA: MIT Press.

———. 2003. *Economic Growth,* 2nd ed. Cambridge, MA: MIT Press.

Bates, R. H. 1981. *Markets and States in Africa: The Political Basis of Agricultural Policies.* Berkeley: University of California Press.

Baumol, W. 1986. "Productivity Growth, Convergence, and Welfare: What the Long-Run Data Show." *American Economic Review* 76 (December): 1072–1085.

———. 1994. "Multivariate Growth Patterns: Contagion and Common Forces as Possible Sources of Convergence." In *Convergence of Productivity, Cross-National Studies and Historical Evidence,* ed. W. Baumol, R. Nelson, and E. Wolf, 62–85. New York: Oxford University Press.

Becker, G. S. 1975. *Human Capital: A Theoretical and Empirical Analysis, with Special Reference to Education,* 2nd ed. New York: Columbia University Press.

———. 1992. "Education, Labor Force Quality, and the Economy: The Adam Smith Address." *Business Economics* 27 (1): 7–12.

Benavente, J. M. 2006. "Wine Production in Chile." In *Technology, Adaptation, and Exports: How Some Developing Countries Got It Right,* ed. V. Chandra, 225–242. Washington, DC: World Bank.

Bernanke, B. S. 2004. "The Great Moderation." Remarks at the meetings of the Eastern Economic Association, Washington, DC, February 20.

Besley, T., and S. Coate. 1998. "Sources of Inefficiency in a Representative Democracy: A Dynamic Analysis." *American Economic Review* 88: 139–156.

Bhagwati, J., and S. Chakravarty. 1969. "Contributions to Indian Economic Analysis: A Survey." *American Economic Review* 59 (4): 1–73.

Bhatnagar, S. 2006. "India's Software Industry." In *Technology, Adaptation, and Exports: How Some Developing Countries Got It Right,* ed. V. Chandra, 49–82. Washington, DC: World Bank.

Biney, A. 2008. "The Legacy of Kwame Nkrumah in Retrospect." *Journal of Pan African Studies* 2 (3): 129–159.

Birdsall, N., and A. de la Torre. 2001. *Washington Contentious: Economic Policies for Social Equity in Latin America.* Washington, DC: Carnegie Endowment for International Peace and Inter-American Dialogue.

Blanchard, O., and J. Simon. 2001. "The Long and Large Decline in U.S. Output Volatility." *Brookings Papers on Economic Activity* 32 (1): 135–164.

Blanchard, O., G. Dell'Ariccia, and P. Mauro. 2010. "Rethinking Macroeconomic Policy." IMF Staff Position Note. International Monetary Fund, Washington, DC.

Blanchard, O., R. Dornbusch, P. Krugman, R. Layard, and L. Summers. 1991. *Reform in Eastern Europe.* Cambridge, MA: MIT Press.

Blanchard, O., M. Boycko, M. Dabrowski, R. Dornbusch, R. Layard, and A. Shleifer. 1993. *Post-Communist Reform: Pain and Progress.* Cambridge, MA: MIT Press.

Blanchflower, D. 2009. "The Future of Monetary Policy." Open lecture at the University of Cardiff, Wales, March 24.

Blankenburg, S., J. G. Palma, and F. Tregenna. 2008. "Structuralism." In *The New Palgrave Dictionary of Economics,* 2nd ed., Vol. 8, ed. S. N. Durlauf and L. E. Blume, 69–74. London: Macmillan.

Blomström, M., R. E. Lipsey, and M. Zejan. 1994. "What Explains the Growth of Developing Countries?" In *Convergence of Productivity, Cross-National Studies and Historical Evidence,* ed. W. J. Baumol, R. R. Nelson, and E. N. Wolff, 243–261. New York: Oxford University Press.

Bold, B. 1982. *Famous Problems of Geometry and How to Solve Them.* New York: Dover.

Bourguignon, F. 2006. "Economic Growth: Heterogeneity and Firm-Level Disaggregation." PREM Lecture, World Bank, Washington, DC, May.

Brady, D. H., and M. Spence. 2009. "Leadership and Politics: A Perspective from the Growth Commission." *Oxford Review of Economic Policy* 25 (2): 205–218.

———. 2010. "The Ingredients of Growth." *Stanford Social Innovation Review* 8 (2): 34–39. http://www.ssireview.org/articles/entry/the_ingredients_of_growth. Accessed February 8, 2012.

Braudel, F. 1984. *The Perspective of the World: Civilization and Capitalism, Fifteenth–Eighteenth Century,* Vol. 3. New York: Harper and Row.

Broad, W. J. 1992. *Teller's War: The Top-Secret Story Behind the Star Wars Deception.* New York: Simon and Schuster.

Calderón, C., E. Moral-Benito, and L. Servén. 2009. "Is Infrastructure Capital Productive? A Dynamic Heterogeneous Approach." World Bank and Centro de Estudios Monetarios y Financieros, Washington, DC, and Madrid.

Cameron, D. 2010. "East End Tech City." Speech, East London, November 4. www.number10.gov.uk/news/east-end-tech-city-speech.

Cameron, R. 1993. *A Concise Economic History of the World,* 2nd ed. Oxford, England: Oxford University Press.

Caprio, G., and P. Honohan. 2001. *Finance for Growth: Policy Choices in a Volatile World.* New York: Oxford University Press.

Carlyle, T. 1849. "Occasional Discourse on the Negro Question." *Fraser's Magazine* (December): 670–679.

Carneiro, P., and J. J. Heckman. 2003. "Human Capital Policy." IZA Discussion Paper 821. Institute for the Study of Labor, Bonn, Germany.

Carroll, L. 1865 [1897]. *Alice's Adventures in Wonderland*. London: Macmillan.

Cass, D. 1965. "Optimum Growth in an Aggregative Model of Capital Accumulation." *Review of Economic Studies* 32 (July): 233–240.

Chala, Z. T. 2010. "Economic Significance of Selective Export Promotion on Poverty Reduction and Inter-Industry Growth of Ethiopia." Ph.D. dissertation, Virginia Polytechnic Institute and State University, Blacksburg, VA, June.

Chang, H.-J. 2002. *Kicking Away the Ladder: Development Strategy in Historical Perspective*. London: Anthem.

———. 2007. *Bad Samaritans—Rich Nations, Poor Policies, and the Threat to the Developing World*. London: Random House.

———, ed. 2008a. *Bad Samaritans: The Myth of Free Trade and the Secret History of Capitalism*. New York: Bloomsbury.

———. 2008b. "Lazy Japanese and Thieving Germans: Are Some Cultures Incapable of Economic Development?" In *Bad Samaritans: The Myth of Free Trade and the Secret History of Capitalism*, ed. H.-J. Chang, 167–208. New York: Bloomsbury.

———. 2008c. "State-Owned Enterprise Reform." UN Policy Note 4. United Nations Department of Economic and Social Affairs, New York.

Chenery, H. B. 1958. "The Role of Industrialization in Development Programmes." In *The Economics of Underdevelopment*, ed. A. N. Agarwala and S. P. Singh, 450–471. Bombay: Oxford University Press.

———. 1960. "Patterns of Industrial Growth." *American Economic Review* 50: 624–654.

Chenery, H. B., and M. Bruno, 1962. "Development Alternatives in an Open Economy: The Case of Israel." *Economic Journal* 72: 79–103.

Cheng, C.-Y. 1982. *China's Economic Development: Growth and Structural Change*. Boulder, CO: Westview.

Chu, J. 2009. "Rwanda Rising: A New Model of Economic Development." *Fast Company Magazine* 134 (April): 80–91.

Chuhan-Pole, P., and M. Angwafo, eds. 2011. *Yes Africa Can: Success Stories from a Dynamic Continent*. Washington, DC: World Bank.

CIA (Central Intelligence Agency). n.d. "Burundi." In *The World Factbook*. Washington, DC. https://www.cia.gov/library/publications/the-world-factbook/geos/by.html. Accessed February 8, 2012.

Cipolla, C. M. 1980. *Before the Industrial Revolution: European Society and Economy, 1000–1700*, 2nd ed. New York: Norton.

Clark, G. 2007. *A Farewell to Alms: A Brief Economic History of the World*. Princeton, NJ: Princeton University Press.

Clift, J. 2010. "IMF Explores Contours of Future Macroeconomic Policy." *IMF Survey Magazine*, February 12.

Coase, R. H. 1937. "The Nature of the Firm." *Economica* 4 (16): 386–405.

————. 1960. "The Problem of Social Cost." *Journal of Law and Economics* 3 (1): 1–44.

Collier, P. 2007. *The Bottom Billion: Why the Poorest Countries Are Failing and What Can Be Done about It*. New York: Oxford University Press.

————. 2010. "Why Natural Resources Should Help End Poverty." *New Statesman,* June 28.

Commission of the European Communities. 2005. "Implementing the Community Lisbon Programme: A Policy Framework to Strengthen EU Manufacturing—Towards a More Integrated Approach for Industrial Policy." Communication from the Commission. Brussels, Belgium, October 5.

Commission on Growth and Development. 2008. *The Growth Report: Strategies for Sustained Growth and Inclusive Development*. Washington, DC: World Bank.

————. n.d. "About Us." www.growthcommission.org/index.php?option=com_content&task=view&id=13&Itemid=58. Accessed February 6, 2012.

Convention People's Party. 1962. "Program for Work and Happiness." Central Committee of the Party, Accra, Ghana.

Cooper, F. 2002. *Africa since 1940: The Past of the Present*. Cambridge, England: Cambridge University Press.

Daveri, F., and O. Silva. 2004. "Not Only Nokia: What Finland Tells Us about *New Economy* Growth." *Economic Policy* (April): 117–163.

Deaton, A. 2009. "Instruments of Development: Randomization in the Tropics, and the Search for the Elusive Keys to Economic Development." Working Paper 1128, Woodrow Wilson School of Public and International Affairs, Center for Health and Wellbeing, Princeton University, Princeton, NJ.

de Ferranti, D., G. E. Perry, D. Lederman, and W. F. Maloney. 2002. *From Natural Resources to the Knowledge Economy: Trade and Job Quality*. Washington, DC: World Bank.

de Grauwe, P. 2008. "Cherished Myths Fall Victim to Economic Reality." *Financial Times,* July 22.

DeLong, J. B. 1997. "Slouching Towards Utopia? The Economic History of the Twentieth Century." http://econ161.berkeley.edu/tceh/Slouch_title.html.

Demery, L. 1994. "Côte d'Ivoire: Fettered Adjustment." In *Adjustment in Africa: Lessons from Country Case Studies,* ed. I. Husain and R. Faruqee, 72–152. Washington, DC: World Bank.

Devarajan, S., W. Easterly, and H. Pack. 2002. "Low Investment Is Not the Constraint on African Development." Working Paper 13. Center for Global Development, Washington, DC.

Diamond, L., and M. F. Plattner. 1995. "Introduction." In *Economic Reform and Democracy,* ed. L. Diamond and M. F. Plattner, i–xxii. Baltimore: Johns Hopkins University Press.

Di Maio, M. 2008. "Industrial Policies in Developing Countries: History and Perspectives." Working Paper 48-2008. Department of Finance and Economic Sciences, Macerata University, Macerata, Italy.

Dinh, H. T., V. Palmade, V. Chandra, and F. Cossar. 2012. *Light Manufacturing in Africa: Targeted Policies to Enhance Private Investment and Create Jobs*. Washington, DC: World Bank.

Djik, M. V., and A. Szirmail. 2006. "Industrial Policy and Technology Diffusion: Evidence from Paper Making Machinery in Indonesia." *World Development* 34 (12): 2137–2152.

Du, L., A. Harrison, and G. Jefferson. 2011. "Do Institutions Matter for FDI Spillovers? The Implications of China's 'Special Characteristics.'" Policy Research Working Paper 5757. World Bank, Washington, DC.

Duflo, E. 2004. "Scaling Up and Evaluation." In *Annual World Bank Conference on Development Economics 2004,* ed. F. Bourguignon and B. Pleskovic, 341–349. Washington, DC: World Bank.

Dulfano, I. 2003. "Intel and Costa Rica: A Model for Global Expansion, Economic Development, and Sustainability." *Global Business Languages* 8 (3).

Dutt, A. K., and J. Ros. 2003. "Development Economics and Political Economy." In *Development Economics and Structuralist Macroeconomics: Essays in Honor of Lance Taylor,* ed. A.K. Dutt and J. Ros, 3–28. Northhampton, MA: Edward Elgar.

Easterly, W. R. 2001. "The Lost Decades: Explaining Developing Countries' Stagnation in Spite of Policy Reform, 1980–1998." *Journal of Economic Growth* 6 (2): 135–157.

Easterly, W., and S. Fischer. 1995. "The Soviet Economic Decline." *World Bank Economic Review* 9 (3): 341–371.

The Economist. 2008. "Connectivity and Commitment Pay Dividends in African Transport." October 16.

Eichengreen, B., M. Mussa, G. Dell'Ariccia, E. Detragiache, G. M. Milesi-Ferretti, and A. Tweedie. 1999. *Liberalizing Capital Movements: Some Analytical Issues*. Washington, DC: International Monetary Fund.

Engerman, S. L., and K. L. Sokoloff. 1997. "Factor Endowments, Institutions, and Differential Paths of Growth among New World Economies: A View from Economic Historians of the United States." In *How Latin America Fell Behind,* ed. S. Haber, 260–306. Stanford, CA: Stanford University Press.

European Commission. 1994. *An Industrial Competitiveness Policy for the European Union*. Communication from the Commission to the Council, the European Parliament, the Economic and Social Committee, and the Committee of the Regions. Brussels, Belgium. COM (94) 319 final, September 14.

FIAS (Foreign Investment Advisory Service). 2008. *Special Economic Zones: Perfor-*

mance, Lessons Learned, and Implications for Zone Development. Washington, DC: World Bank.

Fischer, S. 2001. "The Challenge of Globalization in Africa." Remarks at the France–Africa Summit, Yaoundé, January 19. http://www.iie.com/fischer/pdf/Fischer077.pdf. Accessed February 7, 2012.

———. 2003. "Globalization and Its Challenges." Ely Lecture presented at the American Economic Association meetings, Washington, DC, January 3. http://www.iie.com/fischer/pdf/fischer011903.pdf. Accessed February 7, 2012.

Francesco, G., and M. Pagano. 1991. "Can Severe Fiscal Contractions Be Expansionary? Tales of Two Small European Countries." In *NBER Macroeconomics Annual 1990*, ed. O. J. Blanchard and S. Fischer, 75–122. Cambridge, MA: MIT Press.

Freeland, C. 2000. *Sale of the Century: Russia's Wild Ride from Communism to Capitalism.* New York: Crown Business.

Freeman, C., M. Kumhof, D. Laxton, and J. Lee. 2009. "The Case for a Global Fiscal Stimulus." IMF Position Note. International Monetary Fund, Washington, DC.

Furtado, C. 1964. *Development and Underdevelopment.* Los Angeles: University of California Press.

———. 1970. *Economic Development of Latin America.* London: Cambridge University Press.

G-8 (Group of Eight). 2005. "The Gleneagles Communiqué." 31st G-8 Summit, Gleneagles Hotel, Auchterarder, Scotland, July 8.

Galbraith, J. 2002. "Shock without Therapy." *American Prospect,* August 25. http://prospect.org/cs/articles?article=shock_without_therapy. Accessed February 23, 2012.

Gavin, M., and R. Perotti. 1997. "Fiscal Policy in Latin America." In *NBER Macroeconomics Annual 1997,* Vol. 12, ed. B. S. Bernanke and J. Rotemberg, 11–72. Cambridge, MA: MIT Press.

Gelb, A., V. Ramachandran, M. K. Shah, and G. Turner. 2007. "What Matters to African Firms? The Relevance of Perception Data." Policy Research Working Paper 4446. World Bank, Washington, DC.

German Federal Ministry of Economics and Technology. 2010. *In Focus: Germany as a Competitive Industrial Nation.* Berlin.

Gerschenkron, A. 1962. *Economic Backwardness in Historical Perspective: A Book of Essays.* Cambridge, MA: Belknap Press of Harvard University Press.

Gibson, B., 2003. "An Essay on Late Structuralism." In *Development Economics and Structuralist Macroeconomics: Essays in Honor of Lance Taylor,* ed. A. K. Dutt and J. Ros, 52–76. Northampton, MA: Edward Elgar.

Glaeser, E., and A. Shleifer. 2002. "Legal Origins." *Quarterly Journal of Economics* 117 (November): 1193–1229.

Glassburner, B. 2007. *The Economy of Indonesia: Selected Readings.* Jakarta: Equinox.

Gordon, R., and W. Li. 2005. "Tax Structure in Developing Countries: Many Puzzles and a Possible Explanation." NBER Working Paper 11267. National Bureau of Economic Research, Cambridge, MA.

Government of Ghana. 1959. *The Second Development Plan, 1959–64*. Accra: Government Printer.

Greif, A. 1993. "Contract Enforceability and Economic Institutions in Early Trade: The Maghribi Traders' Coalition." *American Economic Review* 83 (3): 525–548.

Grossman, G. M., and E. Helpman. 1994. "Protection for Sale." *American Economic Review* 84 (4): 833–850.

———. 1996. "Electoral Competition and Special Interest Politics." *Review of Economic Studies* 63 (2): 265–286.

———. 2001. *Special Interest Politics*. Cambridge, MA: MIT Press.

Haggard, S., and R. R. Kaufman. 1995. "The Challenges of Consolidation." In *Economic Reform and Democracy*, ed. L. Diamond and M. F. Plattner, 1–12. Baltimore: Johns Hopkins University Press.

Harrison, A., and A. Rodríguez-Clare. 2010. "Trade, Foreign Investment, and Industrial Policy for Developing Countries." In *Handbook of Development Economics*, Vol. 5, ed. D. Rodrik, 4039–4213. Amsterdam: North-Holland.

Hausmann, R., and B. Klinger. 2006. "Structural Transformation and Patterns of Comparative Advantage in the Product Space." CID Working Paper 128. Kennedy School, Center for International Development, Harvard University, Cambridge, MA.

———. 2008. "Growth Diagnostics in Peru." CID Working Paper 181. Kennedy School, Center for International Development, Harvard University, Cambridge, MA.

Hausmann, R., D. Rodrik, and A. Velasco. 2006. "Getting the Diagnostics Right." *Finance and Development* 43 (1): 12–15.

———. 2008. "Growth Diagnostics." In *The Washington Consensus Reconsidered: Towards a New Global Governance*, ed. N. Serra and J. E. Stiglitz, 324–354. New York: Oxford University Press.

Heckman, J. J. 2006. "Skill Formation and the Economics of Investing in Disadvantaged Children." *Science* 312 (5782): 1900–1902.

Heckscher, E. F., and B. Ohlin. 1991. *Heckscher–Ohlin Trade Theory*. Cambridge, MA: MIT Press.

Helpman, E. 2004. *The Mystery of Economic Growth*. Cambridge, MA: Harvard University Press.

Henckel, T., and W. McKibbin. 2010. *The Economics of Infrastructure in a Globalized World: Issues, Lessons, and Future Challenges*. Washington, DC: Brookings Institution.

Her Majesty's Government. 2009. "Going for Growth: Our Future Prosperity." Department for Business Innovation and Skills, London.

Hesse, M. 2008. "Truth: Can You Handle It?" *Washington Post,* April 27.

Hidalgo, C. A., B. Klinger, A.-L. Barabási, and R. Hausmann. 2007. "The Product Space Conditions the Development of Nations." *Science* 317 (5837): 482–487.

Hirschman, A. O. 1958. *The Strategy of Economic Development.* New Haven, CT: Yale University Press.

———. 1982. "The Rise and Decline of Development Economics." In *The Theory and Experience of Economic Development,* ed. M. Gersovitz and W. A. Lewis, 372–390. London: Allen and Unwin.

Hoeffler, A. 1999. "The Augmented Solow Model and the African Growth Debate." Centre for the Study of African Economies, Oxford University, Oxford, England.

Holdren, J. 2011. "America COMPETES Act Keeps America's Leadership on Target." White House press release, January 6.

Honohan, P., and B. Walsh. 2002. "Catching Up with the Leaders: The Irish Hare." *Brookings Papers on Economic Activity* 1: 1–57.

Huntington, S. P. 1992. *The Third Wave: Democratization in the Late Twentieth Century.* Norman: University of Oklahoma Press.

ILO. n.d. "Sectors Covered." International Labour Organization, Geneva, Switzerland. Available at http://www.ilo.org/sector/sectors-covered/lang—en/index.htm. Accessed February 7, 2012.

Ilzetzki, E., and C. A. Vegh. 2008. "Procyclical Fiscal Policy: Truth or Fiction?" NBER Working Paper 14191. National Bureau of Economic Research, Cambridge, MA.

IMF (International Monetary Fund). 2001. *Guidelines for Foreign Exchange Reserves Management.* Washington, DC.

IMF and Republic of Slovenia. 2001. "Article IV, Report 01/76." Washington, DC, May.

———. 2011. *Global Financial Stability Report.* Washington, DC.

Irwin, D. A. 1996. *Against the Tide: An Intellectual History of Free Trade.* Princeton, NJ: Princeton University Press.

Isaacson, W. 2007. *Einstein: His Life and Universe.* New York: Simon and Schuster.

Ito, H. 1980. "Financial Repression." Portland State University, Oregon.

Jamieson, I. 1980. *Capitalism and Culture: A Comparative Analysis of British and American Manufacturing Organizations.* London: Gower.

Jäntti, M., and J. Vartiainen. 2009. "The Finnish Development State and Its Growth Regime." Research Paper 2009/35. United Nations University, Helsinki.

Jalava, J., and M. Pohjola. 2007. "ICT as a Source of Output and Productivity Growth in Finland." Telecommunications Policy 31 (8–9): 463–472.

Jones, B. F., and B. A. Olken. 2005. "Do Leaders Matter? National Leadership and Growth since World War II." *Quarterly Journal of Economics* 120 (3): 835–864.

Jones, C. I. 1998. *Introduction to Economic Growth.* New York: W. W. Norton.

Jones, C. I., and P. M. Romer. 2009. "The New Kaldor Facts: Ideas, Institutions, Population, and Human Capital." NBER Working Paper 15094. National Bureau of Economic Research, Cambridge, MA.

Ju, J., J. Y. Lin, and Y. Wang. 2009. "Endowment Structures, Industrial Dynamics, and Economic Growth." Policy Research Working Paper 5055. World Bank, Washington, DC.

Juppé, A., and M. Rocard. 2009. *Investir por l'avenir: Priorités stratégiques d'investissement et emprunt national.* Report by the Juppé-Rocard Commission on the Grand Emprut, Paris.

Justman, M., and B. Gurion. 1991. "Structuralist Perspective on the Role of Technology in Economic Growth and Development." *World Development* 19 (9): 1167–1183.

Kaldor, N. 1961. "Capital Accumulation and Economic Growth." In *The Theory of Capital,* ed. F. A. Lutz and D. C. Hague, 177–222. New York: St. Martin's Press.

Kanbur, R. 2009. "The Crisis, Economic Development Thinking, and Protecting the Poor." Presentation to the World Bank's Executive Board, Washington, DC, July 7.

Katz, J. 2006. "Salmon Farming in Chile." In *Technology, Adaptation, and Exports: How Some Developing Countries Got It Right,* ed. V. Chandra, 193–224. Washington, DC: World Bank.

Kim, Y. H. 1988. *Higashi ajia kogyoka to sekai shihonshugi* (Industrialisation of East Asia and the world capitalism). Tokyo: Toyo Keizai Shimpo-sha.

Kojima, K. 2000. "The 'Flying Geese' Model of Asian Economic Development: Origin, Theoretical Extensions, and Regional Policy Implications." *Journal of Asian Economies* 11: 375–401.

Koopmans, T. C. 1965. "On the Concept of Optimal Economic Growth." In *Study Week on the Econometric Approach to Development Planning,* ed. Pontificia Accademia Scientiarum, 225–287. Amsterdam: North-Holland.

Kosonen, K. 1992. "Saving and Economic Growth from a Nordic Perspective." In *Social Corporatism,* ed. J. Pekkarinen et al., 178–209. Oxford, England: Clarendon.

Kroeber, A. L., and C. Kluckhohn. 1952. "Culture: A Critical Review of Concepts and Definitions." *Papers of the Peabody Museum of American Archeology and Ethnology* 47 (1): 41–79.

Krueger, A. O. 1974. "The Political Economy of Rent-Seeking Society." *American Economic Review* 64 (3): 291–303.

———. 1992. *Economic Policy Reform in Developing Countries.* Cambridge, MA: Blackwell.

———. 1997. "Trade Policy and Economic Development: How We Learn." *American Economic Review* 87 (1): 1–22.

Krugman, P. 1979. "A Model of Innovation, Technology Transfer, and the World Distribution of Income." *Journal of Political Economy* 87 (2): 253–266.

———. 1991. "Increasing Returns and Economic Geography." *Journal of Political Economy* 99 (3): 483–499.

———. 1993. "Protection in Developing Countries." In *Policymaking in the Open Economy: Concepts and Case Studies in Economic Performance,* ed. R. Dornbusch, 127–148. New York: Oxford University Press.

———. 1996. "Ricardo's Difficult Idea." Paper presented at the Manchester conference on free trade. http://web.mit.edu/krugman/www/ricardo.htm. Accessed February 6, 2012.

———. 2009. *The Return of Depression Economics and the Crisis of 2008.* New York: W. W. Norton.

Kuznets, S. 1966. *Modern Economic Growth: Rate, Structure, and Spread.* New Haven, CT: Yale University Press.

———. 1971. "Modern Economic Growth: Findings and Reflections." Nobel Prize Lecture presented in Stockholm, Sweden, December 11.

Lal, D. 1983. *The Poverty of Development Economics.* Cambridge, MA, and London: Harvard University Press and IEA Hobart.

Landes, D. S. 1969. *The Unbound Prometheus: Technological Change and Industrial Development in Western Europe from 1750 to the Present.* London: Cambridge University Press.

———. 1998. *The Wealth and Poverty of Nations: Why Some Are So Rich and Some So Poor.* New York: Norton.

Larraín, F., L. F. López-Calva, and A. Rodríguez-Clare. 1996. "Intel: A Case Study of Foreign Direct Investment in Central America." In *Economic Development in Central America,* Vol. 1: *Growth and Internationalization,* ed. F. Larraín, Ch. 6. Cambridge, MA: Harvard University Press.

Lau, L. J., Y. Qian, and G. Roland. 2000. "Reforms without Losers: An Interpretation of China's Dual-Track Approach to Transition." *Journal of Political Economy* 108 (1): 120–143.

Leechor, C. 1994. "Ghana: Frontrunner in Adjustment." In *Adjustment in Africa: Lessons from Country Case Studies,* ed. I. Husain and R. Faruqee, 153–192.Washington, DC: World Bank.

Leibenstein, H. 1957. *Economic Backwardness and Economic Growth: Studies in the Theory of Economic Development.* New York: John Wiley and Sons.

Leke, A., S. Lund, C. Roxburgh, and A. van Wamelen. 2010. "What Is Driving Africa's Growth?" *McKinsey Quarterly* (June).

Lewis, W. A. 1954. "Economic Development with Unlimited Supplies of Labor." *Manchester School* 22 (May): 139–191.

Li, J. W., and Y. J. Zheng, eds. 1989. *Technological Progress and the Choice of Industrial Structure.* Beijing: Kexue Chubanshe.

Li, S., C. Luo, and T. Sicular. 2011. "Overview: Income Inequality and Poverty in China, 2002–2007." CIBC Centre for Human Capital and Productivity Working Paper 2011/10, University of Western Ontario, London, Canada.

Li, Y. 1983. *Zhongguo gongye bumen jiegou* (The structure of the Chinese industry). Beijing: China People's University Press.

Lim, W. 2011. "Joint Discovery and Upgrading of Comparative Advantage: Lessons from Korea's Development Experience." In *Postcrisis Growth and Development: A Development Agenda for the G20,* ed. S. Fardoust, Y. Kim, and C. Sepúlveda, 173–226. Washington, DC: World Bank.

Lin, J. Y. 1989. "An Economic Theory of Institutional Change: Induced and Imposed Change." *Cato Journal* 9 (Spring–Summer): 1–32.

———. 1990. "Collectivization and China's Agricultural Crisis in 1959–1961." *Journal of Political Economy* 98 (December): 1228–1252.

———. 1992. "Rural Reforms and Agricultural Growth in China." *American Economic Review* 82 (1): 34–51.

———. 1995. "The Needham Puzzle: Why the Industrial Revolution Did Not Originate in China." *Economic Development and Cultural Change* 41 (2): 269–92.

———. 1997. "Reform and Development: Lessons from Transitional Economies in East Asia." Paper prepared for the Conference Stabilization, Growth, and Transition: Symposium in Memory of Michael Bruno, Jerusalem, November 22–24.

———. 2003. "Development Strategy, Viability, and Economic Convergence." *Economic Development and Cultural Change* 53 (2): 277–308.

———. 2009a. "Beyond Keynesianism: The Necessity of a Globally Coordinated Solution." *Harvard International Review* 31 (2): 14–17.

———. 2009b. *Economic Development and Transition: Thought, Strategy, and Viability.* Cambridge, England: Cambridge University Press.

———. 2011a. *Demystifying the Chinese Economy.* Cambridge, UK: Cambridge University Press.

———. 2011b. *New Structural Economics and Policy.* Washington, DC: World Bank.

———. 2011c. "New Structural Economics: A Framework for Rethinking Economic Development." *World Bank Research Observer* 26 (2): 193–221.

———. 2012. *Benti and Changwu: Dialogues on Methodology in Economics.* New York: Cengage.

Lin, J. Y., and H.-J. Chang. 2009. "DPR Debate: Should Industrial Policy in Developing Countries Conform to Comparative Advantage or Defy It?" *Development Policy Review* 27 (5): 483–502.

Lin, J. Y., and D. Doemeland. 2012. "Beyond Keynesianism: Global Infrastructure Investments in Times of Crisis." Policy Research Working Paper 5940. World Bank, Washington, DC.

Lin, J. Y., and Z. Li. 2008. "Policy Burden, Privatization, and Soft Budget Constraint." *Journal of Comparative Economics* 36: 90–102.

———. 2009. "Development Strategy, Viability, and Economic Distortions in Developing Countries." Policy Research Working Paper 4906. World Bank, Washington DC.

Lin, J. Y., and C. Monga. 2011. "Growth Identification and Facilitation: The Role of the State in the Dynamics of Structural Change." *Development Policy Review* 29 (3): 264–290.

Lin, J. Y., and R. Ren. 2007. "East Asian Miracle Debate Revisited." *Economic Research Journal* 42 (8): 4–12.

Lin, J. Y., and G. Tan. 1999. "Policy Burdens, Accountability, and the Soft Budget Constraint." *American Economic Review, Papers and Proceedings* 89 (2): 426–431.

Lin, J. Y., F. Cai, and Z. Li. 1996. "The Lessons of China's Transition to a Market Economy." *Cato Journal* 16 (2): 201–231.

———. 1998. "Competition, Policy Burdens, and State-Owned Enterprise Reform." *American Economic Review* 88 (2): 422–427.

———. 2003. *China's Miracle: Development Strategy and Economic Reform*, rev. ed. Hong Kong: Chinese University Press.

Lin, J. Y., X. Sun, and Y. Jiang. 2009. "Towards a Theory of Optimal Financial Structure." Policy Research Working Paper 5038. World Bank, Washington, DC.

List, F. 1841 [1930]. *Das Nationale System der Politischen Ökonomie* (The national system of political economy), Vol. 6: *Schriften, Reden, Briefe*, ed. A. Sommer. Berlin: Reinmar Hobbing.

Lucas, R. E. 1988. "On the Mechanics of Economic Development." *Journal of Monetary Economics* 22 (1): 3–42.

———. 1990. "Why Doesn't Capital Flow from Rich to Poor Countries?" *American Economic Review* 80 (2): 92–96.

———. 2002. *Lectures on Economic Growth*. Cambridge, MA: Harvard University Press.

Mabro, R. 1974. *The Egyptian Economy, 1952–1972*. Oxford, England: Clarendon.

Mabro, R., and S. Radwan. 1976. *The Industrialization of Egypt, 1939–1973: Policy and Performance*. Oxford, UK: Clarendon.

Maddison, A. 2001. *The World Economy: A Millennial Perspective*. Paris: Organisation for Economic Co-operation and Development.

———. 2006. *The World Economy*. Paris: Organisation for Economic Co-operation and Development.

———. n.d. "Historical Statistics of the World Economy: 1–2008 AD." www.ggdc.net/ maddison/Historical_Statistics/horizontal-file_02-2010.xls. Accessed February 23, 2012.

Maliranta, M. 2010. "Finland's Path to the Global Productivity Frontier through Creative Destruction." *International Productivity Monitor* 20 (Fall): 68–84.

Mankiw, N. G. 1995. "The Growth of Nations." *Brookings Papers on Economic Activity* 1: 275–326.

———. 2006. "The Macroeconomist as Scientist and Engineer." *Journal of Economic Perspectives* 20 (4): 29–46.

Marshall, A. 1890. *Principles of Economics.* London: Macmillan.

Mathews, J. A. 2006. "Electronics in Taiwan: A Case of Technological Leaning." In *Technology, Adaptation, and Exports: How Some Developing Countries Got It Right,* ed. V. Chandra, 83–126. Washington, DC: World Bank.

McKinnon, R. I. 1973. *Money and Capital in Economic Development.* Washington, DC: Brookings Institution.

Melese, A. 2007. "Triple Role of the Dutch in the Growth of the Cut-Flower Industry in Ethiopia." Unpublished thesis, The Hague, the Netherlands.

Mendes, S. M., E. C. Teixeira, and M. A. Salvato. 2009. "Investimentos em infra-estrutura e produtividade total dos fatores na agricultura Brasileira: 1985–2004." *Revista Brasileira de Economia* 63 (2): 91–102.

Menon, R. 2010. "Markets and Government: Striking a Balance in Singapore." Opening address at the Singapore Economic Policy Forum, Singapore, October 22.

Merlin-Jones, D. 2010. "Time for Turning? Why the Conservatives Need to Rethink Their Industrial Policy (If They Have One)." *Civitas* 7 (January): 1–11.

MIGA (Multilateral Investment Guarantee Agency). 2006. *The Impact of Intel in Costa Rica Investing: Nine Years after the Decision to Invest.* Washington, DC: World Bank Group.

Mill, J. S. 1848. *Principles of Political Economy.* London: Longmans, Green.

Mistry, P. S., and N. Treebhoohun. 2009. *The Export of Tradeable Services in Mauritius: A Commonwealth Case Study in Economic Transformation.* London: Commonwealth Secretariat.

Mkapa, B. 2008. "Leadership for Growth, Development, and Poverty Reduction: An African Viewpoint and Experience." Working Paper 8. Commission on Growth and Development, Washington, DC.

Mokyr, J. 1990. *The Lever of Riches: Technological Creativity and Economic Progress.* New York: Oxford University Press.

Monga, C. 1996. *The Anthropology of Anger: Civil Society and Democracy in Africa.* Boulder, CO: Lynne Rienner.

———. 1997. *L'argent des autres—Banques et petites entreprises en Afrique: Le cas du Cameroun.* Paris: LDGJ-Montchretien.

———. 2006. "Commodities, Mercedes-Benz, and Structural Adjustment: An Episode in West African Economic History." In *Themes in West Africa's History,* ed. E. Akye-ampong, 227–264. Oxford, England: James Currey.

Montiel, P., and L. Servén. 2008. "Real Exchange Rates, Saving, and Growth: Is There a Link?" Background paper for *The Growth Report: Strategies for Sustained Growth and Inclusive Development.* Washington, DC: World Bank.

Mottaleb, K. A., and T. Sonobe. 2011. "An Inquiry into the Rapid Growth of the Garment Industry in Bangladesh." *Economic Development and Cultural Change* 60 (1): 67–89.

Mrak, M., M. Rojec, and C. Silva-Jáuregui. 2004. "Slovenia: From Yugoslavia to the European Union." *Transition Studies Review* 11 (3): 269–272.

Murphy, K. M., A. Shleifer, and R. W. Vishny. 1989. "Industrialization and Big Push." *Journal of Political Economy* 97 (5): 1003–1026.

Myrdal, G. 1957. *Economic Theory and Under-developed Regions.* London: Gerald Duckworth.

———. 1968. *Asian Drama: An Inquiry into the Poverty of Nations.* New York: Twentieth Century Fund.

Naik, G. 2006a. "Bridging the Knowledge Gap in Competitive Agriculture: Grapes in India." In *Technology, Adaptation, and Exports: How Some Developing Countries Got It Right,* ed. V. Chandra, 243–274. Washington, DC: World Bank.

———. 2006b. "Closing the Yield Gap: Maize in India." In *Technology, Adaptation, and Exports: How Some Developing Countries Got It Right,* ed. V. Chandra, 275–300. Washington, DC: World Bank.

Naím, M. 2000. "Washington Consensus or Confusion?" *Foreign Policy* 118 (Spring): 86–103.

Naughton, B. 1995. *Growing Out of Plan: Chinese Economic Reform 1978–1993.* Cambridge, England: Cambridge University Press.

Nelson, R. R., and S. G. Winter, 1982. *An Evolutionary Theory of Economic Change.* Cambridge, MA, Harvard University Press.

Nicholas, T. 2010. "The Role of Independent Invention in U.S. Technological Development, 1880–1930." *Journal of Economic History* 70 (1): 57–82.

Nkrumah, K. 1957. "Independence Day Speech." Accra, Ghana, March 6.

———. 1960. "The Sessional Address." Parliamentary Debates, Accra, Ghana, July 4.

Noland, M., and H. Pack. 2003. *Industrial Policy in an Era of Globalization: Lessons from Asia.* Washington, DC: Peterson Institute for International Economics.

North, D. 1981. *Structure and Change in Economic History.* New York: W. W. Norton.

———. 1990. *Institutions, Institutional Change, and Economic Performance.* Cambridge, England: Cambridge University Press.

———. 1994. "Economic Performance through Time." *American Economic Review* 84 (3): 359–368.

Nurkse, R. 1953. *Problems of Capital Formation in Underdeveloped Countries.* New York: Oxford University Press.

O'Brian, T. M., and A. D. Rodriguez. 2004. "Improving Competitiveness and Market Access for Agricultural Exports through the Development and Application of Food Safety and Quality Standards: The Example of Peruvian Asparagus." Inter-American Institute for Cooperation on Agriculture, Agricultural Health and Food Safety Program, San José, Peru.

Ocampo, J. A., and L. Taylor, 1998. "Trade Liberalization in Developing Economies:

Modest Benefits but Problems with Productivity Growth, Macro Prices, and Income Distribution." *Economic Journal* 108: 1523–1546.

Ocampo, J. A., C. Rada, and L. Taylor. 2009. *Growth and Policy in Developing Countries: A Structuralist Approach.* New York: Columbia University Press.

OECD (Organisation for Economic Co-operation and Development). 2002. *Foreign Direct Investment for Development: Maximizing Benefits, Minimizing Costs.* Paris.

Olson, M. 1982. *The Decline and Fall of Nations: Economic Growth, Stagflation, and Social Rigidities.* New Haven, CT: Yale University Press.

O'Rourke, P. J. 1991. *Parliament of Whores: A Lone Humorist Attempts to Explain the Entire U.S. Government.* New York: Grove.

Osman-Gani, A. M. 2004. "Human Capital Development in Singapore: An Analysis of National Policy Perspectives." *Advances in Developing Human Resources* 6 (3): 276–287.

Ozawa, T. 2005. *Institutions, Industrial Upgrading, and Economic Performance in Japan—The Flying-Geese Paradigm of Catch-up Growth.* Northampton, MA: Edward Elgar.

Pack, H. 2011. "DPR Debate: Growth Identification and Facilitation." *Development Policy Review* 29 (3): 259–310.

Paulson, H. 2008. "Comprehensive Approach to Market Developments." Statement by Secretary of the Treasury Henry Paulson, Washington, DC, September 19.

Perkins, D. H. 1969. *Agricultural Development in China, 1368–1968.* Chicago: Aldine.

———. 1988. "Reforming China's Economic System." *Journal of Economic Literature* 26 (2): 601–645.

Persson, T., and G. Tabellini. 1994. "Is Inequality Harmful to Growth?" *American Economic Review* 38: 765–773.

Piekkola, H. 2007. "Public Funding of R&D and Growth: Firm-Level Evidence from Finland." *Economics of Innovation and New Technology* 16 (3): 195–210.

Pinkovskiy, M., and X. Sala⊠i⊠Martin. 2009. "Parametric Estimations of the World Distribution of Income." NBER Working Paper 15433. National Bureau of Economic Research, Cambridge, MA.

Pomeranz, K. 2000. *The Great Divergence: China, Europe, and the Making of the Modern World Economy.* Princeton, NJ: Princeton University Press.

Porter, M. E. 1990. *The Competitive Advantage of Nations.* New York: Free Press.

Portes, R. 1993. "From Central Planning to a Market Economy." In *Making Markets: Economic Transformation in Eastern Europe and the Post-Soviet States,* ed. S. Islam and M. Mandelbaum. New York: Council on Foreign Relations.

Prebisch, R. 1950. *The Economic Development of Latin America and Its Principal Problems.* New York: United Nations. Reprinted in *Economic Bulletin for Latin America* 7 (1): 1–22.

———. 1959. "Commercial Policy in Underdeveloped Countries." *American Economic Review* 49 (2): 251–273.

Prescott, E. 1999. "Interview with Edward Prescott." In *Conversations with Economists: Interpreting Macroeconomics,* ed. B. Snowdown and H. Vane, 258–269. Northampton, MA: Edward Elgar.

Pritchett, L. 1997. "Divergence, Big Time." *Journal of Economic Perspectives* 11 (3): 3–17.

———. 2001. "Where Has All the Education Gone?" *World Bank Economic Review* 15 (3): 367–391.

Pritchett, L. 2006. "The Quest Continues." *Finance and Development* 43 (1).

Radelet, S. 2010. *Emerging Africa: How 17 Countries Are Leading the Way.* Washington, DC: Center for Global Development.

Ravallion, M. 2009. "Should the Randomistas Rule?" *Economists' Voice* 6 (2): 1–5.

Rawski, T. G. 1979. *Economic Growth and Employment in China.* New York: Oxford University Press.

Rhee, Y. W. 1990. "The Catalyst Model of Development: Lessons from Bangladesh's Success with Garment Exports." *World Development* 18 (2): 333–346.

Rhee, Y. W., and T. Belot. 1990. "Export Catalysts in Low-Income Countries." Discussion Paper 72. World Bank, Washington, DC.

Ricardo, D. 1817. *On The Principles of Political Economy and Taxation.* London: John Murray.

———. 1921. *On the Principles of Political Economy and Taxation,* 3rd ed. London: John Murray.

Rilke, R. M. 1984. *Letters to a Young Poet.* New York: Random House.

Robinson, J. 1933. *The Economics of Imperfect Competition.* London: Macmillan.

———. 1956. *The Accumulation of Capital.* London: Macmillan.

Robinson, J. A., and R. Torvik. 2005. "White Elephants." *Journal of Public Economics* 89: 197–210.

Rocheteau, G. 1982. *Pouvoir financier et indépendance économique en Afrique: Le cas du Sénégal.* Paris: Orstom-Karthala.

Rodrik, D. 2005. "Growth Strategies." In *Handbook of Economic Growth,* Vol. 1, ed. P. Aghion and S. Durlauf, 967–1014. New York: Elsevier.

———. 2006. "Goodbye Washington Consensus, Hello Washington Confusion? A Review of the World Bank's *Economic Growth in the 1990s: Learning from a Decade of Reform.*" *Journal of Economic Literature* 44 (4): 973–987.

———. 2009. "Industrial Policy: Don't Ask Why, Ask How." *Middle East Development Journal* 1 (1): 1–29.

Romalis, J. 2007. "Capital Taxes, Trade Costs, and the Irish Miracle." *Journal of the European Economic Association* 5 (2–3): 459–469.

Romer, P. 1993. "Two Strategies for Economic Development: Using Ideas and Producing Ideas." In *Proceedings of the World Bank Annual Conference on Development Economics 1992*, ed. L. Summers and S. Shah, 63–91. World Bank: Washington, DC.

Romer, C. 2009. "The Case for Fiscal Stimulus: The Likely Effects of the American Recovery and Reinvestment Act." Speech at the University of Chicago, February 27.

Romer, P. M. 1986. "Increasing Returns and Long-Run Growth." *Journal of Political Economy* 95 (5): 1002–1037.

———. 1987. "Growth Based on Increasing Returns Due to Specialization." *American Economic Review* 77 (2): 56–62.

———. 1990. "Endogenous Technological Change." *Journal of Political Economy* 98 (5): S71–S102.

Rosenstein-Rodan, P. N. 1943. "Problems of Industrialisation of Eastern and South-Eastern Europe." *Economic Journal* 53 (210–211): 202–211.

———. 1961. "How to Industrialize an Underdeveloped Area." In *Regional Economic Planning*, ed. W. Isard, 205–211. Paris: Organization for European Economic Co-operation.

Rostow, W. W. 1960. *The Stages of Economic Growth: A Non-Communist Manifesto*. Cambridge, England: Cambridge University Press.

Roubiniand, N., and X. Sala-i-Martin. 1992. "Financial Repression and Economic Growth." *Journal of Development Economics* 39: 5–30.

Sá Barreto, R. C., and E. Almeida. 2009. "A contribuição da pesquisa para convergência e crescimento da renda agropecuária no Brasil." *Revista de Economia e Sociologia Rural* 47 (3): 719–737.

Sachs, J. 1993. *Poland's Jump to the Market Economy*. Cambridge, MA: MIT Press.

Sage, S. F. 1992. *Ancient Sichuan and the Unification of China*. Albany: State University of New York Press.

Salisbury, H. 1992. *The New Emperors: China in the Era of Mao and Deng*. Boston: Little, Brown.

Sawers, L. 2005. "Nontraditional or New Traditional Exports: Ecuador's Flower Boom." *Latin American Research Review* 40 (3): 40–66.

Schopenhauer, A. 1890 [1998]. "Further Psychological Observations." In *Studies in Pessimism: A Series of Essays*, trans. T. B. Saunders. New York: Macmillan.

Schultz, T. W. 1961. "Investments in Human Capital." *American Economic Review* 51 (1): 1–17.

———. 1962. *Investment in Human Beings*. Chicago: University of Chicago Press.

———. 1964. *Transforming Traditional Agriculture*. Chicago: University of Chicago Press.

Schumpeter, J. 1942. *Capitalism, Socialism, and Democracy*. New York: Harper and Row.

Schumpeter, J. A. 1975. *Capitalism, Socialism, and Democracy*, 3rd ed. New York: Harper.

Selim, T. H. 2006. "Monopoly: The Case of Egyptian Steel." *Journal of Business Case Studies* 2 (3): 85–92.

Sen, A. 1960. *The Choice of Technique: An Aspect of the Theory of Planned Economic Development.* Oxford: Blackwell.

Service, R. 2005. *Stalin: A Biography.* Cambridge, MA: Harvard University Press.

Shambaugh, D. 1993. "Deng Xiaoping: The Politician." In "Deng Xiaoping: An Assessment." Special issue, *China Quarterly* 135: 457.

Shaw, E. 1973. *Financial Deepening in Economic Development.* New York: Oxford University Press.

Shiue, C. H., and W. Keller. 2007. "Markets in China and Europe on the Eve of the Industrial Revolution." *American Economic Review* 97 (4): 1189–1216.

Short, P. 2004. *Pol Pot: Anatomy of a Nightmare.* New York: Henry Holt.

Singer, H. 1950. "The Distribution of Gains between Borrowing and Investing Countries." *American Economic Review* 40 (2): 473–485.

Skidelsky, R. 2003. "The Mystery of Growth." *New York Review of Books,* March 13.

Smith, A. 1776. *The Wealth of Nations.* Chicago: University of Chicago Press.

Smith, R. 2010. "Casualties—US vs. NVA/VC." www.rjsmith.com/kia_tbl.html. Accessed February 23, 2012.

Sokoloff, K. L., and S. L. Engerman. 2000. "History Lessons: Institutions, Factor Endowments, and Paths of Development in the New World." *Journal of Economic Perspectives* 14 (3): 217–232.

Solow, R. M. 1969. *Growth Theory: An Exposition.* New York: Oxford University Press.

———. 1998. *Monopolistic Competition and Macroeconomic Theory.* Cambridge, England. Cambridge University Press.

Spar, D. 1998. *Attracting High Technology Investment: Intel's Costa Rica Plan.* FIAS Occasional Paper 11. Washington, DC: World Bank, Foreign Investment Advisory Service.

Spence, M. 2011. *The Next Convergence: The Future of Economic Growth in a Multispeed World.* New York: Farrar, Straus, and Giroux.

State Statistical Bureau. 1987. *Zhongguo gudingzichantouzi tonggiziliao* (China capital construction statistical data, 1950–1985). Beijing: Zhongguo Tongji Chubanshe.

Stiglitz, J. E. 1998. "More Instruments and Broader Goals: Moving toward the Post-Washington Consensus." WIDER Annual Lecture 2. World Institute for Development Economics Research, United Nations University, Helsinki.

———. 2002. *Globalization and Its Discontents.* New York: Norton.

———. 2003. "Challenging the Washington Consensus: Interview with Lindsey Schoenfelder." *Brown Journal of World Affairs* 9 (2): 33–40.

———. 2009. *Freefall: America, Free Markets, and the Sinking of the World Economy.* New York: W. W. Norton.

Subramanian, A., and D. Roy. 2003. "Who Can Explain the Mauritian Miracle? Mede,

Romer, Sachs, or Rodrik?" In *In Search of Prosperity: Analytic Narratives on Economic Growth,* ed. D. Rodrik, 205–243. Princeton, NJ: Princeton University Press.

Sweeney, P. 1999. *The Celtic Tiger: Ireland's Continuing Economic Miracle,* 2nd ed. Dublin: Oak Tree Press.

Taylor, L. 1983. *Structuralist Macroeconomics: Applicable Models for the Third World.* New York: Basic Books.

———. 1991. *Income Distribution, Inflation, and Growth: Lectures in Structuralist Macroeconomics.* Cambridge, MA: MIT Press.

———. 2004. *Reconstructing Macroeconomics: Structuralist Proposals and Critiques of the Mainstream.* Cambridge, MA: Harvard University Press.

Tollison, R. D., and R. D. Congleton, eds. 1995. *The Economic Analysis of Rent-Seeking.* Aldershot, England: Edward Elgar.

Torrens, R. 1815. *Essay on the External Corn Trade.* London: J. Hatchard.

Trebilcock, C. 1981. *The Industrialization of Continental Powers, 1780–1914.* London: Longman.

UNCTAD (United Nations Conference on Trade and Development). 2006. *A Case Study of the Salmon Industry in Chile.* New York.

———. n.d. *UNCTADstat.* Geneva.

Weber, M. 1958. *The Protestant Ethic and the Spirit of Capitalism.* New York: Charles Scribner's Sons.

Whitman, W. B., ed. 2003. *The Quotable Politician.* Guilford, CT: Lyons.

Williamson, J. 2002. "Did the Washington Consensus Fail?" Speech at the Center for Strategic and International Studies, Washington, DC, November 6.

Williamson, O. E. 2000. "The New Institutional Economics: Taking Stock, Looking Ahead." *Journal of Economic Literature* 38 (3): 595–613.

World Bank. 1993. *The East Asian Miracle: Economic Growth and Policy.* Oxford, England: Oxford University Press.

———. 1995. *Bureaucrats in Business: The Economics and Politics of Government Ownership.* Washington, DC.

———. 1996. *World Development Report 1996: From Plan to Market.* Washington, DC.

———. 2002. *Transition: The First Ten Years; Analysis and Lessons for Eastern Europe and the Former Soviet Union.* Washington, DC.

———. 2005. *Economic Growth in the 1990s: Learning from a Decade of Reform.* Washington, DC.

———. 2007. *World Development Report 2008: Agriculture for Development.* Washington, DC.

———. 2009a. "Enhancing Growth and Reducing Poverty in a Volatile World: A Progress Report on the Africa Action Plan." Washington, DC.

———. 2009b. *Global Monitoring Report 2009: A Development Emergency.* Washington, DC.

———. 2010a. *Africa Development Indicators.* Washington, DC.

———. 2010b. *The Little Data Book on Information and Communication Technology 2010.* Washington, DC.

———. 2010c. *World Development Indicators.* Washington, DC.

———. 2011. *World Development Report 2011: Conflict, Security, and Development.* Washington, DC: World Bank.

WTO (World Trade Organization). n.d. "The Case for Open Trade." WTO Trade Resources. www.wto.org/trade_resources/history/wto/wto.htm. Accessed February 6, 2012.

Wu, Y.-L. 1965. *The Economy of Communist China: An Introduction.* New York: Praeger.

Xiaoping, D. 1980. "On the Reform of the System of Party and State Leadership." Speech for a meeting of the Political Bureau of the Central Committee of the Communist Party of China, Beijing, August 18.

———. 1984. *Selected Works of Deng Xiaoping, 1975–1982,* Vol. 2. Beijing: Foreign Language Press.

———. 1992. *Selected Works of Deng Xiaoping, 1938–1965,* Vol. 1. Beijing: Foreign Language Press.

———. 1994. *Selected Works of Deng Xiaoping, 1982–1992,* Vol. 3. Beijing: Foreign Language Press.

Yeboah, K. 1999. "Introducing the Ghana Steel Fund." *Ghanaweb,* November 30.

Yeltsin, B. N. 1990. *Against the Grain: An Autobiography.* New York: Summit Books.

———. 1995. *The Struggle for Russia.* New York: Crown.

———. 2000. *Midnight Diaries.* New York: PublicAffairs.

Young, A. 2010. "The African Growth Miracle." Department of Economics, London School of Economics. mfi.uchicago.edu/publications/papers/real-consumption -measures-for-the-poorer-regions-of-the-world.pdf. Accessed May 22, 2012.

Zagha, R., G. Nankani, and I. Gill. 2006. "Rethinking Growth." *Finance and Development* 43 (March): 7–11.

Zellner, A. 1979. "Causality and Econometrics, Policy and Policymaking." *Carnegie-Rochester Conference Series on Public Policy* 10: 9–54.

Zoellick, R. B. 2010. "Remarks for the High-Level China–Africa Experience-Sharing Program on Special Economic Zones and Infrastructure Development." Beijing, September 14.

INDEX

Page numbers for entries occurring in figures are followed by an *f* and those for entries in notes, by an *n*.